THE PRENTICE HALL
POCKET

Writing
About
Literature

EDWARD A. SHANNON
Ramapo College of New Jersey

Prentice
Hall

Upper Saddle River
New Jersey 07458

Library of Congress Cataloging-in-Publication Data

Shannon, Edward A., (date)
The Prentice Hall pocket guide to writing about literature /
Edward A. Shannon.

p. cm.
ISBN: 0-13-026160-2
1. English language—Rhetoric—Handbooks, manuals, etc.
2. Literature—History and criticism—Theory, etc.   3. Criticism
—Authorship—Handbooks, manuals, etc.   4. Academic
writing—Handbooks, manuals, etc.   5. Literature—Terminology.
6. Criticism—Terminology.   I. Title: Pocket guide to writing
about literature.   II. Title: Writing about literature.   III. Title.
PE1479.C7 S5 2002
808'.0665—dc21
2001019909

Editor in Chief: *Leah Jewell*
Senior Acquisitions Editor: *Carrie Brandon*
Editorial Assistant: *Thomas DeMarco*
Managing Editor: *Mary Rottino*
Production Liaison: *Fran Russello*
Editorial/Production Supervision: *Kim Gueterman*
Prepress and Manufacturing Buyer: *Sherry Lewis*
Cover Director: *Jayne Conte*
Cover Designer: *Bruce Kenselaar*
Cover Art: Henri Matisse, "Composition, fond bleu."
Courtesy of Dr. Jakob Bill © 2000 Succession H. Marisse,
Paris/Artists Rights Society (ARS), New York
Copyeditor: *Donna Mulder*
Marketing Manager: *Rachel Falk*

This book was set in 8/11 Serifa Roman by ElectraGraphics, Inc.
and was printed and bound by R. R. Donnelley & Sons Company.
The cover was printed by Phoenix Color Corp.

© 2002 by Pearson Education, Inc.
Upper Saddle River, New Jersey 07458

Printed in the United States of America
10 9 8 7 6 5 4 3 2 1

ISBN 0-13-026160-2

Prentice-Hall International (UK) Limited, *London*
Prentice-Hall of Australia Pty. Limited, *Sydney*
Prentice-Hall Canada, Inc., *Toronto*
Prentice-Hall Hispanoamericana, S.A., *Mexico*
Prentice-Hall of India Private Limited, *New Delhi*
Prentice-Hall of Japan, Inc., *Tokyo*
Pearson Education Asia Pte. Ltd., *Singapore*
Editora Prentice-Hall do Brasil, Ltda., *Rio de Janeiro*

For Kathleen, Denis, and Patrick,
for always inspiring me

Contents

Acknowledgments

This book could not have been written without the help of many people. I am indebted to my many colleagues who shared their syllabi, assignments, and ideas. In particular, I would like to thank Erik Bledsoe, Daun Daemon, and Lauren Jones. Thanks are due to Lucindy Willis for Chapter 3's section on literary theory. I should also thank all of the professors whose classes I have taken and whose ideas I have absorbed. And most of all, I am in the debt of my students for keeping me excited about literature.

Finally, I would like to thank Kathleen Shannon for all of her help completing this book.

Credits

M. H. ABRAHMS: Excerpt from A GLOSSARY OF LITERARY TERMS, Seventh Edition, by M. H. Abrams, copyright © 1999 by Holt, Rinehart & Winston. Reprinted by permission of the publisher.

J. A. CUDDON: A DICTIONARY OF LITERARY TERMS AND LITERARY THEORY, Third Edition, Blackwell Publishers. Reprinted with permission.

EMILY DICKINSON: "A Bird Came Down the Walk' is reprinted by permission of the publishers and the Trustees of Amherst College from THE POEMS OF EMILY DICKINSON, Thomas H. Johnson, ed., Cambridge, Mass.: The Belknap Press of Harvard University Press. Copyright © 1951, 1955, 1979, by the President and Fellows of Harvard College.

T. S. ELIOT: 6 lines from "The Waste Land" and 10 lines from "The Love Song of J. Alfred Prufrock," from COLLECTED POEMS 1909–1962 by T. S. Eliot. Reprinted by permission of Faber and Faber London.

HUGH HOLMAN AND WILLIAM HARMON: Definitions of "Imagery" and "Archtypes" from A HANDBOOK TO LITERATURE by William Harmon and Hugh Holman copyright © 1996. Reprinted by permission of Prentice Hall, Inc. Upper Saddle River, NJ.

HOUGHTON MIFFLIN: Definition of "literature" copyright © 1996 by Houghton Mifflin Company. Reproduced by permission from THE AMERICAN HERITAGE DICTIONARY OF THE ENGLISH LANGUAGE, Third Edition.

JIM KAPOUN: "Teaching Undergrads WEB Evaluation: A Guide for Library Instruction," C & RL NEWS (July/August 1998): 522–523. Reprinted with permission from the author.

What Is Literature?

1

INTRODUCTION

This book is a guide to writing papers about literature for college classes. The study of literature is a little different than the study of most other subjects. In math and the sciences, there are numbers and facts to memorize, chemical relationships to understand, problems to solve, and experiments to run. These are difficult tasks and challenging fields of study, but the student of math or science can take comfort in the knowledge that more often than not, she is going to be able to come to an answer that is either right or wrong, and that there is going to be a way to test these answers. Even in the study of history, which often demands interpretation and analysis, one can be relatively sure that for some questions, "1945" or "William the Conqueror" is going to be the correct answer every time. Literature is different. In the study of literature, students are often judged not on the memorization of facts or on the success or failure of certain experiments but on the quality of their reading, interpretation, and writing.

Eventually, it all comes down to the writing. However, writing is different than math. One instructor's A paper is another instructor's B. And what looks great on your computer screen at 2 A.M. the day before the paper is due sometimes looks less exemplary when it is returned drenched in red ink. Even our training can sometimes betray us. Students swear on a stack of grammar books that they were taught never to use the pronoun *I*, to begin a sentence with a preposition, end a sentence with a preposition, or even use prepositions, whatever they are. Some know with certainty that all paragraphs are at least five sentences long while others swear three is the magic number. Their high school teachers told them never to write a paper of more than five paragraphs; others told them never to write a paper of less than five paragraphs. Sometimes we end up memorizing so many rules that begin "Always . . ." or "Never . . ." that we forget that rules are there to serve us, not the other way around.

While it is true that judging good writing is terribly subjective, it is possible to learn to write a successful literary analysis paper. This book will briefly look at some strategies for writing papers that are tightly focused, well developed, well organized, and grammatically and stylistically sophisticated. Of course, there are many reasons to write about literature. One may write to better understand a text, to explore the ideas the text examines, to inform others of the value of a text, or any number of other reasons. This book, however, will focus narrowly on the literary analysis written for the college classroom. It will attempt to address some of the persistent questions asked when reading and writing about literature and to suggest a handful of flexible strategies for dealing with common writing situations.

WHAT IS LITERATURE?

You are sitting in your Introduction to Literature class, and the professor walks in and asks, "What is literature?" You consider yourself a reasonably sophisticated student, so you should be able to answer this question, but you pause. "Literature is important writing," someone answers. Your professor responds, "OK, so is the owner's manual for your new car or the Nuclear Nonproliferation Treaty literature?" Another student says, "Literature is writing that reflects a national or cultural identity." "All right," says the professor, "you mean like the Constitution of the United States or the New York State Civil Code?"

"Only certain genres of writing can be literature," interrupts a student, "like books of fiction and poetry." "So Ben Franklin's *Autobiography* and Jefferson's Declaration of Independence are not literature? How did they get into my *Anthology of American Literature?*"

By now several things are clear: The answer to this question is more difficult than you thought it would be, your professor has a sarcastic streak, and you must have ended up in a fictional classroom because I have never heard that much discussion on the first day of class! Well, we cannot do too much about your professor's disposition or the nonreality of your classmates, but we can address the issue of just what literature is. After all, we cannot discuss writing about literature if we cannot even define what it is.

A basic definition of literature is easy to find. The *American Heritage Dictionary* tells me the following:

lit·er·a·ture *n.* Abbr. lit. 1. A body of writings in prose or verse. 2. Imaginative or creative writing, especially of recognized artistic value. 3. The art or occupation of a literary writer. 4. The body of written work produced by scholars or researchers in a given field. 5. Printed material.

Look at number 5: "Printed material." We are not going to get a much simpler definition than that. And it is a fair enough definition; we can see the importance of the root *literate* here: the same root for words such as *literacy* and *literal,* words dealing with words. This definition is probably familiar. We might have heard salespeople offer to send us "literature" about one product or another. They were not offering us epic poems or novels about their products. They wanted to send us "printed material."

But in the classroom, we have a different definition in mind, maybe number 2: "Imaginative or creative writing, especially of recognized artistic value." This definition excludes not only brochures for a new fuel pump or blender but also, it seems, most of the books in our local bookstore or library. Do we consider R. L. Stine's *Goosebumps* books to be literature? A generation of Americans is being raised on these books, being taught to read with them, building fond lifelong memories of hours of reading pleasure curled up with these little books, but most people would probably say, "That's not literature." What about Stephen King's novels? Or self-help books such as *Chicken Soup for the Soul?* These are all "printed material," and since they are widely read, we can assume that *someone* thinks that they are full of "artistic value." Can books such as these be considered literature? A look at some possible definitions of this weighty term may help us decide.

The Generic Definition

Ask students what literature is and you might get a generic definition such as "novels and poems." That is a definition by kind: these kinds of things are literature. Unfortunately, novels include books such as *Goosebumps* that at first glance do not seem to be literature. At least, we do not see *Goosebumps* titles in the *Norton Anthology of American Literature.* Also, that definition omits many texts that are taught in literature classes. Frederick Douglass's *Narrative of the Life of Frederick Douglass, An American Slave* is certainly literature to many, but it is an autobiography, not a novel or poetry. What about other genres? Is detective fiction literature? What about horror stories? Adventure

stories? Romance? Perhaps another definition will answer
these questions.

The Age Definition

Some of my students tell me that literature is "writing
that stands the test of time." This definition has the back-
ing of history behind it, and it includes all those old, important writers such as Shakespeare, Melville, Wordsworth,
Dante, and Chaucer. Unfortunately, the definition is not only
vague, it has a considerable hole in it. First of all, what does
old mean? I teach American literature, and like many a student of American literature before me, I have actually been
told that there is no such thing as American literature because the United States has not had the time to develop a
literary heritage as old and distinguished as, say, Britain's.
This objection at least reminds us that, as Einstein told us,
time is relative. If literature has to be old, then recent writing cannot be literature. This will come as a surprise to Toni
Morrison, a living author who recently was awarded the
Nobel Prize for literature. In fact, since the Nobel Prize for literature is only about one hundred years old, the folks who
claim that American literature is not literature should have
a field day with this upstart little contest!

The other problem with this definition is that it is a bit
vague on just which "old" texts have passed the test of time
and just what that "test" is. *Alice in Wonderland* is pretty
old. Is that literature, even though it is *just* a children's book?
Is Christopher Marlowe's *Doctor Faustus* literature, even
though the only existing texts we have are incomplete (and
parts of those texts may not even have been written by
Marlowe)? Certain scandalous "anonymous" novels of a sexual bent are still read one or two hundred years after publication. Have they "stood the test of time"?

The "Elitist" Definition

Another definition suggests that literature is writing that
was created by our greatest minds. This is a good definition because it does not specify date or genre, so we can include autobiographies such as the one by Douglass and plays
and poems by Shakespeare. Unfortunately, the term *greatest* is certainly as open to debate as *old*. Some readers, for
instance, might look at the work of someone such as Edgar
Allan Poe and ask thoughtful questions such as, "Didn't he
die in the gutter? Can someone who led such a questionable
life really be 'great'?" Recently the literary world was
shocked to find out that Paul de Man, a well-respected lit-

erary critic, had in fact done some profascist writing during World War II. Similarly, readers have accused T. S. Eliot and Ezra Pound of anti-Semitism. Certainly many authors cheated on their spouses, lied, swore, and generally did all of the nasty things people in other walks of life did.

Does this mean that their writing is no longer literature because their minds are not as "great" as we want them to be? Should we let a sexist writer into the "great minds" club? Does an individual's private life negate his or her public statements? We are now relatively certain that Thomas Jefferson fathered a child by one of his slaves. More to the point, we have always known that he owned slaves. Should we now remove the Declaration of Independence and *Notes on the State of Virginia* from our literature anthologies?

And what about books of uncertain authority? *The Autobiography of Malcolm X* is often taught in literature classes. We can assume that this book was written by Malcolm X and that the book is a reflection of his mind, right? Well, Alex Haley is actually the coauthor of this book, and it is, therefore, also a product of his imagination as well. Most people have heard the theories that the author of the Shakespeare plays was not really Shakespeare but the Earl of Oxford or Francis Bacon. If some new evidence crops up that Shakespeare was not the author, do the plays become "less literary" as a consequence? Well, the words on the page do not change, so it really should not matter if they were written by Shakespeare or not. On the other hand, the name *Shakespeare* contains a lot of meaning all by itself. Should we ignore that meaning?

So, definition by genre, age, and author seems to lead us to dead ends. What is this stuff called literature?!

Here is a formal definition of literature as written by literary scholar, J. A. Cuddon, in his *Dictionary of Literary Terms and Literary Criticism*:

> A vague term which usually denotes works which belong to the major genres: epic, drama, lyric, novel, short story, ode. . . . If we describe something as "literature," as opposed to anything else, the term carries with it qualitative connotations which imply that the work in question has superior qualities; that it is well above the ordinary run of written works. For example: "George Eliot's novels are literature, whereas Fleming's Bond books are unquestionably not." (pp. 505–506)

Cuddon is honest enough to admit that the term is vague. But at least we have a better definition than "printed material." The question we return to is: What are the specific "qualitative connotations" and "superior qualities" we need to look for? Who decides which books are literature and which ones are not?

Let us ask one of your imaginary classmates. Someone answers, "Literature is the stuff they teach you in literature classes." Well, here is a practical definition at last. For the student in a literature class, this seems to be about as valid a definition as there is. While taking a given class, the student of literature is obliged to accept and treat some set of texts as having "superior qualities" and, therefore, being literature: Women's Literature Literature of the American West, British Literature, French Literature, Russian Literature, or Russian Women's Prison Literature of the American West Written in French. Whatever the designation, some student somewhere is going to need to treat this stuff as literature for a semester or more.

So, even though we have already discovered a fairly flexible definition of literature, we may want to reconsider our approach. Rather than look for some blanket definition that will tell us which texts are literature and which are not, we may need to look at how our response to a text changes once we have decided that a text is in fact "literary." Should we read Faulkner the way we read the morning paper?

CONSIDERING THE CONTEXT OF OUR READING

For the college student taking a class that requires essay writing and test taking, reading literature is more than a casual reading experience. Perhaps reading literature in a classroom setting is even less than an ideal reading experience. This student is not just reading to explore the text or discover herself or himself in its pages. This student will be asked to document that search and to do so under some fairly specific conditions. There may be a minimum or maximum number of pages to be written. The student will be given some time restrictions—perhaps a week to write a five-page paper, two weeks for a ten-page paper, or one hour for a two-page paper. Perhaps the student will be asked to memorize a new set of terms and to apply them to the seven or eight novels he or she will read in the next three months. Under these conditions, regardless of the text in question, the study of literature becomes less of a pleasure and more of a job.

Since so much will be expected of us in terms of output, we need to think seriously of how we approach the texts we consider as literary, why we approach them at all, and why we (and others) think these texts ought to be read.

In an ideal world, literature would only be considered at leisure and for pleasure, contemplation, and edification. But students in literature classes are not asked to read literary texts for pleasure at their leisure. Professors of literature classes may sometimes act as if every text introduced will bring nothing but pleasure to the lucky one who reads it. But literature professors know that reading these books can be hard work. Ask literature professors if they treat pleasure reading differently from the reading they do in the course of literary research or in preparation for a class. You may hear them answer, "Oh, to be able to read a novel without taking notes!"

Comments such as this remind us that the context under which we encounter a text changes our experience of the text. Many students say, for instance, that they have read something at home and despaired of ever finding meaning or enjoyment in it only to have the work open up after class discussion. What is happening here is not that the book is changing but that as our expectations and attitudes change, we are able to perceive more and more value in the text.

A student is asked to go home and read "The Tell-Tale Heart" by Edgar Allan Poe for a class called American Short Story. She has already read this story in high school and has some vague memories of class discussion about irony, stories of horror, and something called "suspension of disbelief." More recently, the student remembers babysitting a young cousin and watching a cartoon featuring a caricature of Edgar Allan Poe. She is generally familiar with Poe as a writer of horror and as a writer she associated with children and high school. In fact, Poe's big eyes and wild hair have been a familiar sight in this student's life from television, magazines, and elsewhere. Familiarity breeds contempt; consequently, the student approaches Poe with a little reluctance.

The story begins with some pretty over-the-top language:

> TRUE!—nervous—very, very dreadfully nervous I had been and am; but why *will* you say that I am mad? The disease had sharpened my senses—not destroyed—not dulled them. Above all was the sense of hearing acute. I heard all things in the heaven and in the earth. I heard many things in hell.

"Oh, please," the student responds, "this guy in the story is nuts. And the guy who wrote the story probably was, too. Anyone who says that he can prove he isn't crazy by telling you what he heard in hell is crazy." Our student asks, "This is horror?" Compared to the horror films she has seen, with their chain saws and flowing blood and gruesome special effects, this is not scary, especially since she knows how the story is going to end.

The student knows that she is going to have to write a paper about this story, and so far all she can say is that she does not like it very much. She finds it hard to imagine stretching "I didn't like it" into an eight- to ten-page paper with four secondary sources.

In class, however, the professor tells the class that Poe did not write horror, he wrote "terror." This seems a ridiculous distinction to our student. Horror and terror are the same thing as far as she is concerned.

The professor suggests that the modern horror story, especially the horror film, is concerned with getting an immediate, visceral reaction out of the audience. The modern horror film wants everyone screaming at once. The writer of the contemporary horror novel wants readers to slam the book shut and switch on all the lights immediately upon finding the description of the demon or monster. Poe does not do that, so let us call what he writes "terror," the professor suggests. Poe wants a longer, slower reaction from his reader. Poe wants the feelings of dread to build up. There is no sudden shock of horror; in fact, we know that the victim is dead in the first lines of the story.

Okay, she concedes, I guess I see the distinction. But it still is not a scary story, and that is really what matters, not whether the story is horror or terror.

In answer to a question from the professor, a classmate points out that the story was written in the first person. The professor asks how the story might be different if the old man was the narrator or if the story had a third-person narrator.

Someone laughs and says, "It'd be a pretty short story. The old man hears a sound, wakes up, gets killed, and the story's over, and we don't know who did it."

A classmate responds, "Who knows? Look at a few things the narrator says that are questionable, like he hears things in hell, maybe a lot of what he told us isn't true. Maybe the old man knows a lot more than the killer says he does. We only have the word of an insane confessed killer. How do we know he killed the old man or that there is an old man? This might all be a hallucination!"

Our student pipes in, "All this just goes to show that the story is not about the killing at all. It's about the killer—how he sees the world."

What does the story as Poe gave it to us offer that another version of the story would not? "In Poe's version," our previously bored student says, "we don't get what really happened but what this guy *thinks* happened, and he seems a little questionable. In fact, he tells us that his reason for telling the story of the murder of the old man is that it will prove he's sane. It proves pretty much the opposite."

The professor suggests that Poe's use of an "unreliable narrator" has taken a simple little plot of senseless violence and turned it into an exploration of the mind of a madman. This exploration opens up questions about not only this particular madman's perception of reality but everyone's. For instance, one student cites the following lines, describing the killer's slow entry into his victim's room:

> I was never kinder to the old man than during the whole week before I killed him. And every night, about midnight, I turned the latch of his door and opened it—oh so gently! And then, when I had made an opening sufficient for my head, I put in a dark lantern, all closed, closed, that no light shone out, and then I thrust in my head. Oh, you would have laughed to see how cunningly I thrust it in! I moved it slowly—very, very slowly, so that I might not disturb the old man's sleep. It took me an hour to place my whole head within the opening so far that I could see him as he lay upon his bed. Ha! would a madman have been so wise as this?

"Granted," our student admits, "this guy is nuts." The student wonders, "Did it really take him an hour to put his head in the door? Has anyone had the experience of time seeming to move faster or slower because of how they felt emotionally at the time?"

The class continues this discussion. The professor and students mention different ways that they have noticed that their perception of the world can affect their experience of the world. The professor mentions that Poe frequently features characters such as this one, that it is no fluke to find a narrator whom we cannot trust in the work of Edgar Allan Poe. The professor suggests that Poe returns to this kind of narrator because he finds something important in finding someone who sees the world very differently than most of his audience does. One student mentions that her brother is color-blind and cites his color-blindness as an example of how perception is not always universal: two people can look at the same object and see two different things. Consider cultural differences, the professor suggests. Would an accountant raised in the United States in the late twentieth century respond to seeing an eclipse, for instance, the same way a peasant in medieval France would? Would a contemporary astronomer see things any differently than an ancient Chinese emperor would?

One student brings things closer to home when he mentions that his grandmother is always suspicious of clerks at the supermarket. Although this student does not share his grandmother's suspicion, he points out that she frequently finds that she has in fact been "cheated" at the supermarket for small amounts. He believes that his grandmother is not overcharged more often than the average customer, but she is just more aware of all of the minor overcharges. But because she is more aware, she notices the overcharges more often. Therefore, she becomes even more vigilant at the register and a little ruder to the cashiers. Eventually her experience at the supermarket changes to meet her expectations and perceptions. The supermarket has become a place filled with suspicious people who want to rob her.

The professor suggests that the experience of the grandmother is not far from that of the killer in the story. Poe has managed to document a real and observable aspect of human nature. In the short story, he writes about a person living with extreme, pathological paranoia, but in class discussions, students manage to extrapolate that example into observations about their own lives and into discussions of Poe's interest in psychology. They are also able to make a distinction between terror and horror and to see a value in this distinction. Poe's stories are not just scary because someone is murdered but because the story suggests that the reader is not so very different from the killer. Both reader and killer react to the world they perceive, whether those perceptions are accurate or not. The professor asks if our friend's grandmother is wrong about what she "sees" at the supermarket, which of our perceptions are "wrong"? How well do we know the world in which we live?

The reading experience of the class was, in a way, different than the individual experiences of the students in the class. While at first our student approached the text with a very narrow focus, as a vaguely annoying, vaguely familiar assignment, the class approached the story from different points of view. The professor had one set of ideas, another student had the experience of a color-blind sibling, another a paranoid grandmother, and all of these different experiences and points of view influenced the class's reading of the story.

How can we as students change our reading experiences so that we enter class with many possible interpretations? What we put into the text can dictate how much we take out

of it. The professor brought some research and an aware-
ness of the author's other work as well as some specialized
language, and she may have used terms such as *unreliable
narrator, genre, romantic,* and *Gothic* to describe Poe's work.
The students brought a range of personal and educational
experiences to the story. With the observations mentioned
in class and the terms the professor mentioned, our student
feels confident that she can write a paper about "The Tell-
Tale Heart." She realizes that if she had changed her attitude toward the story in the first place, she might have come
away with some of these observations herself. Like Poe's narrator, she can change her experience of the literature by
changing the way she perceives it.

If we begin with the assumption that reading literature
is a chore, then our reading is going to be a chore. If we begin
with the assumption that our reading can be profitable,
chances are it will be profitable. Our student learned that
her attitude has a lot to do with how valuable her classroom
experience can be. Her experience in the classroom illus-
trates that literature can be a springboard for ideas. Those
ideas can be shaped into essays that express the reader's interpretation of literary texts.

2

Reading Literature

OUR PERCEPTION OF LITERATURE AFFECTS OUR READING EXPERIENCE

This book is about writing a particular kind of genre: the essay of literary analysis. Before we can talk about writing a paper, we need to talk about how we gather the information that goes into that paper. In a way, all literature papers are research papers; after all, we must read a literary text to be able to comment on it. It may help us to think of the essay of literary analysis as a research paper. To write a paper such as this, one must do research. No one is born with a handful of Emily Dickinson poems committed to memory; we need to read the poems (i.e., do the research) before we write the paper. When working on a research paper, students should be careful to collect notes and keep track of all of the books and articles they have read for the project.

However, it is easy to be less than careful. Once we start the familiar task of "writing a paper," it is too easy to get into the habits of our most recent writing experience (which may have been writing a statistics or history or business paper) and forget that literature as a field of study has its own rules and conventions and that studying literature is different than studying current events or science and technology or marketing.

Since literary essays depend on the research we do, we should spend some time talking about how we read and what we are reading for.

THE MYTH OF "HIDDEN MEANING"

One of the first concepts we should consider in our attempt to identify what we write about when we write about literature is the nebulous concept of "hidden meaning." Often students say something such as "I read the story but I didn't get the hidden meaning." We might even refer to this aspect of literature as the "deep secret hidden meaning." Let us examine this mysterious phenomenon.

Anyone who has taken a literature course has probably had this experience: You are given a reading assignment, say, a poem. You read the poem, and it describes in beautiful language, say, a bird singing in a tree. You return to class and tell the professor, "That poem is about a bird singing in a tree." The professor smiles a tired, disappointed smile and explains, "Yes, well that's a common misreading. Actually, the poem is about the poet's unresolved feelings of anger toward his mother. But good try!" Here is born the myth of deep secret hidden meaning! Literary works often are not about what they seem to be about; they are about what the teacher says they are about—and only English teachers can figure out what these hidden meanings are.

Well, we should put this to rest: generally speaking, assume that there is no such thing as hidden meaning in literature. Should literary works only be read on a literal level? No. Should we stop looking for symbol and metaphor in literature? No. Should we say literary works do not contain levels of meaning not apparent on first reading? No.

Literary works should be read on literal and figurative levels. Careful readers of literature should look for symbol and metaphor and figurative language of all kinds. Literary works do contain levels of meaning not apparent on first reading. They are just not hidden.

If we read a work of literature assuming that the work contains hidden meaning, then we must assume also that the author has intentionally hidden it. Under this theory, literature becomes a sadistic puzzle in which "famous authors" write works with carefully hidden subtexts that no one is supposed to find. It is the literary equivalent of backward masking on rock and roll records. You can only really appreciate Led Zeppelin if you listen to their music *backward!*

No. Literature is a means by which authors express themselves and by which sophisticated writers and readers communicate with one another. When a work of literature is really touching and powerful, the reader feels that he or she is in the presence of this other person, whether or not that person is living or dead. It is still possible for us to *know* Tolstoy or Austen or Dickens or Homer or Dickinson or Shakespeare because these people chose to express themselves in their work.

But literature is not like a newspaper story or a how-to book. Authors of literary works often deal with complex social, spiritual, and psychological matters. They often communicate these matters in a complex fashion that allows them to say two or three different (even contradictory) things with the same word, phrase, or image.

In Hawthorne's "Young Goodman Brown," set in the days just before the Salem witch trials, a young man walks into the woods and witnesses a disturbing supernatural scene. He meets a man who looks like an older version of himself, carrying a serpent-headed staff. The man is suggested to have supernatural abilities. Brown's wife is named Faith and is said to be a woman of great spiritual integrity. In fact, Goodman says that Faith will ensure his entry into Heaven. Is Hawthorne "hiding" the meaning of his story? Is he being deceitful with us, or is he writing an allegorical story? We can assume that Hawthorne wants his reader to interpret this story and seek meaning beyond the literal level of the plot. Even if Hawthorne did not intend for us to read into the story, these other levels of meaning seem apparent. For "Young Goodman Brown" to work, the reader needs to see meaning beyond the literal, but we should not assume that this meaning has been *hidden* from us.

On one level, "Young Goodman Brown" is a story about a young Puritan who witnesses evidence of witchcraft and lives to tell the tale. On another level, it is an allegory of guilt and a criticism of a closed-minded belief system. Which one is the "real" meaning of the story? Well, which one means more to you? Which meaning will more powerfully affect the reader of your paper on "Young Goodman Brown"? Which one speaks more powerfully to you?

Back to our poem about the bird in the tree. If the poet was skillful enough, or if the images in the poem evoke other images in the reader's mind, the poem can mean many things. It can be a poem about a bird in a tree or about the poet's unresolved anger toward his mother or about the Russian Revolution or the history of rock and roll! Some of these readings will resonate with many readers, some with only a few. Hopefully all of the variant readings will bring some satisfaction and pleasure to the readers. Perhaps all are valid readings. Perhaps all of these meanings were intended by the poet. But these meanings are not hidden—they are on view for those who care to see them.

But that might mean changing the way we read.

One wonderfully succinct description of what reading a literary text is all about comes to us from the novelist Paul Auster. In his autobiography, *The Invention of Solitude,* he wonders aloud about the difficulty of turning the real events of his life into the narrative he recounts in his book:

If a man says to you, "I'm going to Jerusalem," you think
to yourself: how nice, he's going to Jerusalem. But if a
character in a novel were to speak those same words,
"I'm going to Jerusalem," your response is not the same.
You think, to begin with, of Jerusalem itself: its history,
its religious role, its function as a mythical place. You
would think of the past, of the present (politics; which is
also to think of the recent past), and of the future—as in
the phrase: "Next year in Jerusalem." On top of that, you
would integrate these thoughts into whatever you already
know about the character who is going to Jerusalem and
use this synthesis to draw further conclusions, refine perceptions, think more cogently about the book as a whole.
And then, once the work is finished, the last page read
and the book closed, interpretations begin: psychological, historical, sociological, structural, philological, religious, sexual, philosophical, either singly or in various
combinations, depending on your bent.[1]

Interpretation

When we read a literary work of any value, it is necessary to *interpret* that work. According to M. H. Abrams, "to interpret a work
of literature is to specify the meanings of its language by analysis, paraphrase, and commentary; usually, such interpretation focuses on especially obscure, ambiguous, or figurative passages.
In a broader sense, to interpret a work of literature is to make clear
the artistic features and purport in the overall work of which language serves as the medium. Interpretation in this sense includes
the analysis of such matters as the work's genre, component elements, structure, theme, and effects."[2]

Essentially, when we talk about fiction, drama, and dramatic or
lyric poetry, we can say that *interpretation* means finding some
meaning in a work that is greater than either the events (or in the
case of lyric poetry, the speaker's comments or tone) as recounted
or our own entertainment as we read. If we read a James Bond novel
by Ian Fleming, we may expect little interpretive value in the work.
Most readers might safely say that the novel tried to do little more
than make them experience an adrenalin rush or two. There are
likely few "especially obscure, ambiguous, or figurative passages."

However, some critics may make arguments about the novel's
attitudes toward violence, sexuality, and superpower politics or the

---

[1]Paul Auster, *The Invention of Solitude* (New York: Penguin, 1982),
p. 146.

[2]M. H. Abrams, *A Glossary of Literary Terms*, 7th ed. (Fort Worth:
Harcourt Brace, 1999), p. 127.

history of the Cold War. These critics discuss what E. D. Hirsch might refer to as the novel's significance, "what makes the text alive and resonant for diverse readers in diverse times."[3]

But, in a broad sense, we can say that these critics are interpreting the novel, drawing meaning from it that supersedes our concerns for the well-being of the characters, the outcome of the plot, or even the craftsmanship of the novelist. If we read what we may deem a more "serious" work of literature, it may occur to us that there must be some value to the text beyond the plot and characters, especially if the plot and characters are less dynamic than those found in *Dr. No*. In Ernest Hemingway's "Big Two-Hearted River," one can argue, nothing of any consequence happens: there are no car chases, love scenes, or hidden microfilms. A young man goes camping, builds a fire, and catches a fish. No adrenalin there. Many critics, however, have considered the implications of the character's language and actions and even Hemingway's purpose in spending so much time describing such mundane activities as finding bait. Critics suggest that the man's relationship to the natural landscape surrounding him reinvigorates him and that this renewed sense of life is reflected in the descriptions of the scenery and the man's actions. They point out that early in the story, there is a focus on negative images of fire, darkness, and tension. Later in the story, once the young man makes his camp, these images are replaced with images of life, comfort, and order. These critics suggest that Hemingway's story (if not Hemingway himself) wants us to reconsider our own relationship with nature. While the story may not have a moral, this argument goes, it does have *something* to say to the reader. Did Hemingway intend such an interpretation? If it enhances our lives as readers, does it even matter what the author meant or did not mean? When we interpret a work of literature, we seek meaning important in our own lives rather than the meaning important to the characters in the story.

READING FOR COMPREHENSION

Several years ago I was working in a writing lab, helping students finish their papers or get started on essays for composition or literature classes. One student told me he had to write an essay about a short story his instructor had assigned. He told me he had read the story "but not for comprehension." I was not exactly sure what he meant by this, so I asked him a few questions about the story: main characters, settings, plot, and theme. He remembered nothing. Was there something wrong with this man's memory? No.

---

[3]Abrams, loc. cit., p. 129.

Was he lying about having read the story? No. I understood why he could not remember one word of a story he had read the night before.

What student has not had the experience of doing a marathon session of reading just to keep up with the syllabus? Most students have reread the same paragraph ten times only to look at it again and wonder, "What does this say?" We may plod on and finish our homework, but ultimately, we cannot call this *reading*. If our reading is not "for comprehension," then it is for nothing and it is not reading. Doing the reading but being unable to call up a single word or detail of the text does neither the student nor the professor nor the class nor the text any good. The student in my original example may have looked at all of the words in sequence, but it would be a mistake to call what he did reading.

Often what we get out of our reading has as much to do with us and our feelings and situation as to what is actually written on the page. To read effectively, we should consider several contexts: our reading situation and what will be expected of us, our own "critical theories" of literature, what we know about the text in question before we read it, and even how we are feeling that day. Most readers can recall having reread a poem about which they held a low opinion, only to find that the second time through the poem was much better! Did the poet revise the poem when we were not looking? Or did the reader change somehow and become more open to the language and imagery of the poem?

As a graduate student, my first class was called "Restoration Drama." Although these plays were considered classics of British literature, the professor must have noticed that he had an audience that was not willing to give the plays the benefit of the doubt. Perhaps he realized that students in summer school classes (as this one was) needed more prodding than in the regular semester. Perhaps he knew most of us really wanted to study something else and that this class was one of the few summer offerings that fulfilled specific graduation requirements. Perhaps he could simply smell our fear. Whatever the case, he said something that day that I have repeated many times since to my own students: he leaned back in his chair and slowly in a luxurious southern drawl, he reminded us, "Of course, it is not necessary for us to like these plays. Our job is to study them."

In a literature classroom, reading becomes work. In our leisure time we may lose ourselves in a good book or poem. But as students of literature, we do not always have that luxury. We need to be engaged readers. We must approach a text, highlighter in hand, conscious of the fact that our reading will be evaluated by a third party: our professor. With this in mind, it is important for us to develop reading skills that are appropriate to the task at hand.

Critical Theory

One of the more intimidating aspects of literary studies these days is contemporary critical theory. There are several critical theories competing for attention in the world of literary studies these days: New Criticism (which is actually one of the older theories), New Historicism, feminism, deconstruction, Marxism, and others. These theories can be very confusing, and the jargon the theories generate can be intimidating. We do not need to discuss these theories here (see Chapter 3 for a fuller discussion of these theories). However, it will do us good to define the broad term *critical theory* and recognize that on some level we all must develop a critical theory of our own to be effective readers.

Of course, developing a critical theory takes a while, and before we begin, we need to understand just what a critical theory is. We often think of criticism as being a bad thing. No one wants to be criticized, after all, but criticism is not necessarily all bad. To be critical is to practice careful, exact evaluation and judgment. To practice literary criticism, broadly speaking, is to make discriminating judgments and evaluations of literary works. To do these things well, it serves us to have a set of ideas we can take from one text to another rather than read each new text as our first literary text.

For instance, as a professor of literature, I have one critical theory of literature that is at the base of all other critical theories of literature: I believe fiction, poetry, and drama are able to preserve and communicate complex, important ideas; in fact, I might say that this is the primary value of literary texts. This theory is different from the casual reader who may believe that fiction, poetry, and drama are primarily valuable as works of entertainment and escapism. If my primary theory of literature is that it should be seen as entertainment and escapism, I will not have a very high opinion of those works that do not immediately entertain or those works that deal with unpleasant subject matter. If I hold the former theory, that literature can preserve and communicate complex, important ideas, then I will not necessarily be looking for entertainment from every text. So I may have a broader acceptance of subject matter and style than the reader who is looking for entertainment.

When we approach a text with a particular critical theory, we read with a set of ideas in our heads, which we then apply to the text. If I believe that the only valuable literature is that which focuses only on the pleasant aspects of life, I will be highly suspicious of texts that deal with the confrontation and moral ambiguity we often find in life. If I believe that stories should serve first and foremost as models of behavior, then my response to texts will depend on how admirable a story's characters are. A story that ends with the bad guys winning will strike me as particularly weak and poorly executed, even dangerous and irresponsible.

As Chapter 3 will make clear, there is a variety of sophisticated theories we will likely encounter as we become better readers and students of literature. We may even adopt one of these theories to guide us through a lifetime of reading. In the meantime, it is important to understand that we likely have already developed theories that guide us as we attempt to comprehend or judge texts.

BEFORE YOU READ
Establishing a Reading Context in the Classroom

One skill needed to read effectively as a student in a literature class is recognizing how reading as a student is different than reading as a "civilian." Students in a literature course are having their reading directed by the professor, the reading list, the English department's policy, the editors of literature anthologies, and any number of other factors. These limitations may seem severe, and certainly we would all rather be left alone. However, it is worthwhile to think about what factors exist in a literature class that we might actually be able to take advantage of as we attempt to become better readers (and hopefully A students as well).

TAKING ADVANTAGE OF AVAILABLE RESOURCES
Your Syllabus

Imagine you have just been given a reading assignment. It is your first day in your literature class and you are still getting your bearings. You have every reason to believe that you will be asked to demonstrate your mastery of the reading you have been assigned. You may be asked to write an essay, you may be facing a pop quiz, perhaps an eventual midterm or final exam. This is not an exercise in pleasure reading. Even if you end up enjoying the literature, you know that this is, as we have said, work. Before you begin reading, then, it benefits you to familiarize yourself with the assignment, your texts, and your instructor's expectations.

First, what is the precise nature of the assignment? Have you been asked to take notes or prepare questions for the next day? Check the syllabus. Is there a paper due a week or so down the road? It benefits you to consider that your professor may have a broader plan in mind than an isolated reading assignment. Has the syllabus been divided thematically? Is it arranged chronologically or by some other method? Is there no syllabus at all? Have you been asked to read anything else besides the poem, short story, or novel? Does the text provide an introduction or a short biography of the author? Pay attention to any ancillary reading material that may shed light on the major assignments.

KNOW YOUR TEXTBOOKS

Have you purchased the assigned text or have you picked up a different edition? Sometimes students save a little money by buying or borrowing older editions or used copies of a text from a different publishing house. Make sure that your edition is not substantially different from that which the professor ordered for the class. For instance, if you are expected to read the introduction to the book, you may need to borrow a classmate's copy and photocopy the necessary pages. That information may show up on an exam, but more importantly, it may give you a necessary insight into the literature.

Are you reading individual paperback novels or are you working from an anthology of some sort? If the latter, check the appendices. Does the book feature a glossary or advice on reading and writing about literature? Some students can go an entire semester without realizing how many useful materials are right at their fingertips.

Useful Resources Found in Many Literary Texts

Afterword.   An afterword is a short addition or concluding section at the end of a literary work, often dealing with the future of its characters. This is also called an epilogue. An afterword may also be commentary by the author about the work and its composition.

Appendices.   An appendix is a collection of supplementary material, usually at the end of a book. Many of the items on this list would be found in an appendix.

Author Biographies.   Often, anthologies and other texts offer short introductions to each author whose work is included in the book. These biographical sketches offer insight into the author's experience but also often give the novice some idea of the critical reputation of the author and the text in question. Does this person write funny stories? Horror stories? Did she write during the Enlightenment? Is he a southerner? Also, these little essays often contain a bibliography of criticism, which may be helpful when it is time to do a research paper. The biographies often precede the work of the author in question, but they may also be included as an appendix.

Bibliography. A good anthology will often include a bibliography in the appendix or following each writer's work. When assigned a research paper on a given writer or period of literary history, students may balk at the legwork that faces them: the library catalog, the book stacks, and electronic databases. However, one can often begin research without leaving the classroom. For example, Emory Elliott's *American Literature: A Prentice Hall Anthology* features a short "Suggested Readings" list after the introductory essay discussing each author. The list for poet Hart Crane includes editions of Crane's poetry for further reading of the poetry as well as several titles of biographies and studies of the poet's work, dating from the twenties to the present.

Footnotes (or Endnotes). These are short notes that explain or comment on the text. Most anthologies that cover literature across historical periods contain footnotes. Although they may seem distracting, footnotes offer quick definitions of obscure or antiquated terms or translations of foreign words and phrases. Although readers often complain of intrusive notes in texts such as Shakespeare's plays, few can deny that it is helpful to have a handy reference to Elizabethan culture at your fingertips while perusing the bard's work.

Glossary. A glossary is an alphabetical listing of difficult terms often included in textbooks and anthologies of literature. A glossary is a useful tool to expedite the reading of difficult texts.

Index. An alphabetical list of important topics treated in a text, an index is often found in textbooks and also included in other kinds of books. The index is often an overlooked resource in research. Imagine you are writing a paper about Puritan writers in America. You want to discuss the family lives of these people, but you do not have time to read an entire book about the history of the colonial era. Turn to the index and look for key words that may be related to your topic: *family, children, marriage,* and so forth. This way, you read only the sections you have time for and only the sections most likely to be of service to you and your topic.

Introduction. An essay preceding the main body of a book, the introduction states an author's (or editor's) major theme.

Sometimes an introduction will be supplied by someone other than the author. In the case of a classic work of literature, the introduction may be supplied by a scholar who has studied the work in question. Such an introduction may feature not only commentary on the text but the names of other scholarly texts about the work in question. An introduction is often a useful summary not only of the work it introduces but also of the critical history of that work. Therefore, the introduction is a useful tool for the student embarking on a term paper. In a work such as an anthology of literature each selection is often preceded by a short introductory essay, which introduces the author, offers a brief biography, a summary of the author's career, and a commentary on the work included in the anthology. Again, although often ignored by students, this introductory essay can be invaluable to the reader confronted with a difficult piece or a work written in an era with which the student is unfamiliar.

Table of Contents.   A list of the chapters in a textbook or works in an anthology is found in the table of contents. We learned about this in the first grade, but we often forget how important a table of contents can be in helping us navigate a text. This is especially true when we are doing research for an essay. In such a case, we are not expected to read the entire book but to merely seek the information pertinent to our topic. In this day of the Internet, we often forget that books have long been designed to be user friendly. Like the index, the table of contents is a print equivalent of an Internet search engine.

Considering Historical and Biographical Contexts

Much of the information contained in these introductions, footnotes, and so forth, speak to the historical and biographical contexts of the literature they discuss. You may want to consider when the work you are reading was written and what is known about the author. It is important to mention here that some people will tell you that such information is not necessary for an understanding of a literary text. In fact, they will argue, it could be detrimental because such background information may create self-fulfilling expectations in the mind of the reader. For instance, if you are reading Jane Eyre by Charlotte Brontë, you may say, "Oh, that's a woman's book" or "That's a Victorian novel" and set about to look for only the women's or Victorian issues in the book. Is Allen Ginsberg's "Howl" a gay poem? A Jewish poem? A Beat poem? Such hard and fast, all-encompassing labels are indeed limiting.

On the other hand, if you are reading a work of literature that is one or two hundred (or more) years old, you should be ready for some obvious problems with the language of the text and the manners of the characters. Of course, the meanings of words change from era to era. Anyone who has studied Shakespeare knows that his plays are filled with double entendres and bawdy humor. However, much of that humor is lost on the reader not familiar with Elizabethans' pronunciation and their fascination with puns on *cuckold*.

For instance, *Much Ado About Nothing* contains the following exchange between Beatrice, her cousin Hero, and Hero's servant Margaret:

HERO: These gloves the Count sent me, they are an excellent perfume.
BEATRICE: I am stuff'd, cousin, I cannot smell.
MARGARET: A maid and stuff'd! There's goodly catching of a cold! (III.iv. 64–66)

Did you catch the "naughty" play on "stuff'd"? No? Well, it is easy to miss. Fortunately, most editions of Shakespeare include footnotes that explain such passages. The reader of Shakespeare would do well to recall that although Shakespeare's works are nearly universal in their commentary on human relationships, their language is rooted in a very specific time and place that was very different from our own. Taking some time to consider the historical context of a literary work is often necessary for us to fully comprehend and appreciate the text.

READING IN CONTEXT

In Chapter 1, I mention the professor who looks forward to summer reading so she can put down her pen. But why is she holding a pen in the first place? Consider the student in the writing center, the one who read but "not for comprehension." I asked to see the assignment sheet the professor had given to the class. He could not find it, but he knew he was supposed to compare the story to another story. Which story? He was not sure. How long was the paper supposed to be? When was it due? Was it to be written to a specific audience? Should he mention the ideas that had come up previously in class? Did he need to do any research? Did he need to produce a rough draft with his paper? Did it have to be written in MLA format or APA or some other documentation format?

Before the student sat down to read, what questions could he have asked to prepare himself for the task of reading? When was this story written? Who wrote it? Why was it assigned? Did the professor say anything in class to prepare the students? Had the student taken any notes in class?

Not all professors give students written directions for such assignments, but those who do are giving the class specific ideas of what the students ought to do and of how the professor will grade the papers. Such a resource could become an important part of a student's *reading* as well as his or her *writing*. Even the professor's in-class comments are important and should be written down during class so they can be examined in detail later on.

Approaching a text with some kind of context gives the reader a focus even if the story or poem is difficult to read. A student reading T. S. Eliot's notoriously difficult poem, *The Waste Land* (1922), may well be baffled and bewildered the first time through, but if the student has been told in class to look for "water imagery," then at least he or she has a focus for note taking and class discussion.

Our student struggles through the poem, dutifully reading the footnotes and generally feeling lost. She reads a few lines that are particularly confusing:

> Madame Sosostris, Famous clairvoyante,
> Had a bad cold, nevertheless
> Is known to be the wisest woman in Europe,
> With a wicked pack of cards. Here, said she
> Is your card, the drowned Phoenician Sailor.
> (Those are pearls that were in his eyes. Look!)

"What's going on here?" our student wonders. "The characters keep changing, and I'm lost." But she makes a note in her margin about the "Phoenician Sailor." Sailors work on the ocean; does that count as water imagery? And wait, a few lines later, "Fear death by water." Although she's not ready to write a paper about the poem, by using her class notes, she is able to start reading the poem with somewhat of a critical eye. And she will have at least one question for class tomorrow.

If she had not taken note of the professor's comment about water imagery, she would have felt even more lost in the poem. Now she knows what to look for in preparation for tomorrow's class discussion and lecture. Having a specific guide like that can be invaluable to the student dealing with a difficult text. Take advantage of it!

Imagery

Imagery is a term frequently used in literary analysis and discussion. It seems a fairly straightforward term, but what does it mean? Is it just another word for description? Kathleen Morner and

Ralph Rausch say imagery is "the making of 'pictures with words,' the pictorial quality of a literary work achieved through a collection of images. In a broader sense, *imagery* is often used as synonymous with figure of speech or figurative language (simile, metaphor, or symbol)."[4]

When we speak of imagery, we are not discussing just description, the physical facts we need to understand the action of a story. (For example, did the killer walk with a limp? Was the sky overcast the morning before the big storm that shipwrecked our hero?) Imagery tends to denote the more figurative turns of phrase in literature, language that gives us an emotional or metaphorical "picture" of something as well as a physical picture.

ANNOTATING LITERARY TEXTS

through the senses (me)

Back to our noncomprehender: The pages of his short story collection were a pristine white! The only marks on the page were the words of the short story he was asked to read. Had this student stopped to underline a character's name or at least jot the occasional "huh?" in the margin, he would have remembered *something* about the story and he would have been ready to start working on his paper rather than to start rereading the story in a quiet corner of the writing lab.

Reading is an interpretive act, even if the texts we read are not "literary" texts, such as the James Bond novel we discussed earlier. The words on the page are composed of letters, which are visual symbols intended to stir in our memories the sounds we know are associated with them. *S* makes a "ssss" sound, *T* makes a "tuh" sound, and so on. When we read, we put these symbols together unconsciously and create words, which are themselves symbols. Our minds decipher these symbols as well, and the text "speaks" to us. All of these complicated processes unfold in the twinkling of an eye as we scan the page. Still, as this process indicates, reading is a complicated task. If we choose to read a sophisticated text, such as a poem, novel, or play, we complicate this process further. Now we need to consider why characters act the way they do, why settings are described as they are, and perhaps why certain elements that ought to be present are not.

If we wish to make sense of complicated texts, we need to do more than look at the words; we need to interact with them. Annotating a literary text allows us to reinforce the words themselves and our responses to them. Consider the

[4]Kathleen Morner and Ralph Rausch, *NTC's Dictionary of Literary Terms* (Chicago: NTC, 1991), p. 105.

mechanics of annotation. When we read a text without a pen or pencil in hand, we can get quite a bit out of the text. When we read with a pen or pencil, underlining confusing or interesting passages, we essentially read and reread at the same time. Our experience of the text is doubled. Most students in literature classes have had the experience of slogging through a long piece of prose or poetry only to realize in class that they cannot remember a single detail from the work in question. As class goes on and other students talk and the professor asks questions, the work comes back but never as vividly or quickly as we might like.

Many of those same students can also testify to another kind of reading experience. Imagine being in the same situation; you've done the reading (without annotating) but because of overwork, a tight schedule, and a tough reading selection, you remember nothing of the piece. Class begins, however, not with discussion but with the class writing a journal entry. You begin with a few hems and haws, but after a while, you write a journal entry that is part summary and part reaction. Class discussion follows, but this time, you not only understand most of it, you manage to contribute to it.

You discovered that *writing* can be an integral part of *reading*. The act of writing can be a powerful learning tool. Writing an in-class journal entry can help you remember and even understand a difficult reading assignment. In the same way, writing notes (in your text or notebook) to yourself or as you read can help you not only remember but more fully understand the text you read. And, of course, we all know that writing can be a tool to enhance learning as well as a way to demonstrate how much we have learned. Think of how often you have been asked to complete writing assignments that seemed too elemental to be of any use. How often have you ended up learning something writing those annoying little papers?

Some Guidelines for Annotating a Literary Text

When I was an undergraduate student, a professor told my class that we had to write in the margins of our books if we ever wanted to learn anything.

But I really did not know how to write in my books. The professor had passed around a photocopied page of one of his books, and his margin notes struck me as profoundly on the mark. In the margin of his book were the very issues and ideas he had mentioned in class. How could I match this brilliance? Well, I realized that since I was not teaching the class I would not have to. My notes only had to be for me. So I gave it a try. My attempts ended up in two particular kinds of failure. The first was that on some readings, *nothing* struck me as important enough to underline, and the second was that on other readings, *everything* struck me as important enough to underline.

So, I had to finesse my note taking. Eventually, I came to the conclusion that there were at least four categories of information worthy of annotation by the serious reader. These four categories can be summed up in the following questions:

What is confusing?

What is repeated?

What is familiar?

What is strange?

What Is Confusing?

Often we can react to a new literary text by feeling as if we are just not intelligent enough to understand it. Other times we may feel that the author and his or her supporters are the ones who are not quite so bright. Ask any graduate student who has just looked into *Ulysses* for the first time; it is a common reaction. Why is this so hard? Am I dumb? What is wrong with me?

Too often, readers dismiss these questions, but such reactions are honest and valuable. We can pursue these immediate reactions until we find exactly what it is about this particular text we are having trouble with. Is it the diction? Are there words we do not recognize or that are being used in an unfamiliar way? Is it the author's style? Is this text written in an experimental style? Is it possible that the author wants the readers to be a little confused at a certain point in the text? Is there something about the setting we need to know? If this is a novel about deep-sea fishing, is there some way we can familiarize ourselves with the jargon of this profession? Was the text written at some point in the recent or distant past? Are we missing what the author assumed would be some obvious topical references?

If we do not understand a particular text, there are likely specific reasons for this confusion. If we simply give up and say, "This book stinks," or "I'm dumb," we abandon an important resource: our own confusion, and yes, even our own ignorance. Both of these so-called "deficits" can help us to become better readers.

I was teaching a poem by Walt Whitman to a classroom full of tired, anxious students nearing the ends of their ropes and the end of the semester. One student, exasperated with the poetry, told me that Whitman was just no good and that his poem "Crossing Brooklyn Ferry" just did not make any sense. "What do you mean?" I asked. "Where in the poem does he not make sense?" The student pointed to one line and read "It avails not, time nor place—distance avails not." "That doesn't make any sense," he said. So I asked him, "What does 'avails' mean?" He said, "I dunno."

What do you think? Is this why the poem made no sense to him, or is it just that Whitman really is a no-talent poet and the world was just waiting for this student to point that out? Once we defined the word, the line began to make sense to the student. That does not mean that the entire poem unfolded before him in that instant, but it was a start.

When reading a literary work, it is important for us to make a distinction between writing that makes no sense because of what is lacking in the work and writing that makes no sense because of what is missing in our vocabulary and experience. In this case, given Whitman's status as a world-famous poet (often considered America's finest), it seems only fair to give him a chance. It was a bit silly for my student to decide that, since he did not "get" one poem, he would write Whitman off as a rotten poet. He may decide after reading Whitman's poetry that the praise is undeserved, but the man's reputation at least demands that we look for what is valuable in the text.

Earlier in this chapter we defined and talked about interpretation. Part of our definition of that term focused on "especially obscure, ambiguous, or figurative passages." We discussed other issues regarding interpretation and we will talk about more later. Right now, let us consider the importance of the stuff we barely understand. When I was a high school student, we were asked to read selections from *Beowulf* and Chaucer's *Canterbury Tales*. As you might imagine, we were not terribly thrilled with these assignments. Both of these works were written in a language that only slightly resembled our own twentieth-century American English. In other words, we were dumbfounded.

Our teacher made us do all the reading, but he also gave us little treats. Our textbook gave us Beowulf and Chaucer. The teacher gave us public readings with translations and commentary. I remember when he described Beowulf ripping the arm off of the monster Grendel. Not satisfied with the text of the poem, he stopped to add details about snapping bones and ripping muscles. I admit that as a high school boy, I loved snapping bones and ripping muscles.

When it came time to read Chaucer, we got the added treat of his reading of "The Miller's Tale," notorious as one of the dirtiest of the *Canterbury Tales.* Again, we got the story and all the translations so we could follow all of the action and understand all the scatological humor.

What was really wonderful about this teacher was that he made it perfectly acceptable for us to admit that we did not understand the texts we were reading. Better still, he explained it all to us. Unfortunately, such a teacher cannot be at our sides throughout our reading lives. It is our job to pay enough attention to a text so that we know exactly where we get lost in a text.

It makes perfect sense that a reader will not understand everything he or she comes across, especially the texts that are assigned and, therefore, are not the ones we necessarily want to read. Also, many works of literature are famous for their experimental qualities; some texts, such as Joyce's *Ulysses,* are famous for confusing people who have devoted their lives to literature. It is not incumbent upon every reader to "get" every book stuck under his or her nose, nor is it incumbent upon us to like them once they are explained.

However, careful readers can unlock texts that confuse them by becoming more—rather than less—engaged with these confusing texts (and passages in texts).

What Is Repeated?

For the student beginning to think about annotating a text, one thing that we can look for in a text, regardless of our relationship to the text or how much background we do or do not have on it, is the development of *patterns* in the text. This is a pretty vague term, and that is fine because we are looking for any kind of pattern: a key word that gets repeated, a kind of imagery that shows up more than once, patterns of character behavior, recurring names, similar settings or activities associated with some character or object mentioned in the work.

Think broadly about art and you may find that patterns are an important part of most kinds of art. Surreal and abstract painting is often jarring because it does not give us the patterns we enjoy.

Music relies on patterns. A rock and roll song without a strong beat might end up sounding like a lot of noise. A song with a strong beat but no melody will get stuck in your head for days. The patterns within an individual work of art are

sometimes so subtle as to be invisible. A painting of a group
of soldiers raising a flag will no doubt contain many lines
pointing to the flag: the colonel's arm as he points to the
oncoming troops, the arc of an explosion, the flagpole itself.
You may not consciously notice it, but the pattern of lines
pointing to the flag has gotten your attention.

Or think about a heavy metal song that opens up with a
barrage of screeching guitars. Why are we not surprised?
Because we know this pattern, the guitar solo, the cacoph-
ony of the drums, soon the singer will begin to attack family values. Do you think the video will feature explosions?
Patterns come in many guises.

These kinds of patterns point to the conventions of the
form. We know how heavy metal songs work because they
all sort of do the same thing. That is why we can identify
some songs as "heavy metal songs." But what if the song
broke off into some quiet, subdued strings? What if the singer
began to list his favorite Disney films or sing about the political situation in Luxembourg? We would be taken aback
because a familiar pattern had been disrupted. One pattern
is specific to the form in question: loud guitar noises replaced
with subdued strings—we stop and look at the stereo speaker. What happened? Another pattern broken deals with subject matter: international politics from a party band? What
is this? Perhaps "The Guns of Luxembourg" will not end
up as our all-time favorite metal tune, but it sure got our
attention.

The same is true in literature—only without the loud guitars. Patterns build genres, patterns build individual works,
patterns keep our attention. The disruption of these patterns
can shock us out of quiet reverie into more intense observation. Let us read the Emily Dickinson poem "A Bird came
down the Walk" (also known as poem #328, ca. 1862) with
the idea of the importance of patterns in mind.

Assume we have been asked to read some of Emily
Dickinson's poetry for the purpose of writing an explication
paper, that is, a paper that attempts to make plain some
of the more subtle meanings of a poem. As M. H. Abrams
said, "to interpret a work of literature is to *specify the meanings of its language by analysis, paraphrase, and commentary.*"[5] So, our paper will not be an exhaustive research
project attempting to place Emily Dickinson's poems into
some specific historical or critical tradition. We do not need
to compare her work to that of another poet or to tell our

[5]Abrams, loc. cit., p. 127.

reader what the poem has to say about the Battle of Fort
Sumter or the Industrial Revolution. We just need to write
down what the poem seems to be saying to us. Sounds simple enough, right?

> A Bird came down the Walk—
> He did not know I saw—
> He bit an Angelworm in halves
> And ate the fellow, raw,
>
> And then he drank a Dew
> From a convenient Grass—
> And then hopped sidewise to the Wall
> To let a Beetle pass—
>
> He glanced with rapid eyes
> That hurried all around—
> They looked like frightened Beads, I thought—
> He stirred his Velvet Head
>
> Like one in danger, Cautious,
> I offered him a crumb
> And he unrolled his feathers
> And rowed him softer home—
>
> Than Oars divide the Ocean,
> Too silver for a seam—
> Or Butterflies, off Banks of Noon
> Leap, plashless as they swim

A first reading of this poem may remind us why Dickinson
has managed to get her reputation as a difficult poet. Only
one word, *plashless,* seems unfamiliar. And even if our footnote had not told us that it meant "splashless," we would
have gotten that soon enough, right? So we understand all
the words—what is the problem? Something about the poem
defies an immediate interpretation. We can look at the poem
again—stanza by stanza—this time with our pens ready to
annotate the poem.

Denotation/Connotation

When we talk about what a word *means,* there are actually at
least two kinds of meaning we need to discuss: denotative and
connotative. The *denotative* meaning of a word refers to the precise or literal meaning of a word, without emotional baggage or
popular associations. When we talk of *connotative* meanings, we
talk of the meanings that have come to be associated with the
word or the images it may conjure up in a reader's mind.

*images

For instance, the words *gay* and *awesome* have in recent years picked up connotative meanings so strong that many people have trouble imagining using the words denotatively. Do we use *gay* to denote happiness anymore? Is a new action movie *awesome* in the same sense that an erupting volcano is?

Again, Morner and Rausch neatly sum up the importance of this distinction: "Scientists attempt to hold words to their precise meanings; writers, especially poets, rely on connotations to evoke responses in their readers."[6] To read literature—especially poetry—we want to be sensitive to the connotative meanings of words. In "When Lilacs Last in the Dooryard Bloom'd," his poem for President Lincoln, Walt Whitman writes,

> Ever returning spring, trinity sure to me you bring,
> Lilac blooming perennial and drooping star in the west,
> And thought of him I love.

Denotatively Whitman has made a simple point. In the spring, three events occur: lilacs bloom, Venus is visible in the western skies, and we mark the anniversary of Lincoln's April murder. But why use the word *trinity* (so rich in religious meaning) if not to elevate Lincoln in our imagination? The connotative meaning of *trinity* reinforces the estimation Whitman has of the slain president. This is no mere secular figure but a man almost divine. And Whitman manages to say all this with one word.

How does an intelligent reader handle the issue of denotation and connotation in a literary text? Pick up a dictionary! Often a text that seems inscrutable can be made to open up if we understand the author's diction both denotatively and connotatively. As we said about the line from another Whitman poem, "It avails not, time nor place—distance avails not." If we do not know what *avails* means, we cannot be expected to understand what the poet wants us to think about time and distance. Before we reject a poem as meaningless, we need to consider the possibility that we, the readers are at fault, not the poet. In fact, one of the great values of literature is that it increases not just our vocabulary but our ability to articulate the experiences of our lives: It gives us language, metaphor, simile, symbol, and other tools to express ourselves.

Here we should comment on the value of rereading a work of literature. As we have already commented, a literary work is not like a newspaper article or work of general nonfiction. If a newspaper report does not seem clear to us upon a first reading, we can consider the article something

---

[6]Morner and Rausch, loc. cit., p. 44.

of a failure. Its task is to deliver information quickly and efficiently. That is not the job of literature. Works of real literary value reveal more and more to us upon subsequent readings.

If a first reading leaves us cold, we owe it to the work and to ourselves to take a second look. Why do we owe it to the work? In the case of Emily Dickinson, we are dealing with an artist of the highest order, someone whose poetry is celebrated the world over. Does that mean we have to like it? No, but since so many have gotten so much from her poems, it seems they deserve at least a second reading. Why do we owe it to ourselves? Also, great poetry challenges the reader. Dickinson stimulates our curiosity. Hopefully, a complete reading of the poem will give us a greater insight into the poet, into nature, or even into ourselves. And then there is the issue of that paper we have to write.

> A Bird came down the Walk—
> He did not know I saw—   *weird punctuation*
> He bit an Angelworm in halves
> And ate the fellow, <u>raw</u>,   *nasty word choice*

speaker is not seen by bird

There does not seem to be much in this stanza to annotate. But Dickinson is using rhyme, and that limits her word choice quite a bit. With this in mind, it seems that every detail must be in the poem for a reason. A poet working under tight formal rules has to work hard to make every line fit not just the content of her expression but the form as well. So, the line "He did not know I saw" rates a comment, since most of the stanza is about the bird and this line is really more about the speaker. A pattern is established and broken really in just the first four lines. The second comment, about the word *raw,* does not really speak to patterns, but the word jumps off the page and catches our reader's attention. But, all in all, the stanza makes sense: The speaker is out in a park or garden (there is a "walk" here, implying a man-made locale). She sees a bird eat a worm.

> And then he drank a <u>Dew</u>   *why the uppercase letters?*
> From a convenient <u>Grass</u>—
> And then hopped sidewise to the <u>Wall</u>
> To let a <u>Beetle</u> pass—

doesn't eat the beetle

these 2 stanzas are very straightforward descriptions of simple actions

Again, this stanza is very straightforward. As our reader felt a little confused on reading the whole poem without taking notes, he makes a little note on the simplicity of the first two stanzas. If the individual stanzas are so easy

to read, why is the whole poem such a mystery? The only
other note he makes is that the bird does not eat the beetle. This seems a little odd because up until now the bird has
only been seen eating and drinking. Again, a pattern seems
disrupted.

> He glanced with rapid eyes   *not eating—looking*
> That hurried all around—
> *speaker isn't*   They looked like frightened
> *sure*   Beads, I thought—
> He stirred his Velvet Head   *simile: "like"*
>   *no rhyme!*

Interesting. This stanza makes us aware of a pattern we
had not really paid attention to before: the poem's rhyme.
In this stanza, the familiar *a-b-a-b-c-d-c-d* pattern ("walk[*a*]-
saw[*b*]-halves[*a*]-raw[*b*]" in stanza 1 and "dew[*c*]-grass[*d*]-
to[*c*]-pass[*d*]" in stanza 2) is gone! Also, the poet uses a
simile—the first use of figurative language in the poem. The
poet also makes us aware that this simile implies the speaker's first sense of confusion: "I thought," she says in the stanza's third line. Up until now, the poem has been all solid
observation. We were never told what the speaker "thought"
happened but what actually did happen. This stanza breaks
some of the poem's patterns: rhyme to unrhymed verse, descriptive language to figurative language, direct observation
to the speaker's opinion of the scene before her.

> *who's in danger? bird*   Like one in <u>danger</u>, Cautious,   *another simile*
> *or speaker?*   I offered him a crumb
> *"unrolled?"*   And he <u>unrolled</u> his feathers
> *third simile—weird*   And <u>rowed</u> him softer home—   *still doesn't*
> *one—do birds "row?"*   *rhyme*

Another interesting stanza—the new patterns continue.
Another stanza of unrhymed verse. This stanza is also filled
with figurative language—two more similes. And like the last
stanza, we get the feeling the speaker is not sure of what
she sees. In the previous stanza she tells us she "thought"
the bird's eyes looked like frightened beads. In this stanza,
she continues to tell us what the bird is "like," not what it
is. Also, the similes are strange. The bird "unrolls" his feath-
ers? He "rows" home? There is nothing wrong with these
images, but they are a little unusual.

Finally, there is an unclear line here. Who is "Like one in
danger, Cautious," the bird or the speaker? Up until now,
each stanza has been a complete unit, like a paragraph. But
the first line of this stanza may be a continuation of the last
line of the previous stanza. But maybe not, too.

fourth simile   <u>Than</u> Oars divide the Ocean,   *stanza not as*
                                                                       structured as first

fifth simile—   Too silver for a seam—   *simile? what kind of seam?*
another simile?   Or <u>Butterflies</u>, off Banks of Noon   *simile? What*
                                                                                banks?

                         Leap, <u>plashless</u> as they swim   *butterflies a*
                                                            metaphor, not a simile.
                                                       Swimming butterflies?

Are the "banks of noon" the sky? that's where butterflies swim.
This poem changes as it goes along. It starts out very easy to
read and ends very hard to figure out. I get the feeling that about midway
through, the speaker starts to get confused or upset about something.

Notice that the poem begins with very few comments
from our reader, but at the end it is covered with comments.
Something is going on here. For one thing, this stanza definitely begins with a "broken" line—one that refers to the action of the previous stanza. "Than Oars divide the Ocean"
is the continuation of the last line of the fourth stanza, describing the bird's wings. So the final three stanzas, unlike
the first two, are not complete units; their meaning sort of
leaches into each other. This change in the poem's structure coincides with some other changes that occur in the
third stanza: the rhyme disappears, description is replaced
with simile and metaphor. Also, the speaker is generally less
sure of herself in the third stanza.

The whole stanza seems to be a metaphor based on the
"oars" comment. The bird vanishes more quickly than a boat,
which would leave a "seam" or a "wake" in the water. Why
the unusual metaphors? Why not just come right out and say
that the bird vanished without a trace?

So far our explication paper is looking pretty good, especially when we consider that our first reading of the poem
ended with confusion. We may not have a general interpretation of the poem, but we have detected a shift in the poem's
tone, and we only managed to make this observation by
rereading and annotating the text of the poem. As our reader notes in his final comment, "about midway through, the
speaker starts to get confused or upset about something."
So we can say in our explication paper that the poem is about
the shift of the speaker's attitude from one of certainty to
one of uncertainty, and that this shift occurs in stanza 3,
when the rhyme disappears. Therefore, we can say, the
rhyme—when it occurs—gives the speaker one kind of tone.
When it vanishes, another tone appears. What happens in
that third stanza that is so significant? Maybe a third reading will give us something solid to go on.

> He glanced with rapid eyes   *not eating—looking*
> That hurried all around—
> *speaker isn't*   They looked like frightened <u>B</u>eads, I thought—
> *sure*
>
> *simile: "like"*   He stirred his <u>V</u>elvet <u>H</u>ead   *no rhyme!*

The bird sees something it seems—at least the focus is on its eyes. What could it see? Perhaps the speaker. Remember in the first stanza, we noted that the bird "did not know [she] saw"? Our reader made a note of that right off, although it did not seem particularly important at the time. What difference does it make if the bird knows it is watched? What has the bird done? It eats a worm, drinks some dew, and lets a beetle pass. Our reader considers that none of this seems terribly important. But then nothing else in the poem seems very important. A bird eats some bugs, sees a person on the walk, and flies away. So what? But the *speaker* thought it was important enough to comment on watching the bird in the first place. Could the bird represent something? The speaker goes out and observes nature. Does the bird represent nature?

What does the speaker learn about nature that is disturbing by the third stanza? That some things live and other things die for no other reason than that a bird is or is not hungry? Why should the speaker care about the lives of bugs, unless we assume the bugs represent something greater than just bugs. Could the speaker be upset because she has seen death in nature and finds it random? Does the bird's action make the speaker feel more or less connected to some kind of natural order? Well, it flies away when it sees her, "like one in danger," so it must see the speaker as an enemy. Is this a poem about the speaker's realization that nature is violent, and that it may not want her to know all its secrets? Maybe that idea of nature concealing its secrets has something to do with the curiously opaque nature of the metaphors at the end of the poem.

That seems to work with our reading of the other elements of the poem: the speaker is confused and upset, and all because the bird spotted her in stanza 3. Our reader's annotation and rereading of the poem have revealed to him a possible paper topic for a poem he originally found too murky to make sense of. The focus on patterns gave our reader somewhere to start with his annotation. But could he have used a different focus for his note taking?

What Is Familiar?

We have seen how annotating can work when a reader focuses on patterns. But, obviously, there are other foci one can choose when annotating literature. For instance, a reader can look for *familiar* elements in a literary work. Edgar Allan Poe wrote in "The Philosophy of Composition" that originality is an "obvious and . . . easily attainable source of interest." If Poe is right and originality is not only essential for good literature but is also easy to attain, how do we explain the fact that writers return to familiar material again and again? We have discussed patterns already; since patterns demand repetition, one might argue that the existence of patterns of any kind in literature is an example of a kind of unoriginality. The existence of genres implies a kind of lack of originality. All Westerns, or all science fiction stories, or all tragedies obviously share traits.

In fact, Poe is not the only one who demands originality in writing. How many times have you heard a teacher tell students to be original and avoid repetition in their writing? When a writer repeats himself or herself to create a pattern, that writer can be called repetitious. Pursuing such patterns is running the risk of losing readers. In other ways, writers are "unoriginal" in their work. They recycle plots and character types, they refer to works they hope their readers are familiar with, and they refer to names and locales readers should already know. Should we condemn writers for being unoriginal, or should we congratulate them for being able to recycle so much without us noticing?

Aside from patterns, a careful reader will hunt for material that is *familiar* in a work. The material may be familiar because the writer is repeating something that has already occurred in the work or because the writer is evoking some element that almost always occurs in a certain genre of writing, or because the author is making an allusion to some text or event.

As we become more knowledgeable readers, allusions will become easier to spot. In the meantime there are often footnotes in texts that point us to allusions. In-class discussion may also shed light on allusions. It is safe to say, for instance, that if an instructor mentions an allusion in class, she thinks it is a significant detail in the text. Why not jot it down in the margin of your text? At the very least, it may show up on the dreaded exam!

Allusion

First of all, it is not an "illusion," so watch your spelling and do not trust your spellcheck! An allusion is a passing or implicit reference to something outside the text. Usually, an allusion takes one of several forms:

1. A reference to another work of literature.
2. A reference to a passage of scripture.
3. A reference to an historical event or personage.
4. A reference to mythology.
5. A reference to the author's own life or experience.

The presence of allusion in a work of literature can be significant to the meaning of the work. An allusion not only transmits a good deal of information in a relatively small package, it tells us something of whom the author considers his or her audience to be. Obviously, an author who relies heavily on allusion is writing to an audience composed of serious readers. For instance, T. S. Eliot's *The Waste Land* refers to Shakespeare, Greek myth, the plays of Sophocles, Hindu sacred writing, and the plays of Thomas Kyd among other texts. In fact, most current editions of *The Waste Land* feature footnotes that identify the various references in the poem. A reader who has not read these other works may feel left out by all of these footnotes and wonder if Eliot is being elitist with all of this word play.

But we can just as easily suggest that Eliot is being very economical. At one point in the poem, Eliot tells us that the speaker is "Tireseus." Readers of Sophocles' *Oedipus Rex* know that Tireseus is a blind seer. Rather than create his own character, a project that may take many lines of poetry, Eliot is able to communicate all an informed reader needs to know with a name. Additionally, the name "Tireseus" evokes a sense of age and majesty, elevating his own poem in the reader's estimation.

Similarly, the use of an allusion can communicate volumes about a character or locale, predicting much of a work's action to come. For instance, in Nathaniel Hawthorne's "Rappaccini's Daughter," we are introduced to a young Italian student named Giovanni Guasconti. In the first paragraph of the tale, Giovanni arrives in Padua and takes a room in a tower. We are told little about the setting, but we are told this:

> The young stranger, who was not unstudied in the great poem of his country, recollected that one of the ancestors of this family, and perhaps an occupant of this very mansion, had been pictured by Dante as a partaker of the immortal agonies of his Inferno.

Why would Hawthorne tell us this rather than give us a simple description of the room? Of all the things to mention, why begin by pointing out that the room brings to mind Dante's *Inferno?* Knowing that a former occupant of these rooms had essentially been condemned to Hell, a reader of this story can effectively predict just how pleasant young Giovanni's stay is likely to be. Hawthorne drops the seed with the reader and counts on the readers to cultivate it in their imaginations.

ARCHETYPES

Another kind of "familiar face" we might search for may be called an *archetype*. Archetypes allow us to tell the same stories again and again, with minor changes of location and character names, of course, but the stories do not change much: the young hero learns to be selfless, the courageous explorer goes where no man has gone before, the forces of good square off against the forces of evil, stodgy family traditions separate young lovers who ultimately die for their love, the father recognizes his son's bravery on his deathbed. We see them everywhere, from myths to epic poems to dramas to children's cartoons.

Astute readers spot these archetypes as they appear and, therefore, can make judgments regarding a work's themes. If the cowboy wears a white hat, we expect him to be a good guy. If he acts like a good guy, we sit back and enjoy a retelling of a familiar story. If he murders the schoolmarm, we jump up in our seats and pay renewed attention to this new twist on an old formula.

To stick with the Western example, think of Clint Eastwood in *Unforgiven*. As we sit down to watch the film, we know a few things. In films such as *Shane* and *The Gunfighter*, screen icons such as Alan Ladd and Gregory Peck have established the legend of the "reluctant gunfighter," the hero who is so good at what he does that he cannot avoid the violence of the West. Inevitably, he is drawn into this world of violence, but we can count on him to act with honor and heroism. In *Unforgiven*, we meet a similar character— and he is played by another screen legend. We know big box-office stars only play good guys, so we think we know what we are in for. However, this hero consistently disappoints and ultimately threatens violence against the families of his enemies. The careful "reader" of this "text" might have expected such deviations from the norm when our hero is hired to protect the "honor" of a group of prostitutes, and when he accepts money from them for his services. When did John Wayne ever let a woman *pay* him for protection? Let us consider the archetype as it appears in Stephen Crane's short story "The Open Boat." We'll read a few paragraphs without annotating and then reread for a closer inspection.

Archetype

Morner and Rausch give us a useful definition of *archetype*:
> A pattern or model of an action (such as lamenting the dead), a character type (rebellious youth), or an image (paradise

as a garden) that recurs consistently enough in life and literature to be considered universal. Although the term *archetype* has long been used in its most general sense, the psychoanalyst C. G. Jung gave it new meaning. He theorized that certain ideas, actions, and images—rivalry between brothers, for example—rise out of early experiences of the human race, pass through the "collective unconscious of mankind," and are present in the subconscious of every individual. According to Jung, these archetypes emerge in the imagery of dreams and also in myths and other literature.

Some archetypes are used so often in certain literary genres that they become conventions, or distinguishing features of the genre. For example, it is conventional for the dying hero of a folk ballad to announce his or her last will and testament.[7]

Archetypes are elements that are so common that we sometimes do not even notice them. Why is the *Star Wars* film series so focused on father/son relationships? Why do we know that the young cowardly recruit in a war film will eventually make some grand sacrifice? We have come to expect certain trajectories in our stories.

THE OPEN BOAT
A Tale Intended To Be After the Fact.
Being the Experience of Four Men
from the Sunk Steamer *Commodore*

None of them knew the color of the sky. Their eyes glanced level, and were fastened upon the waves that swept toward them. These waves were of the hue of slate, save for the tops, which were foaming white and all of the men knew the colors of the sea. The horizon narrowed and widened, and dipped and rose, and at all times its edge was jagged with waves that seemed thrust up in points like rocks.

Many a man ought to have a bathtub larger than the boat which here rode upon the sea. These waves were most wrongfully and barbarously abrupt and tall, and each froth-top was a problem in small boat navigation.

The cook squatted in the bottom and looked with both eyes at the six inches of gunwale which separated him from the ocean. His sleeves were rolled over his fat forearms, and the two flaps of his unbuttoned vest dangled as he bent to bail out the boat. Often he said: "Gawd! That was a narrow clip." As he remarked it he invariably gazed eastward over the broken sea.

[7]Morner and Rausch, loc. cit., pp. 14–15.

The oiler, steering with one of the two oars in the boat, sometimes raised himself suddenly to keep clear of water that swirled in over the stern.

It was a thin little oar and it seemed often ready to snap.

The correspondent, pulling at the other oar, watched the waves and wondered why he was there.

The injured captain, lying in the bow, was at this time buried in that profound dejection and indifference which comes, temporarily at least, to even the bravest and most enduring when, willy nilly, the firm fails, the army loses, the ship goes down. . . .

"Keep'er a little more south, Billie," said he.

" 'A little more south,' sir," said the oiler in the stern.

Our immediate response may be simply to identify the scenario and the plot: four men have been shipwrecked and are in desperate straits. At least three of the men—the oiler, the captain, and the cook—seem to have been part of the crew. One, the correspondent, seems to have been a passenger. At least, it is hard to imagine a "correspondent" being part of the ship's crew.

If our text has an introduction, or if our professor has given an introductory lecture, we may know a bit about Stephen Crane—that he was a journalist, that he endured a shipwreck like this one, that he died young, and that he is often called a naturalist writer. But that is beside the point for now. There is much a careful reader can learn from a close reading even of a text on which we have no background information.

Let us see what a closer reading can unearth—one considering both of our questions: "What is repeated?" and "What is familiar?"

THE OPEN BOAT
A Tale Intended To Be After the Fact.
Being the Experience of Four Men
From the Sunk Steamer *Commodore*

subtitle describes the plot

None of them knew the color of the sky. Their eyes glanced level, and were fastened upon the waves that swept toward them. These waves were of the hue of <u>slate</u>, save for the tops, which were foaming white and all of the men knew the colors of the sea. The horizon narrowed and widened, and dipped and rose, and at all times its edge was <u>jagged</u> with waves that seemed thrust up in points like <u>rocks</u>.   *violent images*

sea is harsh

He mentions color twice—they don't know the color of the sky but they do know the color of the water.

So far we do not see much in the way of archetypes or familiar material, but we see a descriptive pattern established:
Crane focuses on the colors the men do and do not notice.
Also, the sea is described to be rocky and violent. This makes
sense in the context of a story about a shipwreck.

metaphor   Many a man ought to have a bathtub
                 larger than the boat which here rode upon
                 the sea. These waves were most wrong-
                 fully and barbarously abrupt and tall, and
                 each froth-top was a problem in small
                 boat navigation.   *more violent imagery*

character   The cook squatted in the bottom and   *at great*
identified   looked with both eyes at the six inches of *risk*
                 gunwale which separated him from the
                 ocean. His sleeves were rolled over his fat
                 forearms, and the two flaps of his unbut-
                 toned vest dangled as he bent to bail   *boat*
dialect   out the boat. Often he said: "Gawd! That *sinking?*
                 was a narrow clip." As he remarked it he
                 invariably gazed eastward over the bro-
                 ken sea.

Again, nothing much here—one of the characters is identified, we see some dialect, words misspelled to resemble the pronunciation of speakers of a particular region
or social group. Also, the men's precarious position is made
clear.

2nd man identified   The oiler, steering with one of the two
                     oars in the boat, sometimes raised himself
                     suddenly to keep clear of water that
                     swirled in over the stern. It was a thin
                     little oar and it seemed often ready to snap.

                                                    danger
3rd man identified   The correspondent, pulling at the other
                     oar, watched the waves and wondered
                     why he was there.   *correspondent does not*
                 belong here—not crew member
4th man identified   The injured captain, lying in the bow,
                     was at this time buried in that profound
                     dejection and indifference which comes,
                     temporarily at least, to even the bravest
                     and most enduring when, willy nilly, the
                     firm fails, the army loses, the ship goes

> down. . . .   *captain is compared to other "types" of men go-getters who are used to winning*

each man identified in opening of paragraph—focus on identity of each man
we never get names—only "professions"—we know what these men do but not who they are

An interesting observation. Crane compares the captain to other men and implies that we might know this <u>kind</u> of man: the businessman, the soldier, the ship captain. Crane implies that he is dealing with archetypes here—at least in the case of the captain. We may get a similar feeling for the correspondent, who, we are told, does not belong here. This seems to be a reference to the uselessness of his trade in these circumstances; at least, given that we know nothing else about him, it seems a fair guess.

a name—Billie   "Keep 'er a little more south, **Billie**," said he.
        " 'A little more south,' sir,"   *"Billie" is a kid's name*
the oiler = Billie   said the <u>oiler</u> in the stern.

Only one character gets a name—are names important here?

We observe that one character is actually given a name: "Billie the oiler." Since we just commented on the fact that no one is given a name, this seems to be a violation of a pattern Crane had been developing. Reading the rest of the story shows us that only the oiler is given a name. Is this significant?

The other characters are only given job titles, so they seem less distinct; they are not individuals. Billie is more of a "person" by virtue of his name, and the others are more types. In fact, later in the story we might note that the cook always talks about food, while the captain gives orders and the correspondent considers all that goes on around him, essentially writing his story in his head as he awaits rescue.

Rather than introduce individual characters, Crane suggests types he hopes we have encountered before. In fact, we will learn very little about the individual lives of any of these men. We know Billie best, by virtue of his name, but in fact, we know very little about even him. Like "John-Boy Walton" of the television program *The Waltons,* Billie seems to have been given this name for the specific reason that his name will evoke a youthful innocence about the character. When Billie dies at the story's end, his youth underscores the tragedy.

Perhaps this gives us very little to use in an essay, but it is a beginning. A close reading of the entire story, using familiar archetypes as our focus may bring us to an archetypal or perhaps allegorical reading of the story. Crane has implied that he wants us to find familiar elements in the story to build our interpretation. Looking for patterns and familiar elements helped us get a handle on at least the opening of this story.

What Is Strange?

Now this category may seem somewhat . . . strange. When we consider the wide variety of subject matter of literary texts that one might read in a literature class or over the course of one's life, just about every subject is going to be covered. In the context of everything, what can we call strange?

Well, think of a literary work as a composition written by an actual human being rather than an exalted work of *literature*. As Emerson once wrote, "Meek young men grow up in libraries, believing it their duty to accept the views that Cicero, Locke, and Bacon, have given; forgetful that Cicero, Locke, and Bacon, were only young men in libraries when they wrote these books." In your academic career, you will no doubt take a composition class, and your instructor may tell you to proofread your work to look for misspellings or lapses in grammar or logic. You can say you are looking for errors, but you are also looking for material that somehow draws attention to itself. In a piece of college composition, it is often desirable to somehow encourage your reader to forget that she is reading an essay. You want to lull your reader into the illusion that someone is whispering into her ear. One of your goals is to get your reader to agree with you. The other is to get her to put the red pen down; to stop paying attention to the individual words on the page. You want your reader to accept the piece as a whole, so that when she is done, there are no passages underlined with "awkward" or "??" or "what does this mean?" written next to it in the margin.

It is not so different with writers of poetry, fiction, and drama. These writers want you to forget that this is all make-believe. Shakespeare wants you to believe there really is a Romeo. Crane wants you to cry when Billie dies. Dickinson wants you to be physically and emotionally disturbed when the bird flies away. Generally speaking, writers do not want you to stop, look at a line, and say "that's a funny way to say that." So, when you are reading a literary work, and something jumps off the page at you and strikes you as being different from the rest of the text or as being different than other similar texts, it should be noted by the careful reader. This may be a spot where the author is experimenting, where he or she is doing things differently. If a writer takes such a risk, there may well be something of particular value.

A very clear example of what I am talking about can be found in the opening lines of T. S. Eliot's "The Love Song of J. Alfred Prufrock" (1917):

> S'io credessi che mia risposta fosse
> a persona che mai tornasse al mondo
> questa fiamma staria senza piu scosse.
> Ma per cio che giammai di questo fondo
> non torno vivo alcun, s'i'odo il vero,
> senza tema d'infamia ti rispondo.

> Let us go then, you and I,
> When the evening sky is spread out against the sky
> Like a patient etherized upon a table;
> Let us go, through certain half-deserted streets. . . .

Okay, we read a few lines and we're doing well. Of course, the careful reader notices that the opening lines are not in English! So, what do we do? Ignore them? No! Of course not. Learn to read Italian? Maybe, but not right now. We want to check out the footnote our textbook hopefully offers, where we should get a translation:

> "If I thought my reply were to one who could return
> to the world, this flame would stop flickering. But
> since no one returns alive from this pit, if what I
> hear is true, I answer you without fear of dishonor."

A good anthology will often feature footnotes such as this (see "Know Your Textbooks"). We should consider the other information our footnote gives us: that this line is taken from Dante's *Inferno* and that it is spoken when Guido da Montefeltro, "suffering in Hades for his sins, confesses to the poet Dante."

We do not need to go read *The Inferno* to get the gist of all this. This poem opens up with a quote from another literary work. The thrust of the quote is that the speaker will confess only with the knowledge that no one else will ever learn of his sins. This will no doubt be useful to our reading of the poem. How can I be so sure? Well, look how Eliot highlights the information. It is not unusual to open a poem or other literary work with a quotation from another source. But choosing to leave the quotation in a foreign language draws our attention to the lines and makes us slow down to take it all in, even forcing us to go to the footnotes. Does Eliot want to "lull the reader into the illusion that someone is whispering into her ear"? Why complicate things? Let us go back to our annotation:

"The Love Song of J. Alfred Prufrock"

Not a very romantic name—odd for a "love song"

*opening lines are
in Italian*

Reference to Inferno.

*Why open a "love song"
by reminding us
of HELL?!*

> S'io credessi che mia risposta fosse
> a persona che mai tornasse al mondo
> questa fiamma staria senza piu scosse.
> Ma per cio che giammai di questo fondo
> non torno vivo alcun, s'i'odo il vero,
> senza tema d'infamia ti rispondo.

speaker (Prufrock?) is well read: quotes from Dante in Italian

> Let us go then, you and I,
> When the evening sky is spread out against the sky
> Like a patient etherized upon a table;
> Let us go, through certain half-deserted streets. . . .

another pretty nasty image for a "love song"

An astute reader can make some conclusions based on
these lines even before going on to read the rest of the poem.
Like Hawthorne's "Rappaccini's Daughter," the work opens
with a reference to one of history's most celebrated descriptions of eternal damnation. That cannot mean good
things for the characters in this work. Eliot gives us the lines
in Italian. Does that tell us something about this "Prufrock"
person? And what kind of name is "J. Alfred Prufrock" anyway? Our reader notes, "Not a very heroic name—odd for a
'love song.'" Is it the kind of name you expect to see in a love
song? Or does it conjure up images of refinement, like some
stuffy British lord?

Our footnote tells us that the lines from Dante are a confession. Could it be that the poem will have similar qualities?
The first few lines speak about finding a quiet, out-of-the-
way, "half-deserted" place. Does Prufrock want to get away,
where no one will overhear him? And where does he want
to go? He says he wants to find a place where "the evening
sky is spread out against the sky/Like a patient etherized
upon a table." As our reader points out, this image is "pretty nasty" for a love song. I do not recall ever seeing a
Valentine's Day card that echoes this sentiment, but maybe
I have been looking in the wrong places.

Now, as with our previous examples, our reader is still
not ready to write a term paper, but his attention to just those
elements of the work that are unusual begins him on the road
to understanding. Most readers of "Prufrock" agree that the
memorable opening images and the opening quotation set
the stage for the rest of the poem. In fact, the image of "the
evening sky is spread out against the sky/Like a patient

etherized upon a table" is among the most famous in modern poetry.

Let us look at another example from a work of literature in a completely different genre. Jonathan Edwards's famous 1741 sermon, "Sinners in the Hands of an Angry God," reveals not only the religious mind of early Americans but the creative mind of Edwards himself. The following passage from the end of this sermon is filled with bold images of physical manifestations of God's anger. Edwards is careful to point out to his congregation that, although they are not in hell now, they can die at any moment and be sent to their eternal "reward." He uses metaphors of fire, warfare, serpents, and insects and spiders to explain the agonies of hell. Careful readers will make a point of looking at these metaphors. Toward the end, Edwards writes:

> And you children who are unconverted, do not you know that you are going down to hell, to bear the dreadful wrath of that god who is now angry with you every day and every night? Will you be content to be the children of the devil, when so many other children in the land are converted and are become the holy and happy children of the King of kings?

Now, on one level, this is not at all *strange*. Edwards has been pouring on the fire and brimstone for twenty pages by the time he gets to this. But for modern-day readers, this comment is violent in the extreme. We can read again, this time paying attention to our gut response:

> *kids must have been terrified!*
>
> And you <u>children</u> who are unconverted, do not you know that you are <u>going down to hell</u>, to bear the dreadful wrath of that god who is now angry with you every day and every night? Will you be content to be the children of the devil, when so many other children in the land are converted and are become the holy and happy children of the King of kings?

Edwards's theological view is not totally extinct today, but most people will likely be shocked to hear a minister speaking to children like this in modern times. Here is a line that needs to be underlined. We can use this line as a starting point, from whence to develop a thesis about the differences between Edwards's day and ours or to simply discuss Edwards as a man of his times. Either way, this line deserves some ink in the margins.

Let us use our "strange" focus on one more work, a poem by Edwin Arlington Robinson.

Richard Cory (1897)

Whenever Richard Cory went down town,
We people on the pavement looked at him:
He was a gentleman from sole to crown,
Clean favored and imperially slim.

And he was always quietly arrayed,
And he was always human when he talked;
But still he fluttered pulses when he said,
"Good-morning," and he glittered when he walked.

And he was rich—yes richer than a king—
And admirably schooled in every grace:
In fine, we thought that he was everything
To make us wish that we were in his place.

So on we worked, and waited for the light,
And went without meat, and cursed the bread;
And Richard Cory, one calm summer night,
Went home and put a bullet through his head.

Our first response might be "How ironic" or "Why did he do that?" In fact, those two responses are essentially the same response, in a way. Upon reflection, we may come to the conclusion that the poem reminds us that "money can't buy us happiness," and the poem certainly says that. But perhaps a careful rereading of the poem can give us more.

Richard Cory

title is main character's name

Whenever Richard Cory went down <u>town</u>,   *a*
We people on the pavement looked at <u>him</u>:   *b*
He was a gentleman from sole to <u>crown</u>,   *a*
Clean favored and imperially <u>slim</u>.   *b*

simple rhyme scheme

So far there is nothing strange at all about this poem. It seems a very conventional and easy-to-read little character study.

seems at once a "regular guy" and an especially gifted man— reminds me of someone like JFK

And he was always quietly <u>arrayed</u>,   *c*
And he was always human when he talked;   *d*
But still he fluttered pulses when he <u>said</u>,   *c*
"Good-morning," and he glittered when he <u>walked</u>.   *d*

same rhyme scheme

And he was rich—yes richer than a
king—   *e*
And admirably schooled in every <u>grace</u>:   *f*

plural speaker   In fine, <u>we</u> thought that he was
<u>everything</u>   *e*
To make us wish that we were in his
<u>place</u>.   *f*

same rhyme scheme

Our reader has not found much to remark upon, except
that the speaker is plural—"we." Our reader looks up to
the first stanza and notices the use of the phrase "We people on the pavement." This "we" has been the narrative
voice since the opening lines. Will this be a significant
observation?

first two lines of last   So on <u>we</u> worked, and waited for
stanza are about   the <u>light</u>,   *g*
"we," not Cory: "we went" And <u>went</u> without <u>meat</u>, and <u>cursed</u>
"we cursed"   the <u>bread</u>;   *h*
And Richard Cory, one calm summer
<u>night</u>,   *g*
Went home and put a bullet through
his <u>head</u>.   *h*

gross ending—violent and ironic—   *same rhyme*
why did he do it? no reason given!   *scheme*

Our reader has come to some interesting conclusions from
his second reading. This first-person plural point of view has
gotten most of the attention of our second reading. In fact,
Cory has gotten very little attention this reading. Perhaps
the poem is not really about him and his money at all.
Perhaps the poem really wants us to pay attention to the
nameless people watching Cory.

Really, who considers himself or herself a "Richard Cory"?
Even millionaire movie stars envy someone. Could this poem
be about envy? What then do we say when the man we envy
ends his life? What of the speakers' decision not only to go
"without meat" (which they could not afford at any rate),
but to "curse the bread" that they did have and that kept
them alive? The poem still talks about money, but now it
does not seem an empty platitude about money's inability to
buy happiness but about our ability to make ourselves mis-
erable with envy.

We also note that we are not told why Cory did it. Was
he unhappy? Insane? Wanted by the law? A foreign agent
about to be discovered? A member of some suicidal religious
cult? Was it an accident? Robinson does not tell us. Here is

an example of a missing element becoming just as important as the present elements of a literary work.

Our careful rereading and annotating of everything that seemed strange to us has given us several possible lines of inquiry into the poem and several possible theses for a future paper. We moved from thinking of this as a poem about Richard Cory, about whom we thought we knew quite a bit, to a poem about his neighbors, about whom we knew nothing—not even their names. Our second reading reverses all of that. Now, it seems we know volumes about these people, and it is Cory who seems unknowable.

Although this book is about *writing* about literature, in this chapter, we have spent a lot of time discussing reading literature. Our careful, informed, and critical reading can prepare us to make careful, informed, and critical observations about literature. But before those observations can really be convincing and persuasive to a reader, we need to consider our audience, our purpose in writing, and what genre or form our writing should take. Once we have made all of these decisions, we may find that our ideas can change as we adapt them for this or that form or present them to this or that audience. In the next chapter, we will consider the different modes of writing about literature that we may encounter.

What Do We Write When We Write About Literature?

A student in a literature class has been assigned a paper. But what is a paper, anyway? What is the purpose of an assignment such as this? The answers to these questions depend on a variety of conditions. A paper can run the gamut from a writing assignment that asks a student to merely report background data to summarizing the work to asking the student to personally respond to the literature to creating an argument that synthesizes the student's reaction, research about the literature, and material from the literature itself.

Basically, there are four modes of composition:

- Exposition
- Narration
- Description
- Argumentation

Exposition is writing that explains. In a literary work, especially drama, we use the term *exposition* to describe information that a reader (or the audience) must know to understand the work: setting, characters, facts that establish the plot, such as the date. When we write a piece of expository writing, we explain something to a reader who is not already familiar with this information. Therefore, we cannot really call pure exposition an argument.

Exposition may have been a major part of most students' early writing instruction. High school or freshman writing classes may focus on forms of expository writing, such as describing a memorable person or event. These assignments may imply an argument (i.e., this person really is memorable), but the focus is really on the transmission of information rather than any powerful attempt at persuasion. When we write about literature, we often need to include expository passages, including historical research, biographical sketches, or summary.

Narration is writing that recounts events as they unfolded. Narration is often organized chronologically. One seldom encounters or employs narration without also including
description. Obviously narration is an important aspect of
every literary text, although narrative voice in literature often
serves the plot and, therefore, is not necessarily going to
be chronological; plot is not merely a *chronological* series of
events but a recounting of events intended to support the
author's thematic vision. For example, "The Tell-Tale Heart"
begins with the killer in jail, confessing his crime. The plot
then goes on to recount events that occurred in the past,
with the narrator in the present commenting on his actions.

When writing about literature, we may employ narration
ourselves to describe an historical event that affects our reading of the work, or an event in the life of the author, which
we may argue will help readers better understand and respond to the work. We might also, if we are writing in a highly subjective mode, narrate some events in our own lives that
affected our reading of the work—perhaps our first encounter
with a particular author or our initial response to a particular work or an event that we experienced that reminds us
of the work we have read. A reviewer, for instance, may recount her immediate confusion upon reading a work, and
then go on to describe conversations with friends that
brought her around to a work.

Description is the sensual recreation of scenes or individuals. Description depends on faithful observation and precise language. We are less likely to see description used in
isolation than the other forms of composition. In a literary
work, description lets the reader picture the persons and
events the story or poem concerns.

In our own writing about literature, description will be
less important, as we will be borrowing from the texts we
have read and will seldom need to describe physical events
and locations in our analysis of the literature.

Description and Evaluation

It benefits us to understand the subtle distinction between language that merely describes and language that evaluates.

Take a look at the following passage from Edgar Allan Poe's
"The Fall of the House of Usher."

> During the whole of a <u>dull</u>, <u>dark</u>, and <u>soundless</u> day in the
> autumn of the year, when the clouds hung <u>oppressively</u> low
> in the heavens, I had been passing alone, on horseback,
> through a singularly <u>dreary</u> tract of country, and at length

> found myself, as the shades of evening drew on, within view of the melancholy House of Usher.

At first glance, we might call this descriptive language. However, very little is actually described here. Where does this take place? What color is the sky? What kind of trees surround the narrator? Are there trees? What color is his horse? How tall is the rider? We are given no details; we are only told how the speaker feels about his surroundings. We know he feels "oppressed" by his surroundings, that he thinks the surroundings are "dreary," and that he feels like it is "dull and dark." However, we are not offered any concrete, objective language so that we may picture what was actually there that day. We know only how the narrator evaluates the scene.

Good description often both displays and evaluates a scene. In these passages, Poe wants his reader to *feel* more than *see* what is before him. Poe is a master of controlling his reader's emotional response. When dealing with description, be aware of the distinction between offering an objective portrait and a subjective evaluation. For an example of more objective description, let us look at a work by Charles Darwin. In this passage from *The Voyage of the H.M.S. Beagle Round the World,* Darwin describes the dress of people he encounters:

> The dress of the Chilian miner is peculiar and rather picturesque. He wears a very long shirt of some dark-coloured baize, with a leather apron; the whole being fastened round his waist by a bright-coloured sash. His trowsers are very broad, and his small cap of scarlet cloth is made to fit his head closely.

While Darwin begins his introduction of this man with subjective terms such as *peculiar* and *picturesque,* for the most part, he focuses on more objective language: "dark-coloured baize," "leather apron," "trowsers." He focuses on details rather than the emotions the details stir. Darwin describes the people and things he sees and goes on to comment about the significance of the details he reports. But like the scientist he is, he is careful to present as many objective, descriptive details as he can before he shares his observations. Poe and Darwin clearly have different goals for their writing. Poe wants to stir our emotions and Darwin wants to us to share in his observations.

Argumentation is a term with at least two meanings. We may use the word *argument* to describe a complete breakdown of civility and order. When we say we have had an argument, we may be talking about a shouting match or a moment when we lost our temper with a friend or family member.

But argumentation in the context of rhetoric is anything but "uncivil" or angry. An argument in this context is a logical process by which we attempt to determine the truth of a proposition. You may be familiar with the syllogism, the most famous of which we find in Aristotle:

All men are mortal [major premise]

Socrates is a man [minor premise]

Therefore, Socrates is mortal [conclusion]

The syllogism can be a powerful tool to achieve the goal of a true argument. That goal, simply, is to convince an audience to agree with our position. A true syllogism depends on a *major premise* that must always be entirely true. Literary arguments, however, often depend on interpretation, which is by its nature subjective and, therefore, not objectively true. An argument that claims to purport the "true meaning" of Emily Dickinson's "A Bird Came Down the Walk" cannot claim to rest upon a universally accepted major premise. More often, our major premise will be subjective, open to debate, and in need of defense.

In this context, argumentation becomes a much more fluid thing, which may take many forms, and may be based on interpretation, expert opinion, supposition, an ever changing historical record, debatable theoretical presuppositions, and our own personal and subjective readings of texts. The many forms of argument are a great strength and allow for a variety of opinions on topics, literary and otherwise.

Argument

The book review is an example of a literary argument based on something other than an objectively true major premise. The reviewer attempts to explain her response to a work and to convince her readers to adopt this position regarding the text in question. However, a reviewer who writes that Stephen King's new novel is "good" cannot assume the existence of a universally accepted definition of *good*. For instance, a reviewer who is a devotee of the horror story may assume the *major premise* that "horror stories are good." If King's new book is indeed a "horror story," her *minor premise* is easy enough to arrive at, and we can imagine her growing syllogism:

Horror stories are good.
Stephen King's new book is a horror story.

Her *conclusion* is obvious:

Stephen King's new book is good.

The problems with this line of argument are clear. The term *good* is certainly not universally accepted to always mean the same thing. There are plenty of people who are bored with horror stories or who find them too frightening or who find them morally objectionable and, therefore, not "good." Even for those who agree, generally, with the major premise, there may be wide disagreement over what makes a story a "horror" story, and which of those stories are "good" and which are "bad."

Many arguments—like our review—depend on a subjective foundation. Therefore, simple syllogisms cannot supply a reliable framework for an argumentative essay on these subjects. In fact, a well-written review *creates* its own major premise by giving the reader a definition of *good* and any other debatable terms necessary for an understanding of the subject matter. An intelligent review of the Stephen King novel might begin with a discussion of the value of horror stories and a defense of our reviewer's definition of what a "good" horror story is and is not.

Seldom do we find ourselves practicing one of these modes without practicing the others. In most cases, these modes are practiced together in some form or other. Let us examine several of the genres of literary essay and consider how each makes use of exposition, narration, description, and argumentation. The names we assign to each of these genres of essay are not necessarily universal, but we can say that writing about literature in the college classroom will usually boil down to these several tasks. In Chapter 4, we will look at the syllogism in greater depth and consider its strengths and limits as a tool in literary debate.

Although the terms *objective* and *subjective* are often misused and misunderstood, they are perhaps useful here to describe two broad categories of writing exercises assigned in literature classes.

Objective reporting refers to papers written to transmit information, not to support the ideas of the writer of the paper.

Subjective literary analysis refers to papers written to establish and defend an argument about a literary work. These papers seek to argue a position that is not clearly and self-evidently true but that may be true. The writer of the subjective literary analysis essay must make use of the elements of objective reporting to support his or her ideas.

OBJECTIVE REPORTING

Summary

When we summarize a literary work, we present the work in a condensed, concise form. A summary reduces a work to its main points. The writer of a summary demonstrates his understanding of the work's plot. The writer of a summary does not usually comment on the value or quality of the work but merely reports the main facts of the piece. A summary is one of the more objective writing assignments a student in a literature class will be asked to compose.

One important note to make about plot summaries is that students in literature classes are often asked to refrain from writing them. A student asked to write a newspaper-style review of a work may be asked to write a short summary (one that does not reveal the end of the story). The assumption we make about the reader of a review is that she has not read the work in question. This reader wants to know if the work is worth her time.

However, while a student may be asked to write a summary as a separate assignment, or as part of a review, she will likely be asked not to write summaries in the body of her longer papers, such as subjective responses or synthesized arguments. One convention of literary analysis is that the reader is usually already familiar with the work. So a student writing an analytical paper about Ernest Hemingway's "The Short Happy Life of Francis Macomber" does not need to summarize the story for the audience.

Researched Report

A researched report is, like a summary, merely a presentation of facts. The writer of a report is asked to seek out and present information about a topic without pursuing an argument. A report may take the form of a summary of one or several critical works. For instance, a student might be asked to find out how reviewers responded to a novel upon its publication or to find out what contemporary critics are saying about the influence of Dorothy Wordsworth on her brother William's poetry. A report on either of these topics would present the information as found without necessarily integrating that information into a synthesized argument about a particular text or issue. The researched report, like the summary, is a presentation of data.

SUBJECTIVE LITERARY ANALYSIS
Subjective Response

The subjective response is essentially the opposite of the summary. In a subjective response, a writer is asked to share his feelings about a work, not to simply tell us what happened. Like a researched (or synthesized) argument, a subjective response is a paper with a clear, identifiable objective. The subjective response presents an opinion about a work and seeks to make sure the audience comes to share this reaction. The writer of a paper such as this would assume that his audience is composed of readers familiar with the text under scrutiny. A subjective response need not be informed by library research or the opinions of other critics. A subjective response is, as its name implies, highly subjective.

In a paper of this sort, the writer forcefully presents an opinion about a work: its worth, its genre, its similarity to other works, its strengths or its flaws, and encourages the audience to come to share these feelings.

Analysis

In *A Handbook to Literature,* Hugh Holman and William Harmon define the term *analysis* succinctly:

> A method by which a thing is separated into parts, and those parts are given rigorous, logical, detailed scrutiny, resulting in a consistent and relatively complete account of the thing and the principles of their organization.[1]

Analysis, therefore, depends on our ability to break a text into its parts and then reassemble those parts in a new fashion. An analysis of the plot of a mystery story, for instance, may require rearranging the events recounted in the story so they are in chronological order. An analysis of a novel may involve arranging a discussion that first addresses character and then plot and then setting. However, in the novel itself, character, plot, and setting are all introduced slowly and certainly not in distinct groups.

The Review

Similar to the subjective response, the review is a response intended to evaluate a work. However, the review is intended for a reader unfamiliar with the work in question. This is a significant break with most papers written in

[1]William Harmon and C. Hugh Holman, *A Handbook to Literature,* 8th ed. (Upper Saddle River, NJ: Prentice Hall, 1999), pp. 22–23.

literature classes. Traditionally, essays written in literature classes are written under the assumption that the audience of the paper will be familiar with the literary work under discussion.

When an instructor assigns a review, however, the assumption is that the reader of the paper will not have read the literature discussed. In fact, the review serves the reader by letting her know if the literary work is worth reading. Often, we may strongly like or dislike a literary work but be unable to state our opinions on the work in our writing. The review demands that we do so. It also demands that we explain and defend our opinions. It is not enough for us to say we do or do not like the piece; we must demonstrate why our opinions are worthwhile.

The Close Reading

The term *close reading* is borrowed from the branch of literary theory called the New Criticism. The New Critics emerged in the early decades of the twentieth century (and so are now "New" in name only). They wanted to focus attention on the literary work itself rather than on elements outside the text. The close reading ignores such issues as the author of the piece, his or her supposed or stated intentions, the work's historical context, or the feelings of the reader. To this end, these critics advocated minute, detailed attention to the language and structure of a piece of literature. A close reading focuses on such elements as words (denotation and connotation), images, and symbols.

A close reading of a literary work is a form of literary analysis that often relies on no outside research. However, a close reading should differ from the subjective response in that the writer of this kind of paper will support interpretations of images, symbols, and so forth, with passages from the texts and explanations of the writer's interpretations. It is not enough to say "The raven in this poem is symbolic of death." The writer of a successful close reading will explain why a raven should be seen in such a light.

When we do a close reading of a poem, we are said to be explicating the poem, or writing an explication of the poem. This term reminds us that the goal of a close reading is to make explicit in the poem that which had previously been implicit.

The Explication

An explication is a very specific and frequently assigned exercise in literary analysis. In an explication, a writer formally and very closely analyzes (or closely studies) every aspect of a literary text (often a short poem). Structure, style, content, diction, imagery, symbol, and figurative language are all examined and discussed. Often, this mode of paper is assigned in poetry classes.

Researched (or Synthesized) Argument

The researched (or synthesized) argument is the kind of paper most students probably imagine writing when they are told to write a paper or a term paper. Obviously, this kind of essay relies on research, but it is very different from the researched report. When we talk about a synthesized argument, we mean more than simply reporting information. A synthesized argument does in fact synthesize information from various sources: articles in literary journals, biographies of authors, research on historical context, classroom notes, the literary work itself, and the writer's own opinions. In a way, the synthesized argument is a combination of the researched report and the subjective response. Obviously, elements of the close reading can be found in the synthesized argument.

Many kinds of papers that fall under these categories—the comparison/contrast paper, papers that focus on character, theme, and many other kinds of essays—are examples of literary analysis essays. And since any of these papers might make use of some researched information, they could all become research papers.

USING LITERARY THEORY

Most of the assignments mentioned so far begin with the literature in question. However, there is another way to think about writing about literature. An essay about literature can be an intellectual exercise by which a writer demonstrates his or her knowledge of the literature, or it can be an intellectual exercise by which a writer demonstrates his or her knowledge of an approach to literature. In the next few pages, we will look at some of the issues raised by literary theory and consider how these ideas can be incorporated into our writing about literature. This discussion owes a debt to the following works:

Bressler, Charles. *Literary Criticism: An Introduction to Theory and Practice*. 2nd ed. Upper Saddle River, NJ: Prentice Hall, 1999.

Eagleton, Terry. *Marxism and Literary Criticism*. Berkeley: California University Press, 1976.

Fowler, Roger, ed. *A Dictionary of Modern Critical Terms*. Revised. London: Routledge, 1987 (1973).

Guerin, Wilfred et al. *A Handbook of Critical Approaches to Literature*. 2nd ed. New York: Harper, 1979.

Meyer, Michael. *The Bedford Introduction to Literature*. 3rd ed. Boston: Bedford, 1993.

Selden, Raman. *A Reader's Guide to Contemporary Literary Theory*. 2nd ed. Lexington: Kentucky University Press, 1989.

Literary theory is a term that refers to the various schools of thought developed by literary scholars by which we approach literature. Everyone who reads has a literary theory of some sort, although for most of us our theory may go unnamed and unexamined. For instance, a student is asked to read *Jane Eyre* by Charlotte Brontë. He finds the book so boring as to be unreadable. "This stinks," he says as he puts the book down. This student has a rudimentary literary theory. Perhaps his theory is little more than an expression of his taste. Summed up, his theory may read: literature should be exciting.

Once we begin studying literature and looking to it for meaning beyond our personal immediate entertainment, we need to have a theory of what literature can and should do that exceeds the narrow dimensions of what we as individuals do and do not enjoy.

In recent decades, a variety of literary theories have developed, so many that they actually may be very confusing to the neophyte literature student. They depend on some highly specialized language and go by many names: feminist theory, Marxist theory, deconstruction, structuralism, poststructuralism, new historicism, cultural criticism, and the New Criticism mentioned earlier.

This is not a book about literary criticism, so we will not attempt to thoroughly define each school here. For now it may be enough to explain some key differences between the schools and their various applications.

Literary criticism is the analysis and interpretation of texts. There are several schools of literary criticism, but none of them totally reveals the meaning of a text. Think of each critical method (formalist, sociological, psychological, historical, reader-response) as a different kind of film. A black-and-white photo reveals different information than a color photo does. A moving picture is different than a still photo.

X-rays and ultraviolet film reveal very different details. One kind of picture is not necessarily better than another. Each has its place and its value.

Any single object can be photographed in a variety of ways. Which kind of film most accurately depicts that object? Who is to say? The casual photographer will say color glossy film, the artist may say black and white, the physician will say X-rays, the scientist will vote for ultraviolet. In the same way, any given literary text can be approached from a variety of perspectives: historical, biographical, formal, feminist, Marxist, and so on. Is one approach truer than another? It all depends on whom you ask. The student, however, need not answer this question. The student should see the many forms of literary criticism as merely tools for reading and writing about literature.

Formalist Criticism

Formalist criticism focuses primarily on the text alone. You might even consider it a scientific approach, since the reader and author and other extraliterary considerations are of little importance. A formalist critique places the text under a microscope. What occurs outside the work is of little concern; the internal matters of the text are what are important (diction, irony, metaphor, symbol, plot, characterization, narrative technique). External matters (biography, history, politics) are secondary. You probably employed this type of approach if you wrote critical papers such as "The Function of Nature in 'The Open Boat'" or "Symbolism in *Huckleberry Finn*" in high school. The most frequently used varieties of formalist criticism are New Criticism and deconstruction. Although the two theories differ widely, both focus primarily on the work itself and not on the reader's reaction or the historical context of the work.

Questions to Consider in Formalist Criticism

1. How do various elements of the work (plot, character, point of view) create and reinforce its meanings?
2. How are the elements related to the whole?
3. What is the work's major organizing principle?
4. What issues are raised by the work? How does the work's structure resolve those issues?

Sociological Criticism

This critical approach looks at social groups, relationships, and values in literature. It sees a work as a reflection of social conditions or as a product of social conditions. Two sociological approaches include Marxist and feminist. Each of these approaches carries its own political agenda.

Marxist critics see literature as a way of promoting socialistic social and economic ideas. Marxist criticism analyzes literature in terms of the historical conditions that produced it, describing the struggle of individuals to free themselves from oppression and exploitation. Form, therefore, is secondary to a work's content or themes. Marxist critics are not interested in the author/artist since a work is not created by an individual, as such, but by a social group's ideas, values, and aspirations.

Questions to Consider in Marxist Criticism

1. How are class differences presented in the work? Are the characters aware or unaware of the economic and social forces that affect their lives?
2. How do economic conditions determine the characters' lives?
3. What ideological values are explicit or implicit?
4. Does the work explicitly embrace or reject socialism?
5. Does the work criticize class structures?

Feminist critics see their work as a way to address predominant critical perspectives, which are male dominated and patriarchal. Feminist critics wish to replace these dominant perspectives with a female point of view.

Like Marxist criticism, feminist criticism has an overtly political agenda. Feminist criticism places the text in a social context in order to explore how women (in and outside a literary text) have been oppressed by a patriarchal society.

Questions to Consider in Feminist Criticism

1. How are women's lives portrayed in the work? Do the women in the work accept or reject these roles?
2. Are the form and content of the work influenced by the author's gender?
3. What are the relationships between men and women? Are these relationships sources of conflict? Do they provide resolutions to conflicts?

Cultural and Historical Criticism

Historical critics use history as a way of understanding literature. These critics move beyond the writer's life and the literary work itself to the culture (social, religious, political) in which the author composed the work. They view the work in its own time period.

Cultural criticism defines culture as local, partisan, material, and historical. The cultural critic looks at a literary work and investigates the various types of boundaries that a society constructs, as well as the cultural differences within that society, such as those based on social class, gender, and ethnicity.

Questions to Consider in Cultural and Historical Criticism

1. How does the work reflect the period in which it was written?

2. How does the work reflect the period it represents?

3. What literary or historical influences helped to shape the form and content of the work?

4. How important is the historical context (both the work's and your own) to interpreting the work?

Psychological Criticism

Using psychoanalytical theories, the critic analyzes the characters of a literary text as well as the symbolic meanings of objects, events, and language in the text. Psychological critics also examine the motivation of the writer and reader of the work.

Questions to Consider in Psychological Criticism

1. How does the work reflect the author's personal psychology?

2. What do the characters' emotions and behavior reveal about their psychological states? What types of personalities are they?

3. Does the author present psychological matters such as repression, dreams, and desire, either consciously or unconsciously? *ALL*

Reader-Response Criticism

The focus of the reader-response critic is on the reader rather than the work. Reader-response criticism focuses on what texts do to—or in—the mind of the reader, rather than looking at a text as something with properties exclusively its own. It explores the reader's experience of a work; it considers the ideas the reader brought to the text and considers how the text "dealt" with those ideas. Reader-response criticism also considers how cultural and social influences affect the reader's response to a work.

Questions to Consider in Reader-Response Criticism

1. How do you respond to the work?
2. How do your experiences and expectations affect your reading and interpretation?
3. Who is the work's original intended audience? To what extent are you similar or dissimilar to that audience?

IN-CLASS ESSAY EXAM

A common writing assignment of the literature classroom is one we may not think of as a "writing assignment" as such. Midterm and final exams frequently feature essay assignments. Although these in-class writing situations may seem impossible to prepare for, actually there are several strategies that can be pursued outside of class to prepare for the in-class experience. In the chapters to follow we will consider specific strategies for writing papers outside of class. However, many of these strategies are not applicable to the in-class essay and identification exam. Let us stop and consider some specific strategies for the in-class exam. Once we are in the classroom, looking at the test in front of us, there are strategies we can follow that make the best use of our time and effort.

Strategies for Writing on an Exam

First, we must realize that although an exam is one assignment, it will often contain several distinct writing contexts. A typical feature of many exams is the identification section. Here you are given quotations from several of the works the class has covered over the semester and are asked to identify them. Usually, *identify* means name the author and/or title of the work from which the quotation was borrowed and explain the significance of the quoted material.

It is only natural for students to worry about an upcoming exam. In fact, it is their right and privilege to complain about studying. However, they are worrying about the wrong part of the test. Naming the author and/or title is actually relatively easy to study for. It is the "significance" students need to worry about.

To properly prepare for an identification section of an exam, it is generally not necessary to reread all of the assignments. The real task is to study enough to be able to identify not what a particular author wrote but what kind of text a particular author might have written and what kind of text a particular author likely would not have written. Preparing an exam is not an exercise in torture, contrary to some opinions, but an attempt to create a mechanism to evaluate student learning. In a survey class, for instance, where students sample a wide variety of works and genres, hopefully students will have retained a few key quotations—those that have repeatedly come up over the course of the semester. Some of these quotations may even become tiresome to students weary of hearing them repeated by an overzealous professor. In my American literature classes, I know I endlessly repeat John Winthrop's characterization of America as a "city upon a hill" or Emerson's "transparent eyeball" metaphor. It may become boring to hear such phrases repeated, but the students who do not think that these lines will be on the exam after continued repetition are kidding themselves.

Such obvious examples are rare. So where do the other quotations come from? Frequently, the quotations in question will be those that either were the focus of class discussion or exemplify an author's style, genre, and subject matter.

Class Discussion

In the case of quotations mentioned in class discussion, we are reminded again of the importance of note taking, annotating, and of having the assigned text in class. If discussion rolls around to a key line, it is not unusual for a professor to announce something such as: "Look at the last paragraph on page 117. Let's read that together." The professor expects students to turn to that page and start underlining and writing in the margins. Once a student begins annotating like this, studying is no longer a question of rereading a text but of rereading her notes. And the student who can focus on the quotations commented upon by the professor has a head start on anticipating which quotations will be on the exam.

Style, Genre, and Subject Matter

Style is an elusive and sometimes vague concept. Some authors have a very distinctive style whereas others seem to cluster together in a reader's memory. For the student studying for an exam, it may be worthwhile to identify aspects of an author's style when that style seems especially apparent. In American literature, this might mean making the assumption that any quotations containing the words *melancholy, dread, dreary,* and *mad* are probably from Edgar Allan Poe, for instance.

Then there is the question of genre and subject matter. Does one writer focus on religious subjects while another writes about nature and a third explores gender roles? A student trying to balance all of this can make a list of the authors he or she is to be tested on and label each. The student making these notes is not interested in memorizing everything he read but in being able to make educated guesses about the quotations he does not immediately recognize. The first step is to distinguish among the poets, fiction, and nonfiction writers. Then the student makes a few comments about the kinds of things these writers discussed in their work. We start with the syllabus given us at the beginning of the semester.

The first step a student can take is merely listing the names of assigned authors and texts and making a few notes about each:

Anne Bradstreet   Genre: Poetry—God, family, nature. Uses metaphors. Some "feminist" ideas. Poem about her house burning. "I am obnoxious to each carping tongue who says my hand a needle better fits"

Edward Taylor   Genre: Poetry—God, family, nature. Uses metaphors. Like Bradstreet, but more abstract. Less family than Bradstreet. Lots of "nurturing" images about God

Jonathan Edwards   Genre: Sermon. Lots of violent images & metaphors. Tries to scare his audience. Talks a lot about God, but his God is angry and looking to punish. Quote: "and you children. Do you want to go down to hell?" Spider metaphor: "you are like a spider held over a flame"

Mary Rowlandson   Genre: Autobiography. More stuff about God. Lots of violence—describes kidnapping and death of her child. Calls daughter "it" not "she"

Thomas Jefferson   Genre: Politics. "Declaration of Independence" Attacks King George—"When in the course of human events..."

Benjamin Franklin   Genre: Autobiography. Brags a lot. Lots about money and working hard to save money. Includes those lists of virtues. Tells us to use his lists and act like him.

Olaudah Equiano   Genre: Autobiography—slave narrative. Violence, description of travels through Africa. Is sold to Europeans. He sees them as monstrous.

Phyllis Wheatley   Genre: Poetry—God and FREEDOM through religion. Lots of sermonizing. Poems addressed to Students and Geo. Washington. Mentions Africa & race.

Washington Irving   Genre: short story—"Rip Van Winkle" Our first short story. Falls asleep. Lots of stuff about the U.S. Revolution. Important quote: "I don't know who I am or what my name is."

Edgar Allan Poe   *Genres: Poetry, essay, and short stories. key word: MELANCHOLY. His narrators are crazy, drunk, on drugs, or all 3. Lots of rhyming in the poems. "The Bells"... Weird, rhyming names for the women: Ulalume, Lenore, Annabelle Lee, and all the women are dead!*

This student may not have memorized everything he read, but he is ready to avoid simple mistakes. For instance, if he comes across a few lines of poetry, he knows it is either Bradstreet, Taylor, Wheatley, or Poe. And although Bradstreet, Taylor, and Wheatley all write about religious subjects, Poe does not. So any nonreligious poetry is most likely his. Any poetry about Africa is Wheatley's. This is studying by process of elimination, but it is an effective way to cover a lot of information in a short time.

Any quotations from short stories, anything containing conversations or "he said" or "she said" or containing names other than the author's will likely be from Irving or Poe. We might worry about confusing autobiography and fiction, but Rowlandson, Franklin, and Equiano all cover distinct subject matter, and Equiano's will be the only prose to discuss slavery. So chances are that our student will not confuse these three.

I said before that students worry about the wrong part of the test. Students are more likely to lose credit when they attempt to discuss the significance of a quoted passage than they are to lose credit missing an author's name.

Following are a few sample identifications from an exam. Each quotation is followed by one blank space marked "Author and/or title" and one marked "Significance." Let us look at one or two answers to an exam such as this. One of these quotations looks familiar. In fact, we discussed it in our annotating chapter. Let us see how we handle it on an exam:

> "And you, children, who are unconverted, do not you know that you are going down to hell, to bear the dreadful wrath of that God, who is now angry with you every day and every night?"

> Author and/or title: *Jonathan Edwards*
> Significance:

Our student knows that Jonathan Edwards is the author of this line. In his notes he jotted down part of this memorable line. Now he needs to consider an answer for the second half of the question. How about something like this?

Edwards addresses the children in his audience. He suggests that they may go to hell for their sins. He describes God as being very angry at these children and even threatens them with God's revenge.

That answer may have the ring of authority about it, but in reality it tells us nothing about the significance of this quotation. In fact, it is merely a restating of the passage in new, more familiar language. While there is nothing "untrue" in this answer, it simply *does not answer the question*. It does not describe the significance of the quote. Worse, besides identifying Jonathan Edwards as the author, this answer does not even demonstrate that the student who gave this answer has ever seen this line before. Someone who has never read the sermon the line came from could have written this answer. One of the things we want to demonstrate on an exam is that we have done the reading. Let us look at another answer:

> Edwards addresses the children in his audience, whom he treats the same as adults. His sermon is filled with emotional, frightening images. This demonstrates his Puritan background.

This answer starts off the same as the first but goes on to address issues not directly stated in the quotation. This answer places Edwards historically and philosophically ("Puritan") as well as generically ("sermon"). By supplying information in our answer that is not already supplied in the question, we show a knowledge of the material and its context. Even if the professor is looking for some other nugget of information that we have not supplied, this answer demonstrates that this is not our first reading of this material.

Essay Exam

It is more difficult to prepare for the essay exam, of course. The identification portion of the exam is based on more or less specific information: authors and titles. The significance section is less specific, of course, but it is also something easily answered in a few lines. The in-class essay exam can be much longer. Students may be expected to write papers of up to five pages or more, and this writing must all be done in the classroom. Usually the student will not know what information the question will cover. It seems on the surface that it will be impossible to study for this exam. But it is not.

Of course, it is safe to assume that the professor will not reveal the content of the exam before the exam date. However, there are ways to amass information that is applicable to any of several possible essays one might write for such an exam. That is to say, study broadly. Since it is hard to say what your professor may ask you to write about, it is important to be able to write about a variety of topics.

If, for instance, I anticipate writing about Anne Bradstreet, I can study everything possible about Anne Bradstreet's poetry. I can memorize titles and lines of poetry and be ready to write a detailed essay about Bradstreet's poetry. However, if I get to class and see there are no Bradstreet questions, I will be very disappointed! On the other hand, if I prepare to write about a broad topic such as "Puritan writers," I should be ready to discuss Edwards, Bradstreet, or Taylor. By grouping my notes under broader topics, I may sacrifice the kind of detail narrower studying may give me, but that kind of information may have limited value on an exam. So the first step toward preparation for an in-class essay exam is in the studying phase. Study broadly and organize your notes into categories.

However, the real work of preparing for this kind of exam does not begin until you are sitting in the classroom looking at the essay question. Once presented with the actual question, the student can utilize a few strategies to develop an essay that answers the question as fully as possible in the limited time the student has been given.

In large measure, the steps one ought to take in preparing to write an in-class exam are the same that one ought to take when writing an out-of-class exam:

- Read the question carefully.
- Make some notes toward an outline.
- Prepare an outline. Be sure your paper will answer the assigned question; stay on task.
- Draft your essay.
- Leave yourself time to proofread and revise your essay.

Of course, these steps will be highly condensed and specialized. For instance, a student writing a paper out of class should schedule at least a day between outlining and drafting and between drafting and proofreading. That one-day layover allows the student to digest his or her ideas. That much time, however, obviously is not an option for the in-class paper.

Proofreading an out-of-class paper should be a tedious effort, allowing the writer to concentrate on the focus, organization, style, development, spelling, and grammar of the essay. The out-of-class revision should be a major effort. For the in-class paper, the proofreading may be a very quick affair. If the writer has skipped spaces on her test sheet, she will be able to make minor—but not major—revisions.

Still, taking a few simple steps can make the in-class essay exam a less daunting affair. Amend our original list to address the specific tasks of the in-class paper:

■ *Read the question carefully.* Ask your professor to explain any questionable words or phrases. Are you given more than one choice? Choose the question with which you are most comfortable.

■ *Carefully read the entire test.* Does the test provide any information you may need to answer these questions? For instance, can you borrow a quotation from the identification section for use in the essay section?

■ *Make some notes toward an outline.* In an out-of-class situation, these notes may take several pages. On an in-class paper, you will not have that luxury. However, it might be wise to jot down your immediate reaction to the question and any specific information you run the risk of forgetting as you prepare your outline and first draft. For instance, you may want to write down dates, names, titles, and so forth, while they are fresh in your mind. As you begin drafting, you may have trouble calling them up.

■ *Prepare an outline. Be sure your paper will answer the assigned question; stay on task.* You may have a little leeway in answering a question, but it is a good idea to be faithful to the question as written. If you are asked to discuss Poe's fiction, you may be able to discuss his poetry as well as the fiction, but you should not ignore the fiction—that is what you will be judged on. It is easy to forget the specifics of the question as you dig into the work of writing. After you have written your outline, reread the question. Does your thesis statement address the question? Are there key words in the question that you can repeat in your thesis?

■ *Draft your essay.* Follow your outline and write neatly. Do not waste time rewriting for the sake of neatness. If you are writing longhand, write neatly and skip spaces. Allow yourself the opportunity to cross out and replace material upon revision. When you cross out material like this, do so neatly. Make one line through the words you want removed.

■ *Leave yourself time to proofread and revise your essay.* Perhaps one quarter of the time allotted to the drafting of your essay should be set aside for proofreading and revising. Again, at this stage, make sure that you have answered the question as it is written on the exam. Neatly write the new material above the old material. Remember that someone will have to read this. You do not want your paper to be prohibitively difficult to read.

These genres represent a few of the most frequently assigned literature papers. Within each category, of course, are many varieties of papers. But these assignments represent most of the skills and activities involved in discussing and analyzing literary works. In the next chapter, we will look in more detail at the writing process and how best to adapt a few key approaches to these tasks.

In this chapter, we have briefly looked at several frequently assigned genres in literary analysis. In the chapters to follow, we will look at these genres in greater detail. It is important to understand that "writing a paper" could be an introduction to any number of different rhetorical tasks, from summary to analysis to research to the use of literary criticism.

How
Do We Write
What We Write?

We have talked about in-class writing. Now we are ready to begin writing an out-of-class essay. We have talked about the tasks that lead up to writing an essay about literature: about reading and annotating a text, about differentiating between the kinds of literary analysis essays, about doing research, about paying attention to classroom instruction, and reading for comprehension.

Now it is time to put all of that into practice. Unfortunately, talking about writing an essay is easier than actually writing the essay. Staring at that blank sheet of paper or that blank computer screen can be demoralizing. This is the sort of feeling that reinforces itself tenfold. The longer you look at it, the blanker the page gets. But all is not lost. There are strategies for getting started on an essay.

Whenever I talk to a student about a paper he or she wishes to revise, one that received a low grade or that just did not work, I ask some standard questions. Did you read the assignment sheet that described the paper's goals? Did you proofread the paper? Did you have a friend proofread? Then I will point to the first word on page 1 and ask "Is this the first word you wrote when you began this assignment?" If the student answers "yes," then I know that I have identified at least part of the problem.

As a teacher and a tutor, I have spent lots of time with students working on papers for literature classes. I know that one strategy for writing an essay is to sit and stare at a page until the first page begins to gel in the student's mind. Students beginning a paper this way imagine that the whole essay is likely to appear to them in their imagination and flow out on the page. And while they wait for inspiration, they write nothing, unless we count the doodles in the corner or their name on the top of the page.

The student following this path assumes that any writing that is not good enough for the final draft is no good at all. But this is not the case. All of the false starts and abandoned introductions and conclusions and all the misspelled words and dangling modifiers are important. All of that writing is potentially important if you know how to read it. And waiting for the whole paper to be completed in your imagination is like waiting for some mythical goddess to spring full-grown from your forehead. I suppose that there are people who can write like this, by simply waiting for the paper to form in their head, and then copying down what they read in their mind, but I have never met them.

What most writers need to do is stop waiting for the paper to form and start writing, although maybe not the paper itself. Good writing demands prewriting, that is, writing that is not intended to be seen as part of the final draft of your project. When we sit down to do prewriting, we do ourselves a big favor. First, we begin an organized process of discovery and invention. Prewriting allows us to examine our thoughts through organized exercises. It allows us to see on paper the kinds of things we might say in an essay. Perhaps most importantly, prewriting lets us write poorly. Prewriting is a forum in which the writer knows she is free from evaluation, so her ideas can flow unchecked. This can be very liberating. In prewriting she can allow herself to take chances and make statements and comparisons that ordinarily she might not make.

Prewriting can take any number of forms: from a highly structured exercise to random and chaotic scribbling. What all of these exercises have in common is that they are not intended to turn into a final draft but only to supply the raw material for one.

Prewriting can begin long before a student is assigned a paper topic. If we have been annotating as we read, we have already been prewriting. Annotating allows us to preserve our first, fleeting impressions of a literary work. If, on first reading, a character in a novel reminds us of a favorite aunt or a character from another novel or a bunny rabbit, and we jot that down, we are preserving an idea that otherwise may have disappeared. It may seem a meaningless observation at the time, but in the context of an assigned essay, these spontaneous reactions can sometimes prove valuable.

FREEWRITING

Freewriting is what it sounds like: writing without any particular goal. Freewriting allows your ideas to flow unchecked by your conscious or unconscious efforts at editing.

Freewriting is an easy way to produce data: raw information that can be later processed into a more refined composition. For the student who says, "I can't come up with seven pages on a ten-line poem," freewriting opens up the imagination enough to release ideas. Responses should flow freely at this stage. After all, at this stage, the ideas do not need to be "right" or "smart" or even on any particular topic other than "what I thought of the poem." Students fond of freewriting can use the technique throughout the semester and accumulate information for papers long before papers are assigned by keeping a reading journal. See Chapter 5 for a sample freewriting exercise.

Keeping a Reading Journal

Along the same lines but more detailed is the reading journal. Often assigned in literature classes, the reading journal is a good idea whether assigned or not. In a reading journal, we jot down our reactions to what we have read. Reactions can vary in length and form but are usually short and informal. Again, the informality of the journal allows for reactions that might seem inappropriate in a more formal essay. Our immediate response to a literary work may be highly personal, or we may make comparisons to other works that we have no evidence to support. Or we may simply discuss how much (or how little) we enjoyed a given piece. While these observations may never appear word for word in a more formal writing exercise, the journal can become a catalog of ideas for us to consult later.

The reading journal lets us keep a running tally of our ideas and responses to the literature we are reading. But sometimes when we are under the gun and the paper is due tomorrow, we need to be able to jump-start our paper. Perhaps you have been in this very situation. Most of us have sat in front of that blank sheet of paper, trying to fill it. We write a few words, reconsider, scratch them out. We start again. Just one or two words this time. Again, they are no good. Again, we scratch them out. We start again, crumple up the paper, and toss it into the garbage can. One can repeat this process until the garbage can is overflowing with useless ideas. This model of the writer at work has even been mythologized by Hollywood. How many times have we seen that one in a movie? I suppose this myth needs to be updated to the computer age now. And that may save us some paper, but it will not improve our writing.

But once again, the student working like this assumes that the entire paper is going to spontaneously flow in one vivid stream of inspiration. If only we could come up with the first couple of words, it would all work! But composition is rarely that orderly. As I sit working on this chapter of this textbook, I have not yet written the introductory chapter. And while I have a very solid outline for the final chapter, I have not yet decided how to finish this chapter. One of the lessons we learn as we write is that we do not have to compose an essay in the order in which it is to be read. In this respect, an essay is like a motion picture, whose scenes are shot out of order to take advantage of the elements available to a filmmaker. If, for instance, a director needs to shoot both the first and last scenes of her film on a particular beach she is renting at ten thousand dollars a day, she will try to get both scenes shot at the same time. And the beach may only be available to her crew two weeks into her shooting schedule. In this case, the middle of the film is shot first and the beginning and end are shot in the middle. And if she does her job right, no one in the audience will be the wiser. The same freedom is available to the student writing an essay for class: write what you know now and let it all come together later. Once the student writer realizes that she does not need to write an entire paper but the parts of the paper (in any order), the paper becomes less demanding.

A student has been assigned a ten-page essay. He has been asked to write about one story from each of three short story writers he has studied: Flannery O'Connor, Raymond Carver, and Joyce Carol Oates. He enjoyed most of these stories, but ten pages sounds like a lot, and he cannot begin to imagine how he will fill all of those pages. So, he puts it off, he does other work, he keeps reading, he procrastinates. Suddenly the paper is due tomorrow and he is thinking about skipping out of the country on a red-eye flight to Zanzibar.

Imagine a slightly different scenario. A student has been assigned a ten-page essay. He has been asked to write about one story from each of three short story writers he has studied: Flannery O'Connor, Raymond Carver, and Joyce Carol Oates. He enjoyed most of these stories, but ten pages sounds like a lot, and he cannot begin to imagine how he will fill all of those pages. Rather than quaking in fear and trying to imagine the entire paper or making travel plans, he consults his notes and begins to assemble possible sections of a possible paper. He noticed the importance of family in the stories by O'Connor and Oates, so he freewrites what amounts to a mini-paper of maybe two or three pages on that topic. Or he may decide to simply freewrite three separate responses to these short stories—one for each writer. In this way, it is possible to come up with three mini-papers of two or three pages each. If these papers are refined and joined with an introduction and conclusion and linking paragraphs, our student can progress in short order from panic over a ten-page assignment to proofreading the finished product.

Of course, the paper could also be organized around other principles than a comparison of the three authors' work: perhaps the role of women in two of the stories or family relationships or use of symbolism. And the freewriting may be chopped up and rearranged any number of ways. The real benefit to this kind of exercise is not that it produces an instant paper but that it produces information that can then be organized into some kind of paper rather than producing little balls of crumpled paper that fill a wastepaper basket.

Clustering

Freewriting is an exercise designed to generate data without much of a sense of organization. Clustering is the opposite: an exercise designed to generate a sense of organization but without much data. Clustering encourages the writer to look for the connections between a few ideas without creating the kind of proto-rough draft one ends up with after doing some freewriting. The benefit of clustering is that it leads the writer to an outline. And while building an outline may seem like a formality that slows you down when what you really want to do is fill the five to ten pages you have been assigned, an outline is really a valuable tool to creating a coherent and intelligent essay that need not be tossed into the garbage because it does not make any sense. Here is a clustering exercise that tries to make sense of the role of women in Flannery O'Connor's "A Good Man Is Hard to Find":

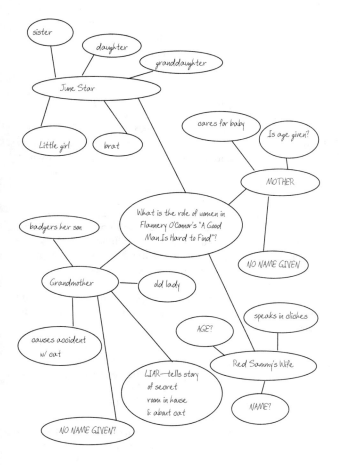

This exercise may look a mess, but it has gotten our writer thinking in an orderly fashion. A clustering exercise allows a writer to create a visual model of his paper. At the center of this little "solar system" is a major idea, or in this case a question: "What is the role of women in Flannery O'Connor's 'A Good Man Is Hard to Find'?" Revolving around this "sun" are smaller "planets" and revolving around these "planets" are "moons." Each of these heavenly bodies is an example from the text or a question. This visual model allows our writer to begin from a very general idea or question and move out to the specifics that may make their way into his paper.

For instance, he began with simple categories: character and gender. His clustering has helped him think of other ways to think about the characters: ages, names, relationships. He may move away from these ideas, but at least he has begun *analyzing* the story, or breaking it down into smaller units.

Outlines

At some point in the seventh or eighth grade, we were probably all taught a very familiar—and rigid—outline format. It involves a series of Roman and Arabic numerals, upper- and lowercase letters. This traditional model is very useful when writing an essay. This outline format allows us to plan the content of a paper before we actually write the paper itself.

These outlines can map out virtually the entire paper, sentence by sentence. For some students, this is a godsend—allowing them to simply flesh out the completed outline, adding a few details and transitions to finish the essay. The outline allows students to think about the relationships between each and every idea in the paper before writing a rough draft.

Imagine a student has been asked to write a paper about Poe's "The Tell-Tale Heart" as a confession. She may write an outline such as this one:

I. "The Tell-Tale Heart" is an ironic confession.
   A. Confessions depend on specific moral codes.
   B. The narrator of "The Tell-Tale Heart" admits he did terrible things.
   C. The narrator's *tone* implies that he knows he has done wrong.
   D. The narrator's *diction* implies that he believes he has done nothing wrong and that telling the story of the crime will exonerate him.
   E. Thesis: The confession in "The Tell-Tale Heart" is ironic, or perhaps not really a confession at all, because it is made by an individual *seemingly* unaware that he has done wrong and will be punished for it.
II. Confessions have certain formal qualities.
   A. They are made by individuals who have violated rules of some kind.
   B. They are made to individuals with power over the person confessing.
      1. You only confess to those who can do something about the confession.
      2. Confessing gives the person to whom you speak power over you, even if that person did not have such power beforehand.

    C. A confession implies a moral or ethical
       framework.
       1. You can only "confess" if you think you've
          done something wrong.
       2. *Wrong* and *right* are moral, ethical, and/or
          legal terms.

III. The narrator of "The Tell-Tale Heart" observes the
    "formal" qualities of the confession.
    A. The narrator who addresses the reader
       describes the rules he has violated.
    B. The narrator seems to be addressing individuals
       with power over him.
       1. He has mentioned police in the story. We
          may assume that he is addressing this
          confession to those police officers or their
          superiors.
       2. He also addresses us, the readers of the story.
          We have the power to judge him.
    C. The narrator has committed a specific crime:
       murder.
       1. He describes how he has killed and butchered
          the old man. He does not seem to entirely
          understand that he has done something
          wrong, and his desire to put himself at risk by
          confessing implies this.
       2. He is likely in the custody of the police—they
          are charged with arresting those who violate
          moral, ethical, and legal codes.
    D. On a "formal" and legal level, the narrator is
       confessing.

IV. However, the narrator seems unaware of the
    ethical, moral, and legal consequences of his
    actions.
    A. The narrator offers little motive for killing the old
       man.
       1. He says he loved the old man.
       2. He says he killed him because of his eye.
          a. Narrator calls the eye evil.
          b. The eye is likely covered with a cataract.
    B. The narrator says that his confession should
       prove his sanity, but it does the opposite.
       1. Sane people do not kill for such trivial causes.
       2. Sane people fear the consequences of
          breaking the law.
    C. Although the narrator makes a legal confession,
       he has not truly demonstrated that he knows he
       has done wrong.

V. Since Poe does not simply follow the crime-confession-consequences pattern, this story may be about something other than this one crime.
   A. The narrator seems to think that we (the readers) will sympathize with him.
   B. The narrator seems to think that everyone sees things the way he does.
   C. Conclusion: Rather than reestablish order at the end, the confession makes for less order.
      1. The story uses the confession structure to demonstrate how little real "order" there is in the world.
      2. The narrator does not really understand his world.
         a. There is a distance between his *tone* and his *diction.*
         b. This distance reveals his madness.
      3. He thinks we will agree with him—maybe we do not really understand the world, either. We may be as "mad" in our own way as the narrator is.

Okay, she has turned out a reasonable outline here, and it is easy to imagine how she could turn this into an essay of about four or five pages. The outline, as practiced here, is a useful tool for turning initial ideas into completed essays.

But many writers do not work this way. They find the form too structured and formal. They have trouble remembering when to use the "I" or the "1."

It can be intimidating. For some students, the outline is so elaborate that it becomes a ritual that becomes an end in itself, and completing the outline supersedes completing the paper. Students hung up on whether to move from uppercase "A" to number "1" or letter "b" have missed the point. An outline allows us to see the skeleton of an essay and to consider how to best flesh out that skeleton. But the skeleton does not have to look just like the one Miss Fishbeck wrote on the board all those years ago in the fifth grade. The Roman numerals and so forth are *means* to an *end.* The end matters more than the means here, so find your own style of outline.

Even writers who cannot keep the "A" and the "a" straight can use an outline that is much less formal. Such an outline might look something like this:

Paragraph 1: Thesis: the confession in "The Tell-Tale Heart" is ironic, or perhaps not really a confession at all, because it is made by an individual seemingly unaware that he has done wrong and will be punished for it.

Paragraph 2: define confession: formal, legal aspects

Paragraph 3: define confession: moral aspects

Paragraph 4: narrator does confess formally

Paragraph 5: narrator does not confess morallyg

Paragraph 6: narrator tries to show he's sane and innocent—really shows he's crazy & guilty: <u>ironic</u>

Paragraph 7: Poe doesn't want to just gross us out—he wants us to think about what's right and wrong and why we think that

Paragraph 8: Conclusion: Poe isn't just a horror writer—he's asking moral questions

This is an outline of sorts. This writer has drawn a box to indicate a paragraph or a "chunk" of the paper and jotted in the ideas he wants to cover in that section. You will notice that although both plans start at about the same place, they end up in different places. The first outline ends up discussing "order" and "disorder"; the second ends up discussing Poe as a writer of more than horror fiction. The first outline looks like a straightforward blueprint of the paper. The second is much rougher. The paragraphs are not fully developed as they are in the first outline. Of course, that is fine. A writer need not follow a very rigid plan. If the writer changes his mind halfway through the paper, he just scribbles out the old box and draws a new one.

Others might find this mode very confusing. What is important, however, is not that a writer chooses one or the other but that he or she realizes that there is a variety of ways to plan a paper. Remember that the format you choose to plan your paper will change the shape of your paper. Planning a paper allows the writer to imagine a draft before it is written. If you can imagine your paper, you can edit it and rearrange it before even putting pen to paper or sitting down at the keyboard.

UNDERSTANDING YOUR AUDIENCE AND MAKING LOGICAL ARGUMENTS ABOUT LITERATURE

Literature is an art; therefore, our reaction to it and our analysis of it will often proceed from a subjective point of view. However, although literary analysis is not exactly a science, good literary analysis does demand a solid basis in logic and fact. It is often said that all readers' reactions to a given work of literature are equally valid. There is much truth in this sentiment. Certainly, if a reader responds to William Faulkner's *As I Lay Dying* by saying "I'm depressed" or comments after seeing a production of Shakespeare's *A Midsummer Night's Dream,* "I thought that was really funny," no one could honestly respond by saying "No, you're not depressed" or "No, you didn't think it was funny." Our reactions are our own and as such they are valid and not necessarily in need of support or validation.

However, once we decide to address a public audience regarding our response, we take on the obligation of making sure our responses are logically balanced, factually accurate, generally sound, and supportable. So while everyone has the right to think that, for instance, Kate Chopin's short story "The Story of an Hour" is terrible, no one can assume that stating as much is the same as making a successful argument. Simply stating our opinions is not enough to carry an argument. It is incumbent upon the person making the argument to ensure that the argument makes sense. If, for instance, a reader wants to make the argument that "The Story of an Hour," which chronicles the death of a Victorian-era husband and the unconventional reaction of the less-than-distraught wife, is an immoral story, that is fine.

However, that reader must understand that several obstacles stand in his way. Of course, one obstacle is that the readers of his paper may come to the argument with a very different opinion of the work. In fact, since Chopin's story is held by many to be a minor classic of American literature, it is safe to assume that many readers of his paper will be inclined to disagree with him from the start. And if they disagree with his first sentence, he may have trouble getting them to read the second. Since he cannot assume that simply saying " 'The Story of an Hour' is an immoral story" will result in his readers immediately dismissing the story, he has to develop a strategy that will allow him to approach this audience and convince them to abandon their ideas and adopt his. Half of this strategy will involve understanding just who his audience is and the other half will involve understanding just what an argument is. Read Kate Chopin's "The Story of an Hour" and imagine a response to it.

The Story of an Hour
(1894)
by Kate Chopin

Knowing that Mrs. Mallard was afflicted with a heart trouble, great care was taken to break to her as gently as possible the news of her husband's death.

It was her sister Josephine who told her, in broken sentences, veiled hints that revealed in half concealing. Her husband's friend Richards was there, too, near her. It was he who had been in the newspaper office when intelligence of the railroad disaster was received, with Brently Mallard's name leading the list of "killed." He had only taken the time to assure himself of its truth by a second telegram, and had hastened to forestall any less careful, less tender friend in bearing the sad message.

She did not hear the story as many women have heard the same, with a paralyzed inability to accept its significance. She wept at once, with sudden, wild abandonment, in her sister's arms. When the storm of grief had spent itself she went away to her room alone. She would have no one follow her.

There stood, facing the open window, a comfortable, roomy armchair. Into this she sank, pressed down by a physical exhaustion that haunted her body and seemed to reach into her soul.

She could see in the open square before her house the tops of trees that were all aquiver with the new spring life. The delicious breath of rain was in the air. In the street below a peddler was crying his wares. The notes of a distant song which some one was singing reached her faintly, and countless sparrows were twittering in the eaves.

There were patches of blue sky showing here and there through the clouds that had met and piled one above the other in the west facing her window.

She sat with her head thrown back upon the cushion of the chair, quite motionless, except when a sob came up into her throat and shook her, as a child who has cried itself to sleep continues to sob in its dreams.

She was young, with a fair, calm face, whose lines bespoke repression and even a certain strength. But now there was a dull stare in her eyes, whose gaze was fixed away off yonder on one of those patches of blue sky. It was not a glance of reflection, but rather indicated a suspension of intelligent thought.

There was something coming to her and she was waiting for it, fearfully. What was it? She did not know; it was too subtle and elusive to name. But she felt it, creeping out of the sky, reaching toward her through the sounds, the scents, the color that filled the air.

Now her bosom rose and fell tumultuously. She was beginning to recognize this thing that was approaching to possess her, and she was striving to beat it back with her will—as powerless as her two white slender hands would have been.

When she abandoned herself a little whispered word escaped her slightly parted lips. She said it over and over under her breath: "free, free, free!" The vacant stare and the look of terror that had followed it went from her eyes. They stayed keen and bright. Her pulses beat fast, and the coursing blood warmed and relaxed every inch of her body.

She did not stop to ask if it were or were not a monstrous joy that held her. A clear and exalted perception enabled her to dismiss the suggestion as trivial.

She knew that she would weep again when she saw the kind, tender hands folded in death; the face that had never looked save with love upon her, fixed and gray and dead. But she saw beyond that bitter moment a long procession of years to come that would belong to her absolutely. And she opened and spread her arms out to them in welcome.

There would be no one to live for during those coming years; she would live for herself. There would be no powerful will bending hers in that blind persistence with which men and women believe they have a right to impose a private will upon a fellow-creature. A kind intention or a cruel intention made the act seem no less a crime as she looked upon it in that brief moment of illumination. And yet she had loved him—sometimes. Often she had not. What did it matter! What could love, the unsolved mystery, count for in face of this possession of self-assertion which she suddenly recognized as the strongest impulse of her being!

"Free! Body and soul free!" she kept whispering.

Josephine was kneeling before the closed door with her lips to the keyhole, imploring for admission. "Louise, open the door! I beg, open the door—you will make yourself ill. What are you doing Louise? For heaven's sake open the door."

"Go away. I am not making myself ill." No; she was drinking in a very elixir of life through that open window.

Her fancy was running riot along those days ahead of her. Spring days, and summer days, and all sorts of days that would be her own. She breathed a quick prayer that life might be long. It was only yesterday she had thought with a shudder that life might be long.

She arose at length and opened the door to her sister's importunities. There was a feverish triumph in her eyes, and she carried herself unwittingly like a goddess of Victory. She clasped her sister's waist, and together they descended the stairs. Richards stood waiting for them at the bottom.

Some one was opening the front door with a latchkey. It was Brently Mallard who entered, a little travel-stained, composedly carrying his grip-sack and umbrella. He had been far from the scene of the accident, and did not even know there had been one. He stood amazed at Josephine's piercing cry; at Richards' quick motion to screen him from the view of his wife.

But Richards was too late.

When the doctors came they said she had died of heart disease—of joy that kills.

Defining Audience

When writing about literature, especially when writing literary argument or literary analysis, we make several assumptions about our audience. One of the key assumptions we often make is that our audience is made of more than one reader. Actually, we often know that this assumption is false. In a literature class, the "real-life" audience is obviously the professor who assigned this paper to the class. Why not write as if Professor Smith is the only one likely to read this paper? That is the truth is it not? Well, that probably is the truth, but it is not always the best strategy.

Who Is in Our Audience?

In literary analysis, we often imagine an audience composed of many readers, not merely our professor. This convention of classroom rhetoric has tradition on its side. Since this tradition has deep roots, our professor will likely be expecting a paper not exclusively addressed to her.

Another reason to imagine a wider audience is that such a strategy will allow the writer to avoid errors of omission. If a student is writing only to Professor Smith, he may tend to assume certain shared information. If Professor Smith has spent time defining *allegory* in class, why does our student need to define it in his paper? Well, that kind of omission may lead to lazy writing in the future. Our student may even proceed with a faulty definition if he feels no need to articulate the term in his paper. It is in this student's best interest to supply his readers with whatever key information he feels they may need to understand his paper. Of course, he does not want to have to reinvent the wheel with every paper, but it is wisest to conceive of an audience that may need to be reminded of some familiar information from time to time rather than let the professor supply information on her own. And, of course, in the classroom, the person grading the paper also wants the student to demonstrate what he has learned.

Since we assume we are addressing an audience greater than simply our professor or our class, it is best to refrain from referring to the classroom context of our reading unless such references strongly support our position. It is counterproductive to include a phrase such as "Our class has read three Faulkner novels so far . . . " or "As we said in class. . . . "

We should try to write as if we were addressing someone we have not met. We should take a professional tone and avoid personal references *unless* they help us support our argument.

What Does Our Audience Know About the Text?

We also assume that our audience is familiar with the text. If we write a paper about William Faulkner's *As I Lay Dying,* we assume our audience has read the novel. Therefore, it is not necessary for us to summarize the novel for the audience. Remember, we want to strike a balance between the "broad audience" of our imagination and the "real-life" audience of our professor; we always have to consider her reaction to the paper. And, of course, it is safe to assume that the person who assigned the paper has read whatever work of literature the class has read.

We also assume, if we are making an argument concerning a fuller understanding of a literary work, that we must be talking to someone who has some understanding of the work. How can a reader unfamiliar with a text seek a fuller understanding of it?

However, we still quote the text. Why bother if the audience has read the work? At least two reasons.

First, we assume the audience has *read* the work. We do not assume they have *memorized* it. Selective use of quoted passages reminds our reader of important events or comments made in the work. Also, since we are explaining our view of the work, it is possible that certain passages we found to be especially important were overlooked by our reader. It is our job to shed light on those passages that lead to the fuller understanding to which we have come.

Second, we want to display our expertise. Frequent quoting shows the reader that we are familiar with the works we discuss. And, again, our real-life reader is our professor. She wants us to demonstrate our mastery of the class material.

What Does Our Audience Think About the Text?

While we assume our audience knows the text we discuss, we do not assume that they came to the same conclusions about it that we have. In fact, it is likely that our readers never considered our position or that they did consider our position only to dismiss it. It is likely we are dealing with an opposition audience we must convince to accept our views. In fact, the safest approach to take in an argumentative paper is to assume that your readers disagree with you. After all, your goal is to shore up support for your position.

To return to our Kate Chopin story, if our reader wants to ensure that immoral works such as "The Story of an Hour" lose their readership, he wants to deal first and foremost with those who approve of the story and are likely to recommend it to others. If he begins his work assuming that he will be talking to like-minded people, only like-minded people will listen to him. If he assumes that he will be speaking to both those who agree and disagree with him, he will be able to get his ideas to the converted and unconverted alike. And remember, like-minded people do not need convincing. Hence, an effective literary analysis paper will make reference to (and attempt to defeat) counterarguments, or contrary positions.

Why Should I Respect My Opposition Audience?

One of the benefits of taking such care imagining an audience is that the writer will hopefully begin to develop some respect for these imaginary people and their ideas. If our student is outraged by "The Story of an Hour," it may be impossible for him to imagine that anyone could possibly enjoy it. Many papers proceed from such a point of view. They often begin with outright attacks on the work in question. Imagine our student has decided to take such a rhetorical position. He may begin his paper with a frontal assault on the story he finds so disagreeable:

> Kate Chopin's short story "The Story of an Hour" treats the sacred institution of marriage with flagrant disregard. Chopin's works were considered morally unacceptable by readers in the 1890s, and they are morally unacceptable today. Readers who applaud Kate Chopin as a fine writer have made a decision to give in to the worst kind of moral relativism, all in the name of feminism.

This paper has a lot of passion. It is angry and full of fire. Here is a person who clearly takes literature seriously. Perhaps this writer's passion will intrigue a fan of "The Story of an Hour" so much that he or she will keep reading and ultimately switch sides. Knowing how people tend to stick to their guns, however, I rather doubt it. In fact, since the final sentence directly attacks those readers, I imagine many have stopped reading. Another introduction, one that assumes that readers who favor Chopin have some kind of valid reason to like the story (and, therefore, a valid reason to disagree with the author of this paper), may actually treat those readers with respect and convince them to read for a few pages. Since showing respect for our audience and their diverse opinions can benefit him rhetorically, it is worth this writer's while to consider their point of view.

Also, in the interest of humility, it might be a good idea for him to remember that he might not know everything, and that it is indeed possible that he is mistaken or at least overstating the truth when he states his position. It benefits him and his cause to go back to the germ of his idea and ask where it came from. Once he does that, he can consider the logical and factual value of the idea.

Why Do I Need to Know About Logic to Make an Argument?

As I said earlier, literature is an art, and discussion of art is often going to proceed along subjective and personal lines. But when communicating our ideas to others, we need to scrutinize the logical and factual basis of our arguments. Everyone has an opinion, but few can articulate their opinions well enough to convince others their opinions are worth listening to. For instance, consider the reader who sticks to his guns in the face of contravening factual evidence. If we read a mystery novel and come to the early conclusion that the butler did it, it may disappoint us to find out that actually the killer was the maid or the reclusive heiress. No amount of arguing on your part can change the plot. Or it may be that you believe that the motives ascribed to the maid are suspect. Imagine that the omniscient third-person narrator tells us, "The maid always hated Mr. Smythe-Bristol because he had insisted on supporting the wrong football team." We may have trouble picturing a maid who doubles as a football hooligan, but if the omniscient third-person narrator tells us that is the case, it must be so! We might argue that the butler is the better choice for a killer or that the novel is flawed because it overlooked this prime plot twist or that the motive is out of character, but we cannot really argue that the novel ended differently than it did.

This is a broad example, but just as this argument needs to be approached with scrutiny, so too must any argument that hopes to be taken seriously. There are various reasons why many literary analysis arguments are doomed to failure from the start, from mistakes in point of fact to overconfidence in theory. But often it boils down to mistakes in logic. A reader may misread a text and proceed to make a flawed argument that only works if we all misread together. These arguments can be mended simply by discovering the error.

Mistakes made because of adherence to one theory can be more difficult because we may be such fervent believers in a pet theory that no amount of argument can sway us. For instance, readers of poetry often subscribe to the theory that poetry is much more personal than prose and, therefore, all poetry should be read as autobiographical. Readers of Edgar Allan Poe, Emily Dickinson, and Walt Whitman often take this approach. All of the women in Poe's poetry are really his wife and all the mourning lovers are him; all of Dickinson's poems can be chalked up to a failed romance with a minister; all of Whitman's poems detail his sex life.

These kinds of statements may not seem to be theoretical errors, but in fact they are. The theory is "poetry is autobiography." And although that theory may be accurate in some cases, it is not universal. These errors cannot stand up to close logical scrutiny.

What Is a Syllogism?

Logic is a small word but it conjures up big ideas and often big misunderstandings. Basically, logic is the study of the principles of reasoning. When we consider logic, we study the form of propositions as much as their substance. So, when we apply logical scrutiny to one of our ideas, we need to distance ourselves from the idea long enough to think about the *structure* and not the *content* of the argument.

One classical logical structure used in argumentation is the syllogism. Aside from Mr. Spock and Sherlock Holmes, syllogistic reasoning may be the first thing we think of when we think of the word *logic*. Whenever a TV detective reasons from the general to the specific to come to his deduction, we are witnessing the use of a syllogism. Syllogisms are a form of deductive reasoning consisting of a major premise, a minor premise, and a conclusion. Deductive reasoning is the process by which we reach a conclusion following from stated premises. Or we might say like the TV detective that we are reasoning from the general to the specific.

We looked at Aristotle's famous syllogism in Chapter 3. Let us revisit that ancient argument:

> All men are mortal.
>
> Socrates is a man.
>
> Therefore, Socrates is mortal.

This syllogism is a three-part argument, consisting of a major premise, a minor premise, and a conclusion. We can label this syllogism thus:

> All men are mortal. [major premise]
>
> Socrates is a man. [minor premise]
>
> Therefore, Socrates is mortal. [conclusion]

The syllogism is certainly a useful construct, and with it we can unravel many a faulty argument. Now, we will apply the syllogistic form to our friend's argument about "The Story of an Hour" and see if it passes logical muster. Here is the thesis:

> Kate Chopin's short story "The Story of an Hour" treats the sacred institution of marriage with flagrant disregard. Chopin's works were considered morally unacceptable by readers in the 1890s, and they are morally unacceptable today. Readers who applaud Kate Chopin as a fine writer have made a decision to give in to the worst kind of moral relativism, all in the name of feminism.

We might notice that there is a lot to deal with here: marriage, feminism, Chopin's career, and one hundred years of history. How do we turn this introduction into a syllogism? The basic argument perhaps can be summed up like this:

> "The Story of an Hour" is morally unacceptable literature because it treats the sacred institution of marriage with disrespect.

To find the syllogism, we can trace back from the conclusion to the minor premise and then to the major premise. The conclusion is clear enough:

"The Story of an Hour" is morally unacceptable.

Why does our writer come to this conclusion? Because the story treats the sacred institution of marriage with disrespect. This conclusion seems to proceed from a clear minor premise:

> Since "The Story of an Hour" treats the sacred institution of marriage with disrespect, it is morally unacceptable.

But where is the major premise? Nowhere to be found! What we have here, then, is not a syllogism but an *enthymeme,* or a syllogism that leaves out one of the premises. We often encounter enthymemes in situations in which the major premise can be taken for granted or is widely accepted. For instance, we can agree with the statement, "Murderers should be punished" without running through a major premise such as "murder is wrong."

The unspoken major premise of this argument must read something like this:

> Literature that treats the sacred institution of marriage with disrespect is morally unacceptable.

If that is the case, then the syllogism on which this paper is built is something such as the following:

> Major Premise: Literature that treats the sacred institution of marriage with disrespect is morally unacceptable.
>
> Minor Premise: "The Story of an Hour" treats the sacred institution of marriage with disrespect.
>
> Conclusion: Therefore, "The Story of an Hour" is morally unacceptable.

So we have tested the thesis and it seems to be logically acceptable or valid. Not only that but we have learned something about the thesis as well. It is based on strong feelings about the institution of marriage in general, not just as depicted in this story.

Can readers object to the student's response to the story on these grounds? Does marriage need to be defended or will most readers generally agree that marriage is important enough that its value need not be articulated? Well, the story has a very solid reputation (it appears in many collections of important fiction, for instance). So, apparently, someone feels the story is valuable. Maybe our writer needs to establish his basis for objection.

While the argument is valid—that is to say, the syllogism works—many disagree with it. They must be wrong, though, because the syllogism works, right? No. It is possible for a syllogism to be valid and still untrue. Consider this syllogism:

> All Americans wear cowboy hats.
>
> Edward A. Shannon is an American.
>
> Therefore, Edward A. Shannon wears a cowboy hat.

As with our previous syllogisms, we are dealing with "classes" or groups of things: mortals, men, works of literature, Americans. In a syllogism, we work from the large group (mortals, men, literature that treats marriage with disrespect, Americans) to the particular (Socrates, "The Story of an Hour," Edward A. Shannon). The syllogisms seem to work, but they can only be called "true" if all the premises are true. In this latest syllogism, we can see the line of reasoning, but we know that the major premise is false. In the Chopin argument, the reasoning looks fine, but only if we accept that major premise. The many readers who enjoy "The Story of an Hour" may not necessarily accept that *all literature that treats the sacred institution of marriage with disrespect is morally unacceptable* the way that they accept that *all men are mortal.* Since our writer ultimately wants to convince others that he is right about "The Story of an Hour," he needs to examine his major and minor premises.

Has marriage changed since the story was written in 1894 and today? Is all criticism of marriage disrespectful? Is the story really criticizing marriage at all? Is that question worth exploring? Is there evidence in the text to suggest that our writer is wrong, and that the story does not demean marriage? Is there evidence to show that criticizing marriage as an institution is not the same as disrespecting marriage?

In "The Story of an Hour," the heroine, Mrs. Louise Mallard, feels a sudden rush of freedom when she learns of her husband's death. Chopin writes that Mrs. Mallard feels a sense of "joy" upon hearing the news. Does that mean that she is some kind of cold-hearted psuedo-murderer? Can she be defended? Think about what is in the text. Once she is hidden in her room, the heroine says to herself, "free, free, free!" That seems pretty cold, although not entirely malevolent. She does not say, "Aha! My scheme worked! Now I can run off with Richards!" She does not seem to want her husband dead, but she does not seem to wish him back, either. Her response is extremely unusual.

Why would she speak about her husband like that? She seems to think he is a decent fellow. In fact, the story's narrator later tells us:

> She knew that she would weep again when she saw the
> kind, tender hands folded in death; the face that had never
> looked save with love upon her, fixed and gray and dead.

Why does Mrs. Mallard not make up her mind? These ideas
also run through her mind:

> And yet she had loved him—sometimes. Often she had
> not. What did it matter! What could love, the unsolved
> mystery, count for in face of this possession of self-
> assertion which she suddenly recognized as the strongest
> impulse of her being!

Why does she love him so little? And how can she say love
does not matter? Marriage is supposed to be built on love;
was that not always the case?

Our writer might look at the date of the story's publication and ask himself if our contemporary definition of marriage is accurate for the marriage Chopin describes. Were
arranged marriages in fashion at the time? Were marriage
bonds based on love or mutual need and respect? Did women
have much say in who or when they married? What rights
did they have in the marriage? Women only got the vote in
the United States in 1920. What was life like twenty-six years
before that?

Does the writer believe that marriage today should more
closely resemble marriage as it was in 1894? How equal could
this marriage have been? Maybe the freedom she looks forward to is freedom from nineteenth-century rules of marriage, not from Brently Mallard, her husband, about whom
she has some warm personal feelings. Remember, she is sad
to think of his "tender hands folded in death" and "the face
that had never looked save with love upon her, fixed and gray
and dead." She loves this man. But does she love being married? She thinks:

> There would be no one to live for during those coming
> years; she would live for herself. There would be no pow-
> erful will bending hers in that blind persistence with
> which men and women believe they have a right to im-
> pose a private will upon a fellow-creature. A kind inten-
> tion or a cruel intention made the act seem no less a crime
> as she looked upon it in that brief moment of illumination.

Maybe these feelings about marriage account for Louise's
less than loving response to her husband's apparent death
and her disappointment at his return. Our reader was responding then, not to the evidence in the text but to his own

emotions. And an argument built on emotional response is going to be weaker than one built on evidence.

In fact, given the evidence of the text, Chopin seems to be criticizing an institution very different from the institution of marriage we know today. Is the word *criticize* different from *disrespect*? Can one be critical of an institution without being disrespectful of it? Perhaps our writer needs to reexamine his syllogism:

> Major Premise: Literature that treats the sacred institution of marriage with disrespect is morally unacceptable.
>
> Minor Premise: "The Story of an Hour" treats the sacred institution of marriage with disrespect.
>
> Conclusion: Therefore, "The Story of an Hour" is morally unacceptable.

Is it possible that his reconsideration of his response, the text, and historical context has helped him uncover a logical flaw? Well, he started out saying that "The Story of an Hour" is morally unacceptable, and now he almost sympathizes with Mrs. Mallard's feelings, although he still holds marriage to be sacred. The problem he has here is one of definition. He assumed that *marriage* only had one meaning, but now he sees at least two definitions for *marriage:* marriage in the late nineteenth century and marriage in the early twenty-first century. Also, he wrongly assumed that criticism was tantamount to disrespect. In essence, his problem was that his definitions were too broad. With more specific language, he can perhaps draft another thesis that reflects both his respect for marriage and his understanding of the value of social criticism:

> Kate Chopin's "The Story of an Hour" is a morally challenging story. It asks us to consider the sacred institution of marriage from the point of view of someone who suffered under its inequities. Chopin's story is ultimately a work of social criticism that attempts to criticize an institution many hold sacred. Chopin manages to do so without showing disregard for the ideals of love and loyalty that marriage should support.

Maybe he has turned this thesis around too far. Is it impossible to believe that a reader could completely change his mind about a story in this way? Actually, that is one of the beauties of literature. Literature is about feelings and subjective responses more than it is about logic. Through literature we can experience a variety of responses. However, when we begin to discuss our reaction to the literature, we must consider not only the logic of the work of literature but also our response to it. Effective literary analysis often forces us to analyze not just the work of literature but our responses to it. This process can be as intellectually satisfying as it is emotionally frustrating.

The preceding example shows how a faulty definition can lead to a faulty argument. Since the literature we read is often from a bygone era, we often run into this problem. Because social convention and the connotation of words are always changing, we may find ourselves responding to ideas that are not exactly what the text is trying to communicate.

A logical fallacy is a flaw in logical reasoning. Sometimes it is a flaw in our syllogism, sometimes a flaw in our information, sometimes a flaw in the kind of authority we seek to support our argument. But there are other ways to develop authority in an argument. Certainly, it is important to show your reader that your ideas are logically sound. It is just as important, however, to make sure that they see that your ideas matter, are interesting and compelling, and have some sort of bearing on the literature and the life of the reader. In other words, a good writer shows the reader that there is something in the essay for the reader.

THE "SO WHAT?" QUESTION

One of the most important rhetorical objectives to consider when writing any essay of importance, especially one with an argumentative agenda, is making the reading of the paper worth the reader's time. What does this mean? After all, we know who is reading the paper and why he or she is reading it. The reader is the professor and the professor is reading the paper to put a grade on it. But to have a really successful paper, we must remember that the reader is also a human being who may find himself or herself bored or distracted. How will we keep the reader reading?

Basically, you need to answer the question: So what? Imagine a given paper successfully argues that, say, Edgar Allan Poe uses symbolism or one of Shakespeare's plays is ironic. The paper may be true and valid, but that does not make it interesting. How can the writer make her reader want to keep reading? She starts by thinking of the needs of the reader. Chapter 5 will try to answer these questions in greater detail, but for now we will consider broad strategies for keeping the reader's interest.

When I was a graduate student, I was working on a paper with a professor. He had seen draft after draft and had approved of what I was saying. But at one point he told me,

"Well, yes, this works, but right now it is just an academic exercise." I really did not understand him at the time. "Of course it is an academic exercise," I thought. It was not until much later that I understood what he meant. I was doing all of the things I was supposed to do, but I was not making any attempt to excite and engage the reader. I wrote as though I understood that it was the reader's obligation to keep reading.

The reader needs to see that the argument matters in some substantive way. The writer needs to show that her argument does more than just answer a question on an essay exam. She needs to write as though she cares about this topic. That may mean using transitional words and phrases that create an organizational strategy in her paper more complicated than *first, second,* and *third.* When introducing a topic, the writer should not just repeat the professor's question. She should rephrase it and make it her own. Creating a *new* thesis allows her to "own" the paper. It also allows her to create an organization for the paper.

The writer needs to understand that the reader's time is valuable. The reader may not need to be entertained, but he does need to be engaged. The writer should open the paper with some comment that shows that the paper will cover a topic in which the reader can find himself or herself.

Writing an Introduction

Generally speaking, there are broad strategies a writer can use to make an introduction effective. Generally, an essay should begin with a full paragraph introduction that builds up to a clear, arguable thesis statement. A paper that opens with a thesis may be too blunt. Imagine, for instance, that the first sentence of a paper reads, "Shakespeare's *A Midsummer Night's Dream* relies on imagery, symbolism, and metaphor." Well, this may be true enough, but it is a bit abrupt. Why talk about Shakespeare? Why this play? Why analyze it? Why metaphors and symbols and irony?

Imagine another introduction, one that leads into the discussion more subtly:

William Shakespeare is probably the most famous writer in the English language. He is held up as one of the greatest writers of all time. Still, contemporary readers of Shakespeare's plays sometimes complain that his antiquated language is difficult to follow and that plays about kings and princes mean very little to Americans. However, Shakespeare is also an entertainer, and this is most obvious in comedies like *A Midsummer's Night Dream*. Although this very funny play does concern kings and princes (and queens and gods), the language is very funny and worth the effort of even modern-day readers, even those who do not care for royalty. The humor of Shakespeare's *A Midsummer Night's Dream* relies on imagery, symbolism, and metaphor.

This introduction tries to be a little more interesting than the first one. This introduction sticks to the same basic thesis, but it also gives the reader a *reason* to be thinking about all those images, symbols, and metaphors.

Building on the Introduction

Subsequent paragraphs should refer to the thesis statement. Make sure each paragraph refers explicitly to the texts you write about. Quotations and paraphrased statements are much more effective than vague references to the texts. Each paragraph should refer explicitly back to the thesis and introductory paragraph(s). The writer can achieve this by repeating key words and phrases that appear in the introduction.

For instance, the rest of our Shakespeare paper should refer back to the ideas the introduction brings up (Shakespeare's lofty reputation, modern readers' difficulties with subject matter and language, comedy, the comic power of the imagery, symbolism, and metaphors). These specific ideas will give the writer of this paper solid foundations for the rest of the paper and a handy structure to build the paper on.

Writing a Conclusion

The conclusion is a notoriously difficult section of the paper. Like the introduction, the conclusion needs to walk the tightrope between broad and general. The essay writer often gets to the conclusion having used up all of the great examples and arguments in the previous paragraphs! Battle fatigue can settle in during those final paragraphs, and many a tired writer has wanted to simply write "That's all, folks!" and hand the paper in!

But the conclusion is an essential part of the essay. The conclusion is the writer's last opportunity to tell the reader why he or she has read the paper. It is the writer's last chance to hammer home the importance of the topic. It is the writer's last chance to answer the question, "So what?"

As with the introduction, the conclusion can be approached with a few broad ideas to guide you. Conclusions should restate the thesis in new, more specific language. The thesis should not merely be cut from the introduction and pasted into the conclusion. In the introduction, we float a possible reading of a text or solution to a problem. The reader has seen no evidence and may have never considered the issue before. By the end of the paper, the reader has seen evidence, thought about the problem, considered and disregarded counterarguments, and worked his or her way through a series of minor arguments. The conclusion should speak to those experiences. By the time the writer has gotten to the conclusion, he should be ready to assert his ideas in bolder, more assertive language.

The conclusion is also the writer's last chance to make the reader look at all of the evidence! Summarize that evidence. Did the reader understand just how many metaphors there were in act 1, scene 1? Should the writer count the ones he cited in the paper? Should he repeat the funniest? Is there one line in particular that needs to be repeated? Perhaps the paper could borrow this line as a title. Then a final repetition at the end of the paper would be doubly appropriate. For these last few sentences, the writer has access to the reader. He needs to take advantage of that access.

Finally, the conclusion should shed a new light on the value of the paper's argument (there is that "so what?" question again!). However, it should not introduce new information. This seems to be a contradiction. However, there is a difference between commenting on an argument that has already been made and engaging in a new argument. Perhaps when the writer restates his thesis, he can take a minute to comment on the importance of coming to an understanding of Shakespeare's plays or the fact that Shakespeare is still a major cultural force. A few comments such as this can reflect positively on the comments a writer has already made without sounding like a whole new set of arguments. Taking time to examine just why this paper was necessary is a way of making sure the paper ultimately proves a point about the text under discussion.

5

Putting It All Together

Throughout this book, we have referred to Edgar Allan Poe's "The Tell-Tale Heart." In this chapter, we will read and annotate the story, look at some sample paper assignments, and read some sample essays about the story. This exercise will illustrate several of the principles this book has tried to demonstrate.

Let us start with what seems to be a simple assignment, a summary. A summary is a more or less objective assignment, remember, in which the writer is asked to merely report information found in the text. We are not asked to respond to the work or to analyze it, merely to describe the action of the text. Still, the summary presents its own challenges. Following is a detailed assignment from an Introduction to Literature class. Read the assignment and begin thinking of the demands the paper makes on the writer of the summary.

Paper Assignment One: The Summary
Due date: _____ 10%

- Make sure that the paper you write conforms to MLA standards. Be sure to document all borrowed material using MLA documentation and parenthetical citation rules. Your mastery of the MLA form will constitute a major portion of your grade. Consult your handout, your notes, and the MLA style guide in the library reserve. You may also consult your grammar text. You may also bring your rough drafts to me for comment.

- Your essay should begin with a short, one-paragraph introduction that introduces the author, title, publication date, and genre of the piece being summarized. Your introduction should end with a clear "thesis" statement. This thesis statement should be phrased as a comprehensive statement regarding the text (see below).

- Subsequent paragraphs should refer to this thesis statement. Make sure each paragraph refers explicitly to the text. Make sure each paragraph refers explicitly back to the thesis.

- Your conclusion paragraph should restate the thesis in new, more specific language. It should summarize your evidence, and it should shed new light on the value of your argument. It should not introduce new information.

- Proofread carefully. Use the *proofreading checklist* on my homepage. Make sure you prove a point about your text. Talk to me if you have questions.

In a short paper (at least 500 words), write a summary of Edgar Allan Poe's "The Tell-Tale Heart." This should be a comprehensive summary. That is, your paper should begin with a major statement about the primary action of the story and then move on to a recounting of the chain of events that informs the story. Imagine you are writing to someone who has not read the story.

This summary should mention every detail that you consider essential to a competent understanding of the story's plot and the primary action with which you begin the paper. Of course, you will omit all details you deem unnecessary to a complete understanding of the plot. You *may* quote the story, but you should not quote extensively.

This summary should include a Work Cited page documenting Poe's story. It should use parenthetical citation if and when it quotes the text. Your paper should feature the heading, title, and page number formats described by the MLA guide.

Your paper should draw no overt, major conclusions; it should simply summarize the story as fully as possible in a small space.

Immediately we notice that this assignment is not merely a summary. The professor has included several specific guidelines for the completion of the project. Before beginning any work on a summary, the writer should make sure he or she understands the assignment. The assignment sheet opens with the following paragraph:

- Make sure that the paper you write conforms to MLA standards. Be sure to document all borrowed material using MLA documentation and parenthetical citation rules. Your mastery of the MLA form will constitute a major portion of your grade. Consult your handout, your notes, and the MLA style guide in the library reserve. You may also consult your grammar text. You may also bring your rough drafts to me for comment.

This assignment makes early reference to MLA documentation standards. The MLA (Modern Language Association) has established standards for documenting research in literary studies. These standards are very familiar to people who study literature. Although many writers think of documentation as an afterthought, this professor *begins* his assignment with a description of what kind of documentation he expects for this paper. This aspect of the paper should arrest the writer's attention; he should track down the resources mentioned. When he proofreads, he should double check to make sure he has documented properly. The professor has also mentioned his willingness to look at rough drafts. The writer should not be afraid to take him up on his offer.

■ Your essay should begin with a short, one-paragraph introduction that introduces the author, title, publication date, and genre of the piece being summarized. Your introduction should end with a clear "thesis" statement. This thesis statement should be phrased as a comprehensive statement regarding the text (see below).

■ Subsequent paragraphs should refer to this thesis statement. Make sure each paragraph refers explicitly to the text. Make sure each paragraph refers explicitly back to the thesis.

■ Your conclusion paragraph should restate the thesis in new, more specific language. It should summarize your evidence, and it should shed a new light on the value of your argument. It should not introduce new information.

■ Proofread carefully. Use the *proofreading checklist* on my homepage. Make sure you prove a point about your text. Talk to me if you have questions.

More specific directions: the professor requests a full introduction with what he calls a "comprehensive" thesis. This introduction must contain several specific elements: "author, title, publication date, and genre." The assignment suggests a specific, multiparagraph structure. The conclusion needs to be more than just the final element in the plot. This paper cannot be written in one long paragraph. This paper demands more than just a sequence of events.

The assignment also makes specific reference to the mechanics of good writing. Reading the assignment closely gives the writer a good idea of the thinking of the person who wrote the assignment and who will be grading the paper.

> In a short paper (at least 500 words*), write a summary
> of Edgar Allan Poe's "The Tell-Tale Heart." This should
> be a comprehensive summary. That is, your paper should
> begin with a major statement about the primary action of
> the story and then move on to a recounting of the chain
> of events that informs the story. Imagine you are writing
> to someone who has not read the story.

The meat of the assignment arrives. We are to write a
summary of "The Tell-Tale Heart." The term *comprehensive*
is defined. In this context, the term is used to describe a
summary that begins with the "key event" of the story and
then proceeds to describe the other major events as they
relate to that key event. This summary is not a simple list
of plot points. In a way, this summary is going to be a kind
of analysis. To truly summarize a work of fiction, one must
analyze the fiction, or break it into its parts. To break a work
of fiction into its major parts, a writer must truly understand
the story; he must have given it some thought and organized its parts in his imagination. He must have given some
thought to what the major rhetorical goals of the story are.
Is the author trying to scare us? Amuse us? Fool us?

> This summary should include a Work Cited page docu-
> menting Poe's story. It should use parenthetical citation
> if and when it quotes the text. Your paper should fea-
> ture the heading, title, and page number formats de-
> scribed by the MLA guide.
>   Your paper should draw no overt, major conclusions;
> it should simply summarize the story as fully as possible
> in a small space.

There is new information here, too. He asks not just for MLA
documentation but also for the formatting of the paper, including pagination and title page. This "summary" assignment seemed simple and straightforward at first, but it has
become clear that even a short paper such as this can be
quite a complicated venture.

  Of course, this assignment is particular to one professor
and one class. However, in any instance when a paper is
assigned, it is wise to gather as much specific information
as possible regarding the instructor's standards and the specific demands of the paper. Often a simple assignment is not
as simple as it seems at first glance.

  Now that our writer has a working understanding of the
assignment, he needs to read the story and draft his paper.
The first object is, of course, to read the story. Hopefully, he
will do this with pen in hand, annotating the tale, looking for

those elements that fall into our four broad categories of annotation: What is confusing? What is repeated? What is familiar? What is strange?

If he reads, but "not for comprehension," he will not be able to accurately summarize the story. However, since he knows he is being asked to summarize, he may want to tailor his note taking to the task. It might be wise to concentrate on summarizing the story as he goes, perhaps in the margin of the book.

THE TELL-TALE HEART
by Edgar Allan Poe
(1843)

date for intro para

TRUE!—nervous—very, very dreadfully nervous I had been and am; but why will you say that I am mad? The disease had sharpened my senses —not destroyed—not dulled them. Above all was the sense of hearing acute. I heard all things in the heaven and in the earth. I heard many things in hell. How, then, am I mad? Hearken! and observe how healthily—how calmly I can tell you the whole story. *first person pov.*

—character's name is not given; says he's not crazy & his story will prove it
—"super-natural" senses

It is impossible to say how first the idea entered my brain; but once conceived, it haunted me day and night. Object there was none. Passion there was none. I loved the old man. He had never wronged me. He had never given me insult. For his gold I had no desire. I think it was his eye! yes, it was this! He had the eye of a vulture—a pale blue eye, with a film over it. Whenever it fell upon me, my blood ran cold; and so by degrees—very gradually—I made up my mind to take the life of the old man, and thus rid myself of the eye forever.

—second character: old man
—narrator says he has no reason to hurt the old man, but he says the man's eye drove him to get rid of the man

A reading of "The Tell-Tale Heart" does not take long, and the notes our reader takes are not terribly detailed. But going through the story with pen in hand allows him to have a sort of "rough draft" of his summary ready before he even sits down to write his paper. Still, the notes will serve as a useful guide when he is ready to write his paper. But before beginning, he needs to answer a key question. Since this is not merely a sequential summary, he needs to begin not with the first event but with the key event in the story. Or, as the assignment sheet puts it, he needs to begin with a "major statement about the primary action of the story and then move on to a recounting of the chain of events that informs the story." There cannot be any question about that, can there? Surely the murder of the old man is the "primary action" of the story. But could there be anything else? Since the story is a confession, could he suggest that the true primary action is the *capture* of the killer? Or is it the moment when he pulls up the floorboards and reveals the evidence of his crime? This is surely the moment for which the story is most famous. Or is the primary action really his recitation of his confession to us the readers? Perhaps his arrest? Or maybe his statements about his sanity?

Well, the writer may finally decide that the murder is indeed the primary action since it is that murder that precipitates the confession and the revelation of the killer's madness. But the nature of this assignment asks that the writer ask this question. Here our earlier comments about summary being a kind of analysis are proven right. To begin summarizing this story, he needs to break the story down and assign relative value to its parts.

Finally, our writer decides that the murder is indeed the "primary action." With that decision made, he begins his rough draft:

> Edgar Allan Poe's "The Tell-Tale Heart" is the story of the brutal murder and dismemberment of an unnamed old man and the subsequent capture and confession of the killer the story is related to us by the killer himself, who like the old man, is never given a name. As the story progresses, it becomes increasingly clear that the killer is insane.
>
> The story opens with the narrator asserts his own sanity. As evidence of his sanity, the narrator cites his keen senses and says he heard everything in heaven, earth and hell. He says his keen senses lead him to the decision to kill the old man, for he has no rational reason to kill the man. It is not anger, jealousy or his greed that prompts the murder, but an obsession with the eye of the old man. The eye is a remarkable "pale blue eye, with a film over it." The killer sets out to get rid of the old man.
>
> Over the course of one week, the killer sneaks into the old man's room each night. The narrator is careful to point out that his slow deliberate actions indicate his intelligence, and therefore his sanity, for, he tells us, "Madmen know nothing." Each of these visits revolve around little more than the narrator shining a light on the old man's closed eye. He finds he cannot kill him, however, unless he sees the eye. The following day he is careful to be polite and friendly to the old man. Again, his kindness to the old man he intends to kill is meant to be seen as evidence of his sanity.

On the eighth night, the old man awakens, and the killer shines his lantern light directly on the old man's eye. After terrorizing the old man, staring at his eye and ignoring his questions, the killer begins to hear the old man's heart beating. Again, this amazing sensory ability is evidence of the man's sanity. The sound of the beating heart drives the killer to a state of "terror" and he finally "drag[s] him to the floor, and pull[s] the heavy bed over him," killing him.

To conceal his crime, the killer dismembers the body, claiming to catch all the blood in a tub. He buries the body beneath his floor boards.

After a while, three policemen arrive to inquire into the whereabouts of the old man. The killer invites the policemen in and talks to them while seated upon the very spot where he had buried the old man. To display his sanity and cleverness, he sits with the police and calmly speaks to them. Eventually, he becomes agitated at a ringing in his ears. He then realizes the sound is not in his ears and that the police must hear it, too. Angered that they do not respond to the sound, the narrator becomes angry and "argue[s] about trifles." Even after his apparent arrest, the killer believes that the police deliberately ignored hearing the sound. Before identifying the sound, he says:

> They heard! —they suspected! —they knew! — they were making a mockery of my horror!—this I thought, and this I think.

Eventually, he tears up the floor boards, reveals the corpse and admits his deed, furious that the police pretend not to hear the sound, which the narrator finally identifies as "the beating of [the dead man's] hideous heart!" The story of the murder of an innocent old man ends where it begins: with the confession of the murderer.

His paper seems to live up to the expectations of the assignment. But, even so, the student may have questions about the paper. His *thesis* (as much as one can have a thesis for a summary) is as follows:

> Edgar Allan Poe's "The Tell-Tale Heart" is the story of the brutal murder and dismemberment of an unnamed old man and the subsequent capture and confession of the killer.

That is certainly a reasonable statement to describe what happens in the story, and the paper is just over 500 words. All of its body paragraphs return to the ideas of murder, concealment, and confession. But has our writer really made the *truest* assessment of the action of the story in his thesis?

As he wrote, it occurred to him that he was relating as true certain comments made by the narrator/killer that clearly were not true: his definition of sanity, his denial of anger at the old man, his claims about his senses. Our reader did not believe the narrator while reading the story; why should he believe him now? Is it not more fair to say that "The Tell-Tale Heart" is about the narrator's revelation of his insanity? Could he rephrase his thesis to show this?

> "The Tell-Tale Heart" is the story of the confession of a mad killer. Although he claims to be sane, his every comment demonstrates his insanity.

This thesis would produce a slightly different paper. The writer would cover the same ground, but he would be moving to a different conclusion: one that demonstrates the killer's madness, not his actions. Still, such a thesis seems a little too close to analysis. It seems that he is making assertions that need to be proven. Our writer is not entirely comfortable with the decision, but he decides to stick with the first thesis. His experience demonstrates that even summary is a kind of analysis and argument. Two different people could read this story, come up with two different summaries, and both could be right, in their own fashion.

If that is the case with a summary, imagine an assignment that asks more than just a recounting of events as they unfold in the plot. If a student is asked to analyze the story, consider his reaction to it, and to come to conclusions of his own, the possibilities become even greater. It is much easier to imagine several possible answers to such a question. Later, we will consider writing such a paper about "The Tell-Tale Heart." But first, our student writer needs to proofread his summary and prepare it to be handed in for a grade.

PROOFREADING FOR CLARITY

Proofreading means more than simply scanning a paper to make sure it more or less means what we think it does. Proofreading should be a slow, thorough process of reading your paper line by line, sentence by sentence, and even word by word. Often, we want to just glance at a paper fifteen minutes before handing it in, but that is a fatal mistake. If we do not slow down and read carefully, the most glaring errors will slip past us. This is true because we know what we *want* the paper to say, so we will often read what should be on the page rather than what actually is on the page; that is one way we hamstring ourselves. Another reason we may do a poor job with our proofreading is that basically we do not want to find any errors.

Imagine a student rushing into a writing lab with a paper and saying, "Can you read this? But don't make any marks on it; it's due in twenty minutes." Well, why does he want the paper read? If he does not want any marks on the paper, he cannot be planning to revise it. This is an extreme example, but this student is not so much different than many of us. When we are done with a first draft, we want it to be perfect. We do not want to go back and do more work on it. But the truth is that most of our best writing is going to happen in revision, and that is certainly true of revising the kind of mechanical errors proofreading can help us weed out.

One of the things I have tried to do for my students is to give them a list of common mechanical and stylistic errors that I find personally frustrating. This list has changed over the years, but at the moment, it looks something like this:

Proofreading Checklist

- *Proofread!* You should proofread your final draft very carefully, reading the essay to yourself (at least twice), out loud, stressing punctuation.

- *Every* essay should have a title—the title of the literary work you are writing about is *not* an appropriate title for your own paper.

- If you refer to <u>any</u> outside work (even assigned class texts), you should include a Work(s) Cited page, which should conform to MLA guidelines! Use proper MLA headings and formatting for every essay.

- When discussing texts, use common present tense and mention author and title early on.

- Try not to begin sentences with phrases such as "It is" and "There was." These constructions lead to wordy sentences.

- Avoid contractions and clichés.

- Use apostrophes appropriately.

- Words and phrases to avoid (they tend to wordiness and vagueness):
  due to
  due to the fact that
  in my opinion
  I think
  I believe
  being as
  being that

- Try to make clear transitions and connections within and between paragraphs.

- Commonly misused and confused words that should get your attention:
  who/ that
  should of/ should have

there/ they're/ their
two/ to/ too
accept/ except
affect/ effect
your/ you're
its/ it's
woman/women

■ Assume you are writing to someone who has read the
work in question; plot summary is usually unnecessary.

   Some of these items may be particular to my tastes. Other
items on this particular list may be completely nonapplicable
to you as a writer. You may never mistake *affect* for *effect*,
but that is not the point. What a list such as this should remind us of is that proofreading often turns up the same errors over and over again. Writers need to train themselves to
spot their own recurring errors. One way to do that is to start
keeping track of the errors that you cannot seem to shake.
Keep a list and read your work, looking for those errors.
   Another tip is to read your paper once for content (Did I
mention the author's name? Did I spell it correctly?) and once
for mechanics. Read the paper aloud, one sentence at a time,
overemphasizing punctuation. For instance, if we look at the
first couple of paragraphs from our friend's "The Tell-Tale
Heart" summary, we may be able to dig out some errors.
   Often when I ask students to proofread their papers (or
their classmates' papers) in class, they spend much of their
time looking for misspellings or circling commas. Other than
that, they often do not know what to look for. And they are
not alone. The standard response I get from new acquain-
tances who learn I am an English teacher is "I'd better watch
my grammar." Most people assume they do not understand
grammar, so they have little idea how to "fix" grammar unless they can identify how it is broken.
   But in point of fact, most adults have a solid grasp of the
grammar of their native language. They may not be able to
identify a dangling modifier, but they usually know when
something *sounds* wrong. And when proofreading, all a
writer really needs to do is revise the sentences that sound
wrong. He need not identify the problems using English
teacher jargon. Leave that to the professionals.
   So if we read the following paragraphs as I suggested,
emphasizing the punctuation, we may hit sentences that
sound in need of revision for clarity's sake. Read aloud, one
sentence at a time, and really "ham up" the punctuation.
When you hit a period or comma, pause much longer than
you ordinarily would. Do you need a pause there at all? When
you hit a question mark, let your voice spiral upward much

more than you ordinarily would. Is this sentence really a question? In this manner, you may not find every error in your writing, but you will find quite a bit:

> Edgar Allan Poe's "The Tell-Tale Heart" is the story of the brutal murder and dismemberment of an unnamed old man and the subsequent capture and confession of the killer the story is related to us by the killer himself, who like the old man, is never given a name. As the story progresses, it becomes increasingly clear that the killer is insane.

How does that sound? I find that I run out of breath reading the first sentence:

> Edgar Allan Poe's "The Tell-Tale Heart" is the story of the brutal murder and dismemberment of an unnamed old man and the subsequent capture and confession of the killer the story is related to us by the killer himself, who like the old man, is never given a name.

An English teacher might call this a run-on or fused sentence. Someone who is not an English teacher might just try to figure out when he or she runs out of breath. It seems to me that happens right around here:

> . . . and confession of the killer the story is related to . . .

The English teacher says that the second independent clause in this run-on begins with "the story is related to . . .". The out-of-breath, amateur proofreader may come to the same conclusion. A feasible revision might read as follows:

> Edgar Allan Poe's "The Tell-Tale Heart" is the story of the brutal murder and dismemberment of an unnamed old man and the subsequent capture and confession of the killer. The story is related to us by the killer himself, who, like the old man, is never given a name.

I could have combined the two sentences with a comma and conjunction or a semicolon, but that first sentence is already a little long. I think my solution is more readable. On to the next paragraph.

> The story opens with the narrator asserts his own sanity. As evidence of his sanity, the narrator cites his keen senses and says he heard everything in heaven, earth and hell. He says his keen senses lead him to the decision to kill the old man, for he has no rational reason to kill the man. It is not anger, jealousy or his greed that prompts the murder, but an obsession with the eye of the old man. The eye is a remarkable "pale blue eye, with a film over it." The killer sets out to get rid of the old man.

As I read this sentence, I get the feeling that there is something funny with that first sentence:

The story opens with the narrator asserts his own sanity.

That phrase, "with the narrator asserts," is just wrong. The English teacher in me says it is a mixed construction. The amateur proofreader says it sounds funny. Let us try it this way:

The story opens with the narrator's assertion of his own sanity.

We have changed the verb "asserts" to a noun, "assertion," and added the possessive "'s" to the noun "narrator." Let us move on:

As evidence of his sanity, the narrator cites his keen senses and says he heard everything in heaven, earth, and hell.

There do not seem to be any punctuation errors here. A careful reader might notice a tense problem, though. The paper begins in present tense, with "cites" and "says" but then moves into past tense with "heard." The paper should be consistent, so our student changes "heard" to "hears." The next couple of sentences yield a similarly subtle problem:

He says his keen senses lead him to the decision to kill the old man, for he has no rational reason to kill the man. It is not anger, jealousy or his greed that prompts the murder, but an obsession with the eye of the old man.

The phrase "anger, jealousy or his greed" does not sound right, does it? If I do not add "his" to "anger" or "jealousy," why do I add it to "greed"? I should cut it. Also, the English teacher says that I really ought to add a comma before the final element in the series, giving me the sentence:

It is not anger, jealousy, or greed that prompts the murder, but an obsession with the eye of the old man.

Wait! How about shortening "eye of the old man" to "old man's eye"? Here is the final revision of the sentence:

It is not anger, jealousy, or greed that prompts the murder, but an obsession with the old man's eye.

Now those last few revisions were subtle, and you might not manage to catch them. But for practical purposes, the kind of proofreading we are discussing here is useful for catching major sentence-level errors, such as the run-on we caught in the first paragraph. Actually, although the revisions we made in the second paragraph make the paper better, the errors in question did not make the paper particularly difficult to understand.

We might want a paper with nary a misplaced comma, but sometimes we need to settle for those errors we can catch. However, proofreading is a learned skill, and most writers find that as they practice on paper after paper, they refine their skills to the point that they catch even the subtler glitches.

PROOFREADING FOR FORMAL CONCERNS

We have spent some time reading our student paper, looking for ways to make the paper more clear and concise. Now let us return our attention to the "formal aspects" of the paper, that is, those elements of the assignment that deal with the final "form" the paper will take when it is handed in for a grade. Remember, although my proofreading checklist mostly deals with elements of writing associated with grammar and style, there are also formal issues mentioned there. For instance, it mentions "MLA guidelines." It also includes the following:

■ When discussing texts, use common present tense and mention author and title early on.

In fact, the assignment sheet our student began with mentions several formal requirements our professor will be looking for. Now, back to that revised paragraph:

> Edgar Allan Poe's "The Tell-Tale Heart" is the story of the brutal murder and dismemberment of an unnamed old man and the subsequent capture and confession of the killer. The story is related to us by the killer himself, who, like the old man, is never given a name. As the story progresses, it becomes increasingly clear that the killer is insane.

This introduction looks good; it seems effective. But does it fulfill the demands of the assignment? Once our student writer started writing the paper, it seems he forgot that the specific assignment he was working on had specific requirements that go beyond something general such as "write a summary." A look at the assignment reveals two specific requirements we have forgotten. The assignment reads: "Make sure that the paper you write conforms to MLA standards."
And:

■ Your essay should begin with a short, one-paragraph introduction that introduces the author, title, publication date, and genre of the piece being summarized. Your introduction should end with a clear "thesis" statement.

So the writer needs to revise the introduction so that it includes the specific information the assignment requests (publication date and genre), and he needs to make sure the paper is written in MLA style. Here is the revised version, written in MLA style, with one-inch margins:

Michael McKeon
Eng. 101
Dr. Shannon
Sept. 14, 2000

"The Tell-Tale Heart": A Summary

Edgar Allan Poe's "The Tell-Tale Heart" is a short story first published in 1843. This horror story tells of the brutal murder and dismemberment of an unnamed old man and the subsequent capture and confession of the killer. The story is related to us by the killer himself, who, like the old man, is never given a name. As the story progresses, it becomes increasingly clear that the killer is insane.

The story opens with the narrator's assertion of his own sanity. As evidence of his sanity, the narrator cites his keen senses and says he hears everything in heaven, earth, and hell. He says his keen senses lead him to the decision to kill the old man, for he has no rational reason to kill the man. It is not anger, jealousy, or greed that prompts the murder, but an obsession with the eye of the old man. The eye is a remarkable "pale blue eye, with a film over it" (Poe 194). The killer sets out to get rid of the old man.

Over the course of one week, the killer sneaks into the old man's room each night. The narrator is careful to point out that his slow, deliberate actions indicate his intelligence and, therefore his sanity, for, he tells us, "Madmen know nothing" (Poe 195). Each of these visits revolves around little more than the narrator shining a light on the old man's closed eye. He finds he cannot kill him, however, unless he sees the eye. The following day he is careful to be polite and friendly to the old man. Again, his kindness to the old man he intends to kill is meant to be seen as evidence of his sanity.

On the eighth night, the old man awakens, and the killer shines his lantern light directly on the old man's eye. After terrorizing the

old man, staring at his eye and ignoring his
questions, the killer begins to hear the old
man's heart beating. Again, this amazing sensory ability is evidence of the man's sanity. The sound of the beating heart drives the
killer to a state of "terror" (197) and he finally "drag[s] [the old man] to the floor, and
pull[s] the heavy bed over him" (197) killing
him.

To conceal his crime, the killer dismembers
the body, claiming to catch all the blood in
a tub. He buries the body beneath his floorboards.

After a while, three policemen arrive to
inquire into the whereabouts of the old man.
The killer invites the policemen in and talks
to them while seated upon the very spot where
he had buried the old man. To display his sanity and cleverness, he sits with the police
and calmly speaks to them. Eventually, he becomes agitated at a ringing in his ears. He
then realizes the sound is not in his ears and
that the police must hear it, too. Angered
that they do not respond to the sound, the
narrator becomes angry and "argue[s] about
trifles" (198). Even after his apparent arrest, the killer believes that the police deliberately ignored hearing the sound. Before
identifying the sound, he says:

They heard! —they suspected! —they knew!
—they were making a mockery of my horror!
—this I thought, and this I think. (198)
Eventually, he tears up the floorboards, reveals the corpse, and admits his deed, furious that the police pretend not to hear the
sound, which the narrator finally identifies
as "the beating of [the dead man's] hideous
heart!" (199). The story of the murder of an
innocent old man ends where it begins: with
the confession of the murderer.

McKeon 3

Work Cited

Poe, Edgar Allan. "The Tell-Tale Heart."
   Selected Writings of Edgar Allan Poe. Ed.
   Edward H. Davidson. Boston: Houghton
   Mifflin, 1956. 194-199.

Our student's MLA-style title page is simple and straight-forward. The paper begins on the next line after the title. In MLA style, the paper does not need a separate title page (or a plastic folder or other trappings of the sort). He includes his name, the class title, his professor's name, and the date in the upper left-hand corner. In the upper right-hand corner he supplies his last name and the page number (notice that this heading appears on the Work Cited page as well). He does not boldface or italicize or underline his title. The entire paper, including the heading on page 1 and the Works Cited page is double-spaced. He has also been careful to use MLA-style parenthetical documentation and has included a Work Cited page. He has also made sure to proofread the paper, looking for logical lapses, factual errors, mechanical errors, and typographical errors.

For a fuller description of MLA style, see Chapter 6. But for now our student has this paper looking presentable. Now that the summary is ready to be handed in, he can get to work on a more challenging project, an analysis paper. The following assignment is also written for the same Introduction to Literature class. It describes a writing project more complex than a summary: an analysis.

Paper Assignment Two: Subjective Analysis
Due date: _____ 15%

■ Make sure that the paper you write conforms to MLA standards. Be sure to document all borrowed material using MLA documentation and parenthetical citation rules. Your mastery of the MLA form will constitute a major portion of your grade. Consult your handout, your notes, and the MLA style guide in the library reserve. You may also consult your grammar text. You may also bring your rough drafts to me for comment.

■ Your essay should begin with at least a full paragraph introduction that concludes with a clear, arguable thesis statement. Subsequent paragraphs should refer to this thesis statement. Make sure each paragraph refers explicitly to the text(s) you discuss (quote and/or paraphrase several times in each paragraph). Make sure each paragraph refers explicitly back to the thesis (repeat key phrases, etc.).

■ Subsequent paragraphs should refer to this thesis statement. Make sure each paragraph refers explicitly to the text. Make sure each paragraph refers explicitly back to the thesis.

■ Your conclusion paragraph should restate the thesis in new, more specific language. It should summarize your evidence, and it should shed new light on the value of your argument. It should not introduce new information.

■ Proofread carefully. Use the <u>proofreading checklist</u> on my homepage. Make sure you <u>prove a point</u> about your text. Talk to me if you have questions.

> In a short paper (at least 1,000 words), write a subjective analysis of Edgar Allan Poe's "The Tell-Tale Heart." You should read the story, consider your response (were you scared? confused? anxious? bored?). Then analyze the story: find out how Poe managed to make you feel the way you felt.
>
> This paper should not be a summary of the plot. Do not simply narrate the events of the story in your own words. Imagine you are writing to someone with a knowledge of Poe and his story. This audience has read the story. They have drawn conclusions about the story. Now have them reconsider their conclusions and adopt yours instead.
>
> To avoid summary, make sure that your paper is organized on some principle other than the plot. Do not walk through the plot describing how you felt page by page. Create a comprehensive thesis, one that describes your overall reaction to the entire story. Next address several major points in the story and show how these aspects of Poe's fiction created the effect that they did.
>
> You should refer to the story frequently. Make sure to quote and/or paraphrase from the story several times in each paragraph of your paper (excluding your introduction and conclusion, which may or may not include quoted passages).
>
> This paper should include a Work Cited page documenting Poe's story. It should include parenthetical citation when it quotes the text. Your paper should feature the heading, title, and page number formats described by the MLA guide.
>
> Your paper should draw a specific conclusion; it should not simply summarize the story.

This assignment is noticeably different from the previous one, but just as obviously, there are some common elements. Like the previous assignment, this one demands a Work Cited page and other MLA format requirements. Like the previous assignment, this one makes certain demands on organization. The professor asks us "to avoid summary."

He also makes the following statements:

> Your essay should begin with at least a full paragraph introduction that concludes with a clear, arguable thesis statement. Subsequent paragraphs should refer to this thesis statement. Make sure each paragraph refers explicitly to the text(s) you discuss (quote and/or paraphrase several times in each paragraph).

These statements again indicate that a clear organization will be an important aspect of this paper. This next comment seems particularly telling:

> Make sure each paragraph refers explicitly back to the thesis (repeat key phrases, etc.).

Here the professor makes a specific suggestion regarding how the paper is organized. He must find this to be particularly important. Otherwise, the first half of the assignment is very similar to that of the first half of the first assignment sheet. Later on, other distinct changes appear.

This paper has a minimum word count of 1,000 words. Obviously, the professor wants more content out of the student this time. The student's opinions must be worth more than mere summary. This paper is worth 15% of the student's grade, whereas the summary was worth only 10%.

Since the professor puts a higher value on analysis, the student should remind himself what analysis means. In Chapter 2, we borrowed a definition from *A Handbook to Literature* by Hugh Holman and William Harmon. They define *analysis* as follows:

> A method by which a thing is separated into parts, and those parts are given rigorous, logical, detailed scrutiny, resulting in a consistent and relatively complete account of the thing and the principles of their organization.[1]

This definition helps us shed light on another comment made in the assignment sheet. Asking us to avoid summary, the professor wrote:

> Do not walk through the plot describing how you felt page by page. Create a comprehensive thesis, one that describes your overall reaction to the entire story. Next address several major points in the story and show how these aspects of Poe's fiction created the effect that they did.

This comment refers to the act of analysis: separating a thing into parts and scrutinizing those parts. Again, our student's close reading of the assignment sheet should help him hone the aspects of his writing that the professor will value most.

Since the phrasing in this assignment tells him that analysis is a "higher-order" task, he needs to address the paper with even greater vigor than he did the summary. Perhaps a rereading of the story is in order. When he initially read the story planning only to summarize, his notes were merely a running summary of the text. Now, however, he is being asked to do more. He is asked to analyze the story and to craft a subjective response. So he may wish to reread, taking new

[1]Holman and Harmon, op. cit., pp. 22–23.

notes with new guidelines for his reading. He needs to again reconsider his basic annotating guidelines: What is confusing? What is repeated? What is familiar? What is strange?

To this list, he will want to add some other key ideas. Remember, he is being asked to analyze the story, or break it into its parts. What are the "parts" of a work of fiction? There is plot, character, dialogue, description, word choice (or diction), and tone to begin with. Of course, he knows that literature often makes use of figurative language, such as metaphor, simile, imagery, and symbolism. With these ideas floating in his mind he can address the story with a more careful eye than he did in his previous reading.

The Tell-Tale Heart
by Edgar Allan Poe
(1843)

5 senses—esp. hearing

True! —nervous —very, very dreadfully nervous I had been and am; but why will you say that I am mad? The disease had sharpened my senses —not destroyed—not dulled them. Above all was the sense of hearing acute. I heard all things in the <u>heaven</u> and in the earth. I heard many things in <u>hell</u>. How, then, am I mad? Hearken! and observe how <u>healthily</u>—how calmly I can tell you the whole story.

says he is sane b/c he can hear hell

first person pov.

real love? not $

motive?

gross

plans murder is he honest

It is impossible to say how first the idea entered my brain; but once conceived, it <u>haunted</u> me day and night. Object there was none. Passion there was none. I <u>loved</u> the old man. He had never <u>wronged</u> me. He had never given me insult. For his <u>gold</u> I had no desire. <u>I think</u> it was <u>his eye! yes</u>, it was this! He had the eye <u>of a vulture</u>—a pale blue eye, with a <u>film</u> over it. Whenever it fell upon me, my blood ran cold; and so by degrees— very gradually—I made up my mind <u>to take the life</u> of the old man, and thus rid myself of the eye forever.

dark language

not revenge

metaphor

about the eye? He seems to decide as he says it. "I think it was his eye. Yes!" Should we believe him?

In these notes, since the student writer is looking for more than a basic plot, he begins to make deeper observations. When he underlines words such as *film* and *vulture,* he identifies unusual aspects of Poe's language. Also, when he pays attention to the ironic use of *healthily,* he is looking at Poe's unusual stylistic decisions. These observations fall into the "what is strange?" category.

defines sanity as intelligence

define??

"thrust": violent word choice

hearing/sight?

Now this is the point. You fancy me mad. Madmen know nothing. But you should have seen me. You should have seen how wisely I proceeded—with what caution—with what foresight—with what dissimulation I went to work! I was never kinder to the old man than during the whole week before I killed him. And every night, about midnight, I turned the latch of his door and opened it—oh so gently! And then, when I had made an opening sufficient for my head, I put in a dark lantern, all closed, closed, that no light shone out, and then I thrust in my head. Oh, you would have laughed to see how cunningly I thrust it in! I moved it slowly—very, very slowly, so that I might not disturb the old man's sleep. It took me an hour to place my whole head within the opening so far that I could see him as he lay upon his bed. Ha! would a madman have been so wise as this? And then, when my head was well in the room, I undid the lantern cautiously—oh, so cautiously—cautiously (for the hinges creaked)—I undid it just so much that a single thin ray fell upon the vulture eye. And this I did for seven long nights—every night just at midnight—but I found the eye always closed; and so it was impossible to do the work; for it was not the old man who vexed me, but but his Evil Eye. And every morning, when the day broke, I went

kindness = sanity? *he's vicious & crazy*

this is funny?

pattern: wise = sane

sound: sense of hearing

whole week

focus on sight

boldly into the chamber, and spoke
courageously to him, calling him by
name in a hearty tone, and inquiring how he has passed the night. So
you see he would have been a very
profound old man, indeed, to suspect that every night, just at twelve,
I looked in upon him while he slept.

he's a stalker!

*lots of language of sight & hearing—no metaphors or similes
smart always means sane to this guy*

8th night

Upon the eighth night I was
more than usually cautious in
opening the door. A watch's minute hand moves more quickly than
did mine. Never before that night
had I felt the extent of my own
powers—of my sagacity. I could
scarcely contain my feelings of
triumph. To think that there I was,
opening the door, little by little,
and he not even to dream of my
secret deeds or thoughts. I fairly
chuckled at the idea; and perhaps
he heard me; for he moved on the
bed suddenly, as if startled. Now
you may think that I drew back—
but no. His room was as black as
pitch with the thick darkness, (for
the shutters were close fastened,
through fear of robbers,) and so I
knew that he could not see the
opening of the door, and I kept
pushing it on steadily, steadily.

sound image?

power trip

define??

hearing

*talks to us
again*

I had my head in, and was
about to open the lantern, when
my thumb slipped upon the tin fastening, and the old man sprang up
in bed, crying out—"Who's there?"

sight/light

hears him

dialogue

I kept quite still and said nothing. For a whole hour I did not
move a muscle, and in the meantime I did not hear him lie down.
He was still sitting up in the bed
listening;—just as I have done,
night after night, hearkening to the
death watches in the wall.

*long time—
believe him?*

sound image

*compares self
& victim
define??*

can you take AN HOUR to move your head in a door? How much is true?

Our student's reading and annotation of the story offers different information this time. When he reads with an eye toward *his own reaction,* he makes different notes than he does when he only wants to summarize. The second time around his notes are as likely to be about *his thoughts* (original information) as about the content of the story (Poe's information). And it is this "original information" that will constitute his reaction paper. He finds our four categories are useful. He has stopped to look at matter in the story that is confusing, such as unfamiliar words ("dissimulation," "sagacity," "death watches") or the narrator's madder claims (he *hears* hell). He has spotted repeated information (or patterns), such as the narrator's definition of sanity (cleverness or wisdom) or Poe's use of sound images (clocks, creaking doors) and light images (the old man's eye, the lantern). He has underlined strange details (like the narrator's ideas on health and love!). However, he has not stopped to note much in the way of familiar information. It seems, in this story anyway, that Poe is not using allusion to refer to texts our student may have read previously.

If he continues reading the story with these kinds of questions in mind, he should end up with a text filled with notes, questions, and underlined passages. Another way to think of that material is as a very rough draft or an outline in progress. So, as he moves on to draft his analysis paper, he already has some of that work done.

His next step is to begin shaping that material into an actual rough draft, which means rereading his notes and putting that information down on paper. He may want to write an outline or do some other form of prewriting. I find that just sitting down and writing off the top of my head is a good way to start such a project. Of course, that only works if I understand that what I am producing is not a final draft, or even a rough draft, but a "predraft."

With this attitude, it is possible to begin work on a paper even if I do not feel ready to begin. If I sit down to write my first or final draft, I have to ask myself: "What is the paper going to be about? How will I organize it? What will I say? How long does it have to be? How many sources do I need?" These are tough questions and they can stop a writer dead in his tracks. However, if all the writer is doing is exploring some ideas that might or might not end up in the paper, then he does not have to worry about any of that. Freewriting might turn up a great idea or it might be junk. Either way, no one ever has to see it but the writer. No one has to worry about spelling, page length, neatness, or anything else. So, with those ideas freeing our writer up, he can look at Poe's story and his notes and begin to explore some ideas.

Freewriting on "The Tell-Tale Heart"

The interesting thing about this story is not really what this guy does but what he says you get the idea that he's talking right to you he's not an artificial sounding guy even though he's nuts it's also interesting that he thinks he's seen some things he just couldn't have seen Does he see the heart beating under the floorboards or just hear it? does the old man's eye really look like he says it does?

it's not even the things he sees but really the things he hears he says he hears a dead man's heart and he says he hears things in hell—i was thinking he really did hear this stuff at first i thought it was a horror story and we would see a demon or something but that never happens He mentions hell, the most terrifying place imaginable and then he just skips over that is the story about what's really scary? there are all kinds of horror movies about demons and devils and hell and the supernatural but Poe scares us with just one crazy guy. is one man's craziness really more scary than hell? most of those movies are awful anyway the special effects are never good enough to make you believe in them I almost like the old 50's and 40's movies that don't try to use special effects anyway. . . .

Freewriting releases the writer from the pressure of deadlines, grading anxiety, grammar rules, and so forth.

One of the dangers of freewriting, however, is that the writer may get stumped and be unable to come up with anything to write about the story. In this case, he might repeat the last sentence or start writing "I need a new idea" or something like that. Most writers find the repetition boring enough to force a new idea onto the page.

Another danger of freewriting is that the writer may wander away from his real concerns. In this example, our student has stopped talking about Poe and started talking about movies. Of course, it is easy enough to get back on track. The writer should stop at the bottom of each page and ask: "Well, is there anything good here?"

And actually, I kind of like that last remark about movies:

most of those movies are awful anyway the special effects are never good enough to make you believe in them I almost like the old 50's and 40's movies that don't try to use special effects anyway. . . .

This is certainly true, and yet Poe's story has had a reputation as a "scary" story for over one hundred years. Perhaps this subjective analysis can explore what makes "The Tell-Tale Heart" so much scarier than splatter flicks such as *Nightmare on Elm Street*.

Perhaps this analytical reading of Poe could focus on this aspect of our student's reaction. Perhaps he can draw on his very subjective fondness for horror movies. He needs to work up an outline; imagine he chooses to write a rough outline, such as the one we saw in Chapter 4. He starts with two key ideas, as he spotted them earlier: horror movies and narration.

Paragraph 1, intro:

—talk about horror movies—lots of blood, not so scary, what does scary even mean?

—Poe's not as bloody as horror movies—do people today see what is scary about Poe?

—what's really scary is how he tells the story. the narration

---

paragraph two:

—the killer controls the story, so we immediately kind of sympathize with him his is the only voice we hear

---

paragraph three:

—he is unreliable, so we do not know what is true and what is not

---

paragraph four:

—he is "realistic" and supernatural at the same time

---

paragraph five:

—the real horror is that he does not even know who he is or why, what he has done is so terrible—that's scarier than lots of blood and guts *paragraph six:*

—and the question at the end is: Is he right to confide in us? are we his kind of people? Poe scares us by making this guy seem kind of reasonable

Of course, our student could also write a more detailed, traditional outline. Let us take a look at the beginnings of such an outline:

I. Introduction
  A. Horror movies
    1. More popular than books today
    2. Very bloody and violent
    3. Not as frightening as they promise to be in spite of the blood and guts
  B. Poe's stories
    1. Compared to horror movies
    2. Not as bloody and violent
    3. Scares us with how the story is told, not the details of the story
  C. Thesis: the narration is effective because the narrator controls the story, is unreliable, makes the story seem both realistic and supernatural, and is unaware of his own evil

He could continue with this more formal outline or move right from his more informal outline into a rough draft. Both avenues have their advantages, depending on how you prefer to work. The formal outline allows the writer to see the paper emerge slowly into its final form. Also, as our student wrote the outline for the introduction, he realized that he had not drafted even a tentative thesis. The formal outline of the introduction ends with a thesis.

He also noticed that what seems like a few loosely related ideas jotted down in the rough outline looks like two discrete categories of information in the formal outline of paragraph 1. Perhaps he may end up writing a two-paragraph introduction to accommodate all of this information.

On to the first draft of the paper:

"The Tell-Tale Heart": A Subjective Analysis

Edgar Allan Poe has a reputation as one of the great horror writers of all time. In fact, if most Americans were asked to name the most famous horror writers, only two names come to mind for most people: Edgar Allan Poe and Stephen King. But Poe is far more famous than King, who is frequently compared to Poe. But more people probably know King from his movies than from his writing. It is horror movies—not novels and stories—where most Americans go to get scared these days. And those movies are very different from Poe's fiction. In the last few decades, the American horror movie has gotten bloodier and bloodier. Movies like the *Nightmare on Elm Street* and *Friday the Thirteenth* series and the films that imitate them are filled with explicit sexuality and gory images of carnage. While Poe's stories can be pretty graphic, it is safe to say that none of them are quite as visceral as the R-rated films teenagers flock to every summer.

To audiences reared on *Night of the Living Dead, Scream, I Spit on Your Grave,* and other gore-fests, Poe's fiction can actually seem rather tame. Certainly, it is hard to imagine a story like "The Tell-Tale Heart" shocking someone who has sat through something like *Cannibalistic Humanoid Underground Dwellers.* So some might suggest that Poe's fiction should no longer be considered "scary." Perhaps in this day and age we are too jaded to call what Poe writes scary. But that is only true if our definition of "horror" is the same as our definition of "shocking." My experience with these films is that I am seldom scared by them (although I am often shocked or "grossed out" by them). I am not afraid to turn off the light after I turn off the VCR or return from the theater. In fact, except for describing my favorite gross-out moment or lackluster performance, I seldom give these films another thought. However, after reading Edgar Allan Poe's "The Tell-Tale Heart," I did find myself wondering about the narrator and his strange tale for hours, even days, after reading the story. Perhaps I was not afraid to turn off the light, but I was not "grossed out" or laughing at the absurdity of the story, either. I would suggest that Poe is a writer of terrifying fiction, and that his stories are scary not because of all of the blood and surprises, but because he is able to communicate to the reader on an even deeper level than that.

In Edgar Allan Poe's "The Tell-Tale Heart," horror is about asking the reader to consider not what is in the story, but what has been left out! To properly analyze Poe's story and find out why it is superior to most of today's horror films, we should start with a definition of "horror" that goes beyond "whatever scares me!" If we think about why people go to horror movies or read scary books, we will see that often they want more than just a shock. In fact, "shock" is an element of fiction other than horror fiction. We are often shocked and thrilled in adventure stories, spy stories, mystery stories, even love stories. Horror stories have to give us more than a shock. Often (but not always) horror stories involve supernatural elements and ask us to imagine that the world does not work exactly as we imagine it does, that we are not quite as in control as we think we are. Horror stories make us feel vulnerable. The best horror stories, I think, are those in which the villain is not all-powerful—in which the bad guy is someone we can believe exists, someone we can almost sympathize with! What's scarier: the giant spider or the mad killer living next door? The scariest stories are the ones that make evil seem real. In Edgar Allan Poe's "The Tell-Tale Heart," the killer is, in a weird way, not such a bad guy. He even seems to think we will understand him. The scary thing is not what he does, but that he thinks we will understand why he did it! Poe's decision to allow the killer to do the talking makes the story a powerful work of horror fiction, because the killer then controls the story, forcing his (and only his) twisted version of events on us. He makes the events seem "realistic" even though we only see some of the events, and he makes us wonder about why he confides in us, of all people.

In Poe's story, the killer controls the narration of the story. One of the things he seems to be after in killing the old man is power. He writes:

> Upon the eighth night I was more than usually cautious in opening the door. A watch's minute hand moves more quickly than did mine. Never before that night had I felt the extent of my own powers—of my sagacity. I could scarcely contain my feelings of triumph.

He shows that he has power by killing the old man, and then again by controlling just how much we know about the events of that night. In fact, he tells us about the killing not because we have forced him to or because we are his judge but because he wants to show off just how clever and sane he is. The famous opening lines tell us this much:

> TRUE! —nervous —very, very dreadfully nervous I had been and am; but why will you say that I am mad? The disease had sharpened my senses —not destroyed— not dulled them. Above all was the sense of hearing acute. I heard all things in the heaven and in the earth. I heard many things in hell. How, then, am I mad? Hearken! and observe how healthily—how calmly I can tell you the whole story.

He is not forced to tell us this, he chooses to tell us. This makes the story very unusual and even uncomfortable. "Why does this lunatic want to talk to me?" the reader might ask. "Let him talk to someone else!" Yet, at the same time, the story is so interesting, that we keep listening. In this way, we are drawn into a gripping story but also into the "clutches" of a madman, who uses his "power" to control what we see and hear of his actions. For as long as we read, this evil man is "triumphant."

Since the killer (who never reveals his name) is in control of the story, we might not stop to wonder about how true his story is. In fact, since he confesses to a capital crime, in a weird way, he becomes kind of trustworthy. After all, if he confesses to murder, why would he lie about anything else? At the same time, we know that he is not telling the entire truth. When he tells us that he "heard many things in hell," we realize that he is obviously insane, so we discount that information. Later in the story, he tells us that he hears the dead man's heart beating beneath the floorboards. He shouts to us that he "felt that [he] must scream or die! and now—again! —hark! louder! louder! louder! louder!" Well, obviously what he hears is not the beating of the dead man's heart. He obviously hears, if anything, his own nervous heart beating as he talks to the police. So we disregard this. But we do tend to believe that he did bury the man and reveal the body just as he claims he did. Why? Is the rest of his story so believable? He claims to have killed the old man for no good reason. He tells us:

> I loved the old man. He had never wronged me. He had never given me insult. For his gold I had no desire. I think it was his eye! yes, it was this! He had the eye of a vulture—a pale blue eye, with a film over it. Whenever it fell upon me, my blood ran cold; and so by degrees—very gradually—I made up my mind to take the life of the old man, and thus rid myself of the eye forever.

Is this so much more believable than hearing things in hell? There are other details that are also questionable. He tells us that he chopped up the body and hid it. His clothes are clean for a simple reason: "There was nothing to wash out—no stain of any kind—no blood-spot whatever. I had been too wary for that. A tub had caught all—ha! ha!" That's an awful lot of blood for us to believe that not even a drop got on his clothes, and I know about blood from all those horror movies I've seen! One of the more disturbing aspects of this story is that we are left to decide how much is true. Much of what we are told is terribly disturbing, but much of what we may consider on our own could be even worse. Perhaps this man is covered in blood when the police arrive? Why not? If he can hear things in hell, maybe he cannot see things on earth! Poe asks us to consider the world from an insane point of view. When we do that, the story takes on truly horrifying aspects!

This unusual point of view offers an appropriate tone for a horror story. Although the story is "realistic" in the sense that everything in it can be explained, it has a supernatural feeling to it. While a contemporary horror film might rely on the simple shocks of a supernatural killer from another dimension, Poe offers us a real-life horror: a friend turned mad killer. But at the same time, the killer is almost supernatural because he believes he has supernatural powers. He also believes that there are other supernatural elements in the world. After all, he fears the old man's "Evil Eye." He claims to have "super senses." "The disease," the narrator tells us, "had sharpened my senses —not destroyed—not dulled them. Above all was the sense of hearing acute." Of course, he can hear things in hell, a supernatural realm. He also claims to have superhuman powers of patience. He moves unnaturally slowly while he stalks his prey:

> Oh, you would have laughed to see how cunningly I thrust it in! I moved it slowly—very, very slowly, so that I might not disturb the old man's sleep. It took me an hour to place my whole head within the opening so far that I could see him as he lay upon his bed. Ha! would a madman have been so wise as this[?]

By creating a madman for a narrator, Poe invites us to travel a dark road into the human mind. He does not "cheat" by creating an unrealistic monster, but he gives us something even better: a monster that is sometimes human, sometimes superhuman, depending on how we look at him, from our point of view or his!

And this observation of the character's "unusual realism" leads us to what makes the story truly frightening. What makes the story scary is that the narrator's view is the only one we have, and as far as he is concerned, there is nothing wrong with anything that he has done. In his world, you kill a kindly old man because of his "evil eye." Poe puts us into a madman's world and gives us no alternative explanation for the events of the story's plot. And to a certain extent, we are comfortable in his world. We read the story, we hang on to see how he kills the man, and how he is captured. Even when we may begin to sympathize with the old man, Poe is quick to get us back into the killer's head:

> Many a night, just at midnight, when all the world
> slept, it has welled up from my own bosom, deepen-
> ing, with its dreadful echo, the terrors that distracted
> me. I say I knew it well. I knew what the old man felt,
> and pitied him, although I chuckled at heart.

We might identify with the old man as the killer eases
into the room; even the killer does. But that warm sentiment is cut off with the killer's chuckle. The horror of
this story is not the shock of the blood and violence or the
hints at supernaturalism, it is in the killer's complete disregard for everything decent. This killer manages to commit a completely pointless, totally brutal and arbitrary
killing for which he is captured within hours. The "realistic" yet horrifying vision of reality we get here puts us
into a madman's head, and lets it all make some kind of
sense. That is more frightening than the ghosts of today's
horror films.

If Edgar Allan Poe's stories do not seem like they have
much in common with the horror films of today, that does
not mean that Poe's stories are not frightening. Maybe it
means that today's writers of horror stories and films have
lost their way. Poe creates a world that is real, and he tells
a story we can easily imagine happening. What's more,
he lets us see this world through the eyes of a crazed killer
who manages to pass as just another "regular guy." This
is not a killer foaming at the mouth or tricked up in a special effects costume. This killer speaks "courageously to
[his victim], calling him by name in a hearty tone, and inquiring how he has passed the night." And most frighteningly, this killer chooses to tell us all his secrets, as if we
are his friends. Worse still, the world he describes is not
so different from ours. Poe scares us not because he shows
us something new, different, and shocking. He shows us
a killer depressingly similar to us, and that's scary!

The first draft of our student's paper is done. He has at
least reached the assigned page limit. In fact, he has gone
beyond it. More important, the body paragraphs do not seem
random. There is a clear organization here, and the opening
of the body paragraphs shows that organization. In the introduction, he writes:

> Poe's decision to allow the killer to do the talking makes
> the story a powerful work of horror fiction, because the
> killer then controls the story, forcing his (and only his)
> twisted version of events on us. He makes the events
> seem "realistic" even though we only see some of the
> events, and he makes us wonder about why he confides
> in us, of all people.

Later paragraphs in the paper refer back to this statement. The next paragraph begins with a restatement of one of the ideas in this thesis statement:

> In Poe's story, the killer controls the narration of the story.

Later paragraphs follow suit, commenting on the narrator, his tone, and the information he chooses to share with us. The next paragraph picks up on the thesis again:

> Since the killer (who never reveals his name) is in control of the story, we might not stop to wonder about how true his story is. In fact, since he confesses to a capital crime, in a weird way, he becomes kind of trustworthy.

Our student follows this pattern with the remaining paragraphs.

> This unusual point of view offers an appropriate tone for a horror story. Although the story is "realistic" in the sense that everything in it can be explained, it has a supernatural feeling to it. While a contemporary horror film might rely on the simple shocks of a supernatural killer from another dimension, Poe offers us a real-life horror: a friend turned mad killer.

And

> And this observation of the character's "unusual realism" leads us to what makes the story truly frightening. What makes the story scary is that the narrator's view is the only one we have, and as far as he is concerned, there is nothing wrong with anything that he has done.

He makes an effort to repeat key terms without simply repeating himself word for word. Repeated and related words and phrases that reappear include "control of the story," "narration," "narrator's view," "unusual point of view," and "supernatural." By reminding his reader of the ideas he used in the opening paragraphs of the paper, he builds a framework that keeps the paper together.

The organization of the paper shows that this is definitely an analysis, not a summary. The paper is not structured on the plot, which could lead to summary. He has arranged the paper according to the qualities of the narrator. By focusing on his voice, he avoids a point-by-point repetition of his first paper. In fact, comparing the two papers, it is clear that summary and analysis are two very different genres. In the summary, our writer assumed he wrote to an audience who had not read the story. His task was to inform them of what happened in the story. In his subjective analysis, our student's task is quite different. A summary asks the writer not to comment on the action or to inject his opinions. An analysis asks him to develop opinions and commentary. The assignment sheet's use of the word *subjective* even highlights that aspect of the assignment. These two papers are, in fact, polar opposites: from objective to subjective, from reporting plot information to avoiding reporting plot information.

Still, what we have here is merely a first draft, and as such it is in need of revision. Let us start with the introduction, which has grown from one paragraph to three. That is not really a problem, necessarily. No rule carved in stone says an introduction must be only one paragraph long. The assignment sheet even allows for longer introductions; the instructions read, "*at least* a full paragraph introduction." One advantage of a longer introduction is that it allows the writer to ease into a subject rather than begin the paper with a blunt thesis statement. A multiparagraph introduction also allows the writer to avoid a five-paragraph paper.

"The Tell-Tale Heart": A Subjective Analysis

Edgar Allan Poe has a reputation as one of the great horror writers of all time. In fact, if most Americans were asked to name the most famous horror writers, only two names come to mind for most people: Edgar Allan Poe and Stephen King. But Poe is far more famous than King, who is frequently compared to Poe. But more people probably know King from his movies than from his writing. It is horror movies—not novels and stories—where most Americans go to get scared these days. And those movies are very different from Poe's fiction. In the last few decades, the American horror movie has gotten bloodier and bloodier. Movies like the *Nightmare on Elm Street* and *Friday the Thirteenth* series and the films that imitate them are filled with explicit sexuality and gory images of carnage. While Poe's stories can be pretty graphic, it is safe to say that none of them are quite as visceral as the R-rated films teenagers flock to every summer.

To audiences reared on *Night of the Living Dead, Scream, I Spit on Your Grave,* and other gore-fests, Poe's fiction can actually seem rather tame. Certainly, it is hard to imagine a story like "The Tell-Tale Heart" shocking someone who has sat through something like *Cannibalistic Humanoid Underground Dwellers.* So some might suggest that Poe's fiction should no longer be considered "scary." Perhaps in this day and age we are too jaded to call what Poe writes scary. But that is only true if our definition of "horror" is the same as our definition of "shocking." My experience with these films is that I am seldom scared by them (although I am often shocked or "grossed out" by them). I am not afraid to turn off the light after I turn off the VCR or return from the theater. In fact, except for describing my favorite gross-out moment or lackluster performance, I seldom give these films another thought. However, after reading Edgar Allan Poe's "The Tell-Tale Heart," I did find myself wondering about the narrator and his strange tale for hours, even days, after reading the story. Perhaps I was not afraid to turn off the light, but I was not "grossed out" or laughing at the absurdity of the story, either. I would suggest that Poe is a writer of terrifying fiction, and that his stories are scary not because of all of the blood and surprises, but because he is able to communicate to the reader on an even deeper level than that.

In Edgar Allan Poe's "The Tell-Tale Heart," horror is about asking the reader to consider not what is in the story, but what has been left out! To properly analyze Poe's story and find out why it is superior to most of today's horror films, we should start with a definition of "horror" that goes beyond "whatever scares me!" If we think about why people go to horror movies or read scary books, we will see that often they want more than just a shock. In fact, "shock" is an element of fiction other than horror fiction. We are often shocked and thrilled in adventure stories, spy stories, mystery stories, even love stories. Horror stories have to give us more than a shock. Often (but not always) horror stories involve supernatural elements and ask us to imagine that the world does not work exactly as we imagine it does, that we are not quite as in control as we think we are. Horror stories make us feel vulnerable. The best horror stories, I think, are those in which the villain is not all-powerful—in which the bad guy is someone we can believe exists, someone we can almost sympathize with! What's scarier: the giant spider or the mad killer living next door? The scariest stories are the ones that make evil seem real. In Edgar Allan Poe's "The Tell-Tale Heart," the killer is, in a weird way, not such a bad guy. He even seems to think we will understand him. The scary thing is not what he does, but that he thinks we will understand why he did it! Poe's decision to allow the killer to do the talking makes the story a powerful work of horror fiction because the killer then controls the story. Forcing his (and only his) twisted version of events on us, he makes the events seem "realistic" even though we only see some of the events, and he makes us wonder about why he confides in us, of all people.

What Is Wrong with a Five-Paragraph Paper, Anyway?

A friend once told me that he had written nothing but five-paragraph papers in college. Even term papers that needed to be ten or twenty pages long ended up being two or three five-paragraph papers strung together. He said if he had to, he could probably figure out how many paragraphs he had written in college. His high school English teacher had taught him the secret of the universe: that you could use the five-paragraph structure for just about any topic. You just needed to have an introduction, three supporting ideas, and a conclusion, and you were off and running.

Now, you may have heard some professors in English and composition complain about the five-paragraph paper. In many composition programs, a movement is afoot to kill this venerable old form. Perhaps you have heard professors complain about the five-paragraph paper. You may wonder why. There is nothing inherently wrong with the five-paragraph paper; it gets the job done. However, it is not the only structure available to writers of college papers. Students should not be afraid to experiment with other structures that allow them to write successful papers. In fact, given the animosity some professors show toward the old five-paragraph workhorse, students may want to show the person grading their papers that they can do the job in more than one way. They may end up learning something about writing once they try to do things differently.

Given its length, it is hard to imagine that our student needs to add information to the introductory paragraphs, but it is just as important to think about what he may cut from the paragraph.

Edgar Allan Poe has a reputation as one of the great horror writers of all time. ~~In fact, if most Americans were asked to name the most famous horror writers, only two names come to mind for most people: Edgar Allan Poe and Stephen King. But Poe is far more famous than King, who is frequently compared to Poe. But more people probably know King from his movies than from his writing.~~ It is horror movies—not novels and stories—where most Americans go to get scared these days. And those movies are very different from Poe's fiction. In the last few decades, the American horror movie has gotten bloodier and bloodier. Movies like the *Nightmare on Elm Street* and *Friday the Thirteenth* series and the films that imitate them are filled with explicit sexuality and gory images of carnage. While Poe's stories can be pretty graphic, it is safe to say that none of them are quite as visceral as the R-rated films teenagers flock to every summer.

Well, it did not take him long to make the inevitable comparison between King and Poe. But as it turns out, he abandons that approach and goes on to talk about horror films and not horror novels like King writes. Since he never gets back to Stephen King in the paper, there seems little reason to leave this in the introduction.

To audiences reared on *Night of the Living Dead, Scream, I Spit on Your Grave,* and other gore-fests, Poe's fiction can actually seem rather tame. Certainly, it is hard to imagine a story like "The Tell-Tale Heart" <u>shocking</u> someone who has sat through something like *Cannibalistic Humanoid Underground Dwellers.* So some might suggest that Poe's fiction should no longer be considered "<u>scary.</u>" Perhaps in this day and age we are too jaded to call what Poe writes <u>scary</u>. But that is only true if our definition of "<u>horror</u>" is the same as our definition of "shocking." <u>My experience</u> with these films is that <u>I</u> am seldom scared by them (although <u>I</u> am often shocked or "grossed out" by them). <u>I am not afraid</u> to turn off the light after I turn off the VCR or return from the theater. In fact, except for describing <u>my</u> favorite gross-out moment or lackluster performance, <u>I</u> seldom give these films another thought. However, after reading Edgar Allan Poe's "The Tell-Tale Heart," <u>I did find myself wondering</u> about the narrator and his strange tale for hours, even days, after reading the story. Perhaps <u>I</u> was not afraid to turn off the light, but <u>I</u> was not "grossed out" or laughing at the absurdity of the story, either. <u>I</u> would suggest that Poe is a writer of <u>terrifying</u> fiction, and that his stories are <u>scary</u> not because of all of the blood and surprises, but because he is able to communicate to the reader on an <u>even deeper</u> level than that.   *too vague? Personal pronouns?*
                                                   What about quotes?

In Edgar Allan Poe's "The Tell-Tale Heart," horror is about asking the reader to consider not what is in the story, but what has been left out! To properly analyze Poe's story and find out why it is superior to most of today's horror films, we should start with a definition of "horror" that goes beyond "whatever scares me!" If we think about why people go to horror movies or read scary books, we will see that often they want more than just a shock. In fact, "shock" is an element of fiction other than horror fiction. We are often shocked and thrilled in adventure stories, spy stories, mystery stories, even love stories. Horror stories have to give us more than a shock. Often (but not always) horror stories involve supernatural elements and ask us to imagine that the world does not work exactly as we imagine it does, that we are not quite as in control as we think we are. Horror stories make us feel vulnerable. The best horror stories, ~~I think~~, are those in which the villain is not all-powerful—in which the bad guy is someone we can believe exists, someone we can almost sympathize with! What's scarier: the giant spider or the mad killer living next door? The scariest stories are the ones that make evil seem real.

¶? In Edgar Allan Poe's "The Tell-Tale Heart," the killer is, in a weird way, not such a bad guy. He even seems to think we will understand him. The scary thing is not what he does, but that he thinks we will understand why he did it! Poe's decision to allow the killer to do the talking makes the story a powerful work of horror fiction, because the killer then controls the story. Forcing his (and only his) twisted version of events on us, he makes the events seem "realistic" even though we only see some of the events, and he makes us wonder about why he confides in us, of all people.

The problem in these paragraphs is that as he tries to define "horror," he moves back and forth between using "scary," "horror," "shocking," and "terrifying." In Chapter 1's discussion of "The Tell-Tale Heart," we discussed the possible different usages of "terror" and "horror." Our writer does need not to engage in that debate here, but he wants to be consistent with his terms. Finally, he does get specific about the definition, and while it may not be the best definition ever, it suits his purposes because it moves away from "shock value" as the only definition of "horror."

He also notices that he uses the personal pronoun *I* pretty frequently. Although many students have been told to never use personal pronouns, this assignment, a "subjective analysis," calls for it. One can also say that in this context, the use of personal pronouns and references to personal experience is effective because it points to the effect of the story's (and the films') techniques. The one spot where our student may have gone too far is the point where he writes "I think" while discussing the best horror stories. While his personal experience may shed light on the techniques Poe uses to affect his reader, his *opinion* is still just an opinion. And while it may be valuable to have his opinion appear in the paper, he does not need to remind his reader that it is merely opinion. Dropping the "I think" from this paragraph makes his opinion on horror stories read more like fact, and fact is more compelling than opinion!

What About Personal Pronouns?

One issue related to the writer's attitude toward his or her audience is the writer's attitude toward himself or herself. Is it wrong to use personal pronouns in an essay of literary analysis? Many students were taught in no uncertain terms never to use "I" in an essay of literary analysis.

It is not *wrong* to refer to yourself (using the pronouns *I* and *my*) in literary analysis, but it is often *counterproductive.* The audience assumes that the paper is the writer's opinion of the work in question. The writer does not need to remind them of that with phrasing like "I think" or "in my opinion." It is often wise to use a more remote voice when writing such an essay.

However, if the writer's personal experience of the work is significant, he or she should go ahead and use it. There is a difference between "It seems to me that *Ironweed* is a sad book, in my opinion" and "I wept when Gerald died." The first emphasizes the subjectivity of the writer's opinion, and the second emphasizes the emotional power of the scene in question.

Another thing he notices is that he has not made any references to the text yet. He does not necessarily have to quote from the story at this point, but he should keep in mind that the assignment explicitly calls for quotations and that a good work of literary analysis will include enough references to the work to show the writer's expertise.

Finally, our writer considers breaking that last paragraph into two paragraphs. That may be a good idea, if it seems that the reader may be losing track of the writer's train of thought as he or she moves through the paper. On to the body of the paper:

> In Poe's story, the killer controls the narration of the story. One of the things he seems to be after in killing the old man is power. He writes:
>
> > Upon the eighth night I was more than usually cautious in opening the door. A watch's minute hand moves more quickly than did mine. Never before that night had I felt the extent of my own powers—of my sagacity. I could scarcely contain my feelings of triumph.
>
> He shows that he has power by killing the old man, and then again by controlling just how much we know about the events of that night. In fact, he tells us about the killing not because we have forced him to or because we are his

judge but because he wants to show off just how clever
and sane he is. The famous opening lines tell us this much:

> TRUE! —nervous —very, very dreadfully nervous I had
> been and am; but why will you say that I am mad? The
> disease had sharpened my senses —not destroyed—
> not dulled them. Above all was the sense of hearing
> acute. I heard all things in the heaven and in the earth.
> I heard many things in hell. How, then, am I mad?
> Hearken! and observe how healthily—how calmly I
> can tell you the whole story.

He is not forced to tell us this, he chooses to tell us. This
makes the story very unusual and even uncomfortable.
"Why does this lunatic want to talk to me?" the reader
might ask. "Let him talk to someone else!" Yet, at the
same time, the story is so interesting, that we keep listening. In this way, we are drawn into a gripping story
but also into the "clutches" of a madman, who uses his
"power" to control what we see and hear of his actions.
For as long as we read, this evil man is "triumphant."

lots of block quotes—is that ok?

He has spotted a grammatical error in the use of an unnecessary comma, but that is hardly the biggest concern
here. The big question for this paragraph is the use of quoted passages. Does he want to rely so heavily on lengthy quotations? The nice thing about these "block quotes" is that
they fill out the paper, helping the student get to that minimum page length that the assignment requires. However,
if the quotations do not make the paper stronger, it does
not matter if he meets his minimum page length—his paper
will suffer from weak writing instead of missing pages. Let
us look at the use of the quoted passages and see if we can
make the paragraph stronger:

> In Poe's story, the killer controls the narration of the
> story. One of the things he seems to be after in killing the
> old man is power. The killer tells us that he feels his power
> over the old man after stalking him for a week. Bragging
> about his stealth he says, "Never before that night had I
> felt the extent of my own powers—of my sagacity." The
> killer sees his ability to sneak into the old man's bedroom
> as a testament to his wisdom and cleverness. He is so full
> of himself that "[he] could scarcely contain [his] feelings
> of triumph." He shows that he has power by killing the
> old man, and then again by controlling just how much we
> know about the events of that night. In fact, he tells us
> about the killing not because we have forced him to or
> because we are his judge but because he wants to show
> off just how clever and sane he is. The famous opening

lines tell us this much. He frames the story as a defense of his sanity. He asks us, "but why will you say that I am mad?" The rest of his tale and the way he tells it is supposed to prove his sanity to us, as he makes clear when he says "Hearken! and observe how healthily—how calmly I can tell you the whole story." He is not forced to tell us this, he chooses to tell us. This makes the story very unusual and even uncomfortable. "Why does this lunatic want to talk to me?" the reader might ask. "Let him talk to someone else!" Yet, at the same time, the story is so interesting that we keep listening. In this way, we are drawn into a gripping story but also into the "clutches" of a madman, who uses his "power" to control what we see and hear of his actions. For as long as we read, this evil man is "triumphant."

As far as page length goes, he still seems safe, but now he has cut out the sections of the passage that he does not need and he is down to the bare essentials. Hopefully, there is less chance that the reader will be distracted from his main ideas by passages from Poe that do not support his observations. Of course, it is sometimes necessary and advantageous to include longer passages but overuse can make a paper seem that it has been "padded." Later in the paper, he includes this "blocked" quotation:

> Of course, he can hear things in hell, a supernatural realm. He also claims to have superhuman powers of patience. He moves unnaturally slowly while he stalks his prey:
>> Oh, you would have laughed to see how cunningly I thrust it in! I moved it slowly—very, very slowly, so that I might not disturb the old man's sleep. It took me an hour to place my whole head within the opening so far that I could see him as he lay upon his bed. Ha! would a madman have been so wise as this[?]
> By creating a madman for a narrator, Poe invites us to travel a dark road into the human mind.

The longer quote is more effective here. The writer wants to demonstrate several things: the killer's violence, his unbalanced tone, and his unusual logic. This passage works well, and there is no reason to cut it down.

So far, revising this paper has caused the writer to look at his organization, his use of evidence, and his grammatical clarity. Further revisions will ensure that he uses other quoted passages with economy and effectiveness, and that the paper contains no major grammatical or stylistic errors. He also needs to make sure that the paper is written in MLA style. Here is the finished draft:

Michael McKeon
Eng. 101
Dr. Shannon
Oct. 9, 2000

"The Tell-Tale Heart":
A Subjective Analysis

Edgar Allan Poe has a reputation as one of the great horror writers of all time. However, It is to horror movies—not novels and stories—where most Americans go to get scared these days. And those movies are very different from Poe's fiction. In the last few decades, the American horror movie has gotten bloodier and bloodier. Movies like the *Nightmare on Elm Street* and *Friday the Thirteenth* series and the films that imitate them are filled with explicit sexuality and gory images of carnage. While Poe's stories can be pretty graphic, it is safe to say that none of them are quite as visceral as the R-rated films teenagers flock to every summer.

To audiences reared on *Night of the Living Dead, Scream, I Spit on Your Grave,* and other gore-fests, Poe's fiction can actually seem rather tame. It is hard to imagine a story like "The Tell-Tale Heart" shocking someone who has sat through something like *Cannibalistic Humanoid Underground Dwellers.* So some might suggest that Poe's fiction should no longer be considered "scary." Perhaps in this day and age we are too jaded to be frightened by Poe. But that is only true if our definition of "horror" is the same as our definition of "shocking." My experience with these films is that I am seldom scared by them (although I am often shocked or "grossed out" by them). I am not afraid to turn off the light after I turn off the VCR or return from the theater. In fact, except for describing my favorite gross-out moment or lackluster performance, I seldom give these films another thought. However, after reading Edgar Allan Poe's "The Tell-Tale Heart," I did find myself wondering

about the narrator and his strange tale for
hours, even days, after reading the story.
Perhaps I was not afraid to turn off the light,
but I was not "grossed out" or laughing at
the absurdity of the story, either. I would
suggest that Poe is a writer of terrifying fiction, and that his stories are scary not because of all of the blood and surprises, but
because he is able to communicate to the
reader on an even deeper level than that.

In Edgar Allan Poe's "The Tell-Tale Heart,"
horror is about asking the reader to consider not what is in the story, but what has been
left out! To properly analyze Poe's story and
find out why it is superior to most of today's
horror films, we should start with a definition of "horror" that goes beyond "whatever
scares me!" If we think about why people go
to horror movies or read scary books, we will
see that often they want more than just a
shock. In fact, "shock" is an element of fiction other than horror fiction. We are often
shocked and thrilled in adventure stories, spy
stories, mystery stories, even love stories.
Horror stories have to give us more than a
shock. Often (but not always) horror stories
involve supernatural elements and ask us to
imagine that the world does not work exactly
as we imagine it does, that we are not quite
as in control as we think we are. Horror stories make us feel vulnerable.

The best horror stories are those in which
the villain is not all-powerful—in which the
bad guy is someone we can believe exists,
someone we can almost sympathize with! What's
scarier: the giant spider or the mad killer
living next door? The scariest stories are the
ones that make evil seem real. In Edgar Allan
Poe's "The Tell-Tale Heart," the killer is,
in a weird way, not such a bad guy. He even
seems to think we will understand him. The
scary thing is not what he does, but that he
thinks we will understand why he did it! Poe's
decision to allow the killer to do the talking

makes the story a powerful work of horror fiction because the killer then controls the
story. Forcing his (and only his) twisted version of events on us, he makes the events seem
"realistic" even though we only see some of
the events, and he makes us wonder about why
he confides in us, of all people.

In Poe's story, the killer controls the narration of the story. One of the things he
seems to be after in killing the old man is
power. The killer tells us that he feels his
power over the old man after stalking him for
a week. Bragging about his stealth he says,
"Never before that night had I felt the extent of my own powers—of my sagacity." The
killer sees his ability to sneak into the old
man's bedroom as a testament to his wisdom and
cleverness. He is so full of himself that
"[he] could scarcely contain [his] feelings
of triumph." He shows that he has power by
killing the old man, and then again by controlling just how much we know about the
events of that night. In fact, he tells us
about the killing not because we have forced
him to or because we are his judge but because he wants to show off just how clever and
sane he is. The famous opening lines tell us
this much. He frames the story as a defense
of his sanity. He asks us, "but why will you
say that I am mad?" The rest of his tale and
the way he tells it is supposed to prove his
sanity to us, as he makes clear when he says
"Hearken! and observe how healthily—how calmly I can tell you the whole story." He is not
forced to tell us this, he chooses to tell us.
This makes the story very unusual and even uncomfortable. "Why does this lunatic want to
talk to me?" the reader might ask. "Let him
talk to someone else!" Yet, at the same time,
the story is so interesting that we keep listening. In this way, we are drawn into a gripping story but also into the "clutches" of
a madman, who uses his "power" to control what
we see and hear of his actions. For as long

as we read, this evil man is "triumphant"
(195).

   Since the killer (who never reveals his
name) is in control of the story, we might not
stop to wonder about how true his story is.
In fact, since he confesses to a capital crime,
in a weird way, he becomes kind of trustworthy. After all, if he confesses to murder,
why would he lie about anything else? At the
same time, we know that he is not telling the
entire truth. When he tells us that he "heard
many things in hell" (194), we realize that
he is obviously insane, so we discount that
information. Later in the story, he tells us
that he hears the dead man's heart beating
beneath the floorboards. He shouts to us that
he "felt that [he] must scream or die! and
now—again! —hark! louder! louder! louder!"
(199). Well, obviously what he hears is not
the beating of the dead man's heart. He obviously hears, if anything, his own nervous heart
beating as he talks to the police. So we disregard this. But we do tend to believe that
he did bury the man and reveal the body just
as he claims he did. Why? Is the rest of his
story so believable? He claims to have killed
the old man for no good reason. He tells us:

   I loved the old man. He had never wronged
   me. He had never given me insult. For his
   gold I had no desire. I think it was his
   eye! yes, it was this! He had the eye of
   a vulture—a pale blue eye, with a film over
   it. Whenever it fell upon me, my blood ran
   cold; and so by degrees—very gradually—I
   made up my mind to take the life of the
   old man, and thus rid myself of the eye forever. (194)

Is this so much more believable than hearing
things in hell? There are other details that
are also questionable. He tells us that he
chopped up the body and hid it. His clothes
are clean for a simple reason: "There was
nothing to wash out—no stain of any kind—no
blood-spot whatever. I had been too wary for

that. A tub had caught all—ha! ha!" (197). That
is an awful lot of blood for us to believe that
not even a drop got on his clothes, and I know
about blood from all those horror movies I have
seen! One of the more disturbing aspects of
this story is that we are left to decide how
much is true. Much of what we are told is terribly disturbing, but much of what we may consider on our own could be even worse. Perhaps
this man is covered in blood when the police
arrive? Why not? If he can hear things in hell,
maybe he cannot see things on earth! Poe asks
us to consider the world from an insane point
of view. When we do that, the story takes on
truly horrifying aspects!

This unusual point of view offers an appropriate tone for a horror story. Although the
story is "realistic" in the sense that everything in it can be explained, it has a supernatural feeling to it. While a contemporary
horror film might rely on the simple shocks of
a supernatural killer from the netherworld, Poe
offers us a real-life horror: a friend turned
mad killer. But at the same time, the killer
is almost supernatural because he believes he
has supernatural powers. He also believes that
there are other supernatural elements in the
world. After all, he fears the old man's "Evil
Eye" (195). He claims to have "super senses."
"The disease," the narrator tells us, "had
sharpened my senses—not destroyed—not dulled
them. Above all was the sense of hearing acute"
(194). He can hear things in hell, a supernatural realm. He also claims to have superhuman powers of patience. He moves unnaturally
slowly while he stalks his prey:

> Oh, you would have laughed to see how cun-
> ningly I thrust it in! I moved it slowly—
> very, very slowly, so that I might not
> disturb the old man's sleep. It took me an
> hour to place my whole head within the open-
> ing so far that I could see him as he lay
> upon his bed. Ha! would a madman have been
> so wise as this[?] (195)

McKeon 6

By creating a madman for a narrator, Poe invites us to travel a dark road into the human mind. He does not "cheat" by creating an unrealistic monster, but he gives us something even better: a monster that is sometimes human, sometimes superhuman, depending on how we look at him, from our point of view or his!

And this observation of the character's "unusual realism" leads us to what makes the story truly frightening. What makes the story scary is that the narrator's view is the only one we have, and as far as he is concerned, there is nothing wrong with anything he has done. In his world, you kill a kindly old man because of his "evil eye." Poe puts us into a madman's world and gives us no alternative explanation for the events of the story's plot. And to a certain extent, we are comfortable in his world. We read the story, we hang on to see how he kills the man, and how he is captured. Even when we may begin to sympathize with the old man, Poe is quick to get us back into the killer's head:

> Many a night, just at midnight, when all the
> world slept, it has welled up from my own
> bosom, deepening, with its dreadful echo, the
> terrors that distracted me. I say I knew it
> well. I knew what the old man felt, and pitied
> him, although I chuckled at heart. (196)

We might identify with the old man as the killer eases into the room; even the killer does. But that warm sentiment is cut off with the killer's chuckle. The horror of this story is not the shock of the blood and violence or the hints at supernaturalism, it is in the killer's complete disregard for everything decent. This killer manages to commit a completely pointless, totally brutal and arbitrary killing for which he is captured within hours. The "realistic" yet horrifying vision of reality we get here puts us into a madman's head, and lets it all make some kind of sense. That is more frightening than the ghosts of today's horror films.

If Edgar Allan Poe's stories do not seem like they have much in common with the horror films of today, that does not mean that Poe's stories are not frightening. Maybe it means that today's writers of horror stories and films have lost their way. Poe creates a world that is real, and he tells a story we can easily imagine happening. What is more, he lets us see this world through the eyes of a crazed killer who manages to pass as just another "regular guy." This is not a killer foaming at the mouth or tricked up in a special effects costume. This killer speaks "courageously to [his victim], calling him by name in a hearty tone, and inquiring how he has passed the night" (195). And most frighteningly, this killer chooses to tell us all his secrets, as if we are his friends. Worse still, the world he describes is not so different from ours. Poe scares us not because he shows us something new, different, and shocking. He shows us a killer depressingly similar to us, and that is frightening.

Work Cited

Poe, Edgar Allan. "The Tell-Tale Heart."
    Selected Writings of Edgar Allan Poe. Ed.
    Edward H. Davidson. Boston: Houghton
    Mifflin, 1956. 194–199.

THE MECHANICS OF WRITING ABOUT LITERATURE

Using Quotations from Other Texts

For most of this chapter, we have looked at some sample essays and considered their "life cycle," from the initial assignment to reading and annotating to freewriting to outlining to first draft to revision. Now that we have looked at the "macroscopic" issues of composition, let us look at some of the "microscopic" issues of dealing with a literary text in a paper such as those we have discussed. Writing a literary analysis paper means writing about something that someone else wrote. Writing a paper like that means quoting frequently from these other texts.

In an essay of literary analysis, the literary texts we discuss are both our subject matter and our evidence. Although we may refer to literary theory or an historical event or our own personal experience, the main evidence we are most likely to cite in such a paper is evidence taken from our primary source (the literary work) or evidence taken from a secondary source (criticism or historical documents or other writing). To be effective, the writer needs to be able to quote other texts regularly and elegantly, or at least clearly.

Borrowing this kind of material and doing it with style and clarity can be quite difficult. After all, when we insert someone else's writing into our own, we pair up what can be two very different writing styles. Also, when we put lines from fiction, drama, or poetry into our paper, we cross genres, mixing imaginative literature with expository or analytical prose. Fortunately, there are several general rules of thumb writers can use as a guide through these rhetorical problems. Some of these rules originate in the MLA standards we have discussed. Others are commonsense general guidelines. Together, they help us write essays that achieve their rhetorical ends by allowing us to incorporate the writing of others into our own prose.

Plagiarism

Of course, when we borrow information and language from another text, we need to give credit to that source. Otherwise, we are guilty of plagiarism. Plagiarism is not *using* someone else's words or ideas. Plagiarism is *claiming authorship* of someone else's words and ideas. For students writing essays about literature, this distinction is important for several reasons. For one, we must borrow someone else's words and ideas when we write about literature. Since "someone else's words and ideas" would work well as a definition for literature, the very practice of writing about literature would be impossible if we could not "borrow" these things. The important distinction here is between giving credit and claiming authorship of someone else's words and ideas.

A plagiarist is one who does not give proper credit for the work he or she has borrowed. We have discussed using MLA documentation to indicate works from which we have borrowed, but writers have more responsibility than to merely list the titles of books, journals, and Web pages from which material is borrowed. Throughout this book material has appeared in quotation marks. These marks indicate either that someone is speaking or that the words in those quotation marks originally appeared in the work of some other writer. I have used quotation marks because it is not enough for me to list book titles at the end of my work. I have an obligation to indicate which individual words I have borrowed from these texts. And it is not merely words for which I must give credit. Borrowed ideas must be marked so my reader will know that I have borrowed and not created these ideas. Of course, it is harder to deal with ideas than it is to deal with words. Fortunately, writers have developed various strategies for conferring proper credit for borrowed materials. These strategies range from specific punctuation marks and documentation forms to more subtle means.

Likewise, plagiarism itself ranges from blatant cheating to accidental plagiarism caused by laziness, ignorance, or inattention to detail. The student who buys a paper off the Internet surely knows that he is doing wrong. Likewise, the student who hands in a homework assignment her roommate completed two semesters ago knows that she will be punished if she is caught. But there are other, less overtly dishonest situations that demand our attention. Should the student who borrows ideas from his professor include the professor's lectures on his Works Cited page? And what about the professor? Are we to believe that she invented all of the information she gives in her lectures? What about the broader society around us? Is it not true that celebrities and politicians regularly employ ghost writers and speech writers? Do not newspaper writers routinely touch up press releases and call them "their stories"? Is that plagiarism? Should that be punished? It is certainly true that we live in a world filled with moral uncertainty. Wilson Mizner said, "When you steal from one author it's plagiarism; if you steal from many, it's research."[2] Happily, it is not our job to clarify

[2]John Bartlett, *Bartlett's Familiar Quotations,* ed. Justin Kaplan, 16th ed. (Boston: Little, Brown, and Co., 1992), p. 631.

all of these moral ambiguities. We merely need to learn the established conventions of citing the works of others in literary analysis. We can fall back on several specific rhetorical conventions to keep us from being accused of plagiarism.

Why Is Plagiarism Such a Problem?   Students often are not only puzzled at just what is and is not considered plagiarism but at the severity of the penalties meted out for the offense. Offenders can receive a zero on an assignment or fail a class for the semester or even be suspended or expelled from school for an act of plagiarism. Students know, however, that many who cheat do not get caught. Some chronic cheaters are so good at their craft, in fact, that they are regularly praised for it! Since "everybody does it," these students may wonder, "Why does it matter?"

Well, first we should draw a distinction between saying "many people cheat" and saying "everybody cheats." We may be aware of many individuals who break the rules but many others do not. More to the point, writing papers and doing homework are tasks intended to build the intellectual power of students. Research has shown, for instance, that the more we write, the better writers we become. If we hire someone to write our papers for us, we may receive an A grade, but we will not learn anything. A student who plagiarizes is like a weightlifter who hires someone else to lift his weights—he is not going to build any muscles that way.

Also, the more we write, the more we recognize how much work goes into this enterprise. It is only just and fair to give that hard work the benefit of simple recognition. We would want recognition for ourselves and our work, after all.

Paraphrasing and Quoting Others' Words

Once we decide to incorporate the work of another writer into our text, we have a series of decisions to make, starting with how to incorporate the work: through direct quotation or paraphrase.

Direct Quotation.   A direct quotation is, of course, the borrowed words of another writer exactly as they appear in the original text. Direct quotation is a useful and effective strategy.

Why Do We Quote?   The writer making a literary argument needs to refer to the text frequently to demonstrate that he or she has a valuable, compelling point. These quotations are her major evidence. If she does not tell us which lines are important, she cannot be sure that we will remember them. If she writes a paper about the irony in Kate Chopin's language but never shows her audience the language then she really cannot prove her point. A lawyer who claims that her client's diary will exonerate him must eventually produce the diary. It is the same with the evidence of Chopin's short story. The writer needs to show her reader the evidence if she wants the reader to believe her!

Using the exact language that appears in the original text is a particularly effective strategy because it demonstrates the writer's familiarity with the text and—to a certain extent—it cannot be disputed. It is one thing to say that "the characters in this novel are often angry." It is another to produce the language of the novel that shows that anger. A reader can dispute your broad assessment of the characters but the reader cannot deny the very words of the text (although he can disagree with your interpretation of those words).

How Much Should I Quote?   The answer to this question is deceptively simple: as much as you need to! Of course, "how much" is enough changes from text to text and argument to argument. Generally, the writer of literary analysis should not be afraid to let the text speak for itself, after selecting the most appropriate passages and key terms best suited to making the essay's argument. As we saw in our sample subjective analysis of Poe's "The Tell-Tale Heart," that does not mean simply dropping long passages into the essay but choosing carefully those select passages that do the most work most effectively.

How Much Is Too Much?   One fear that many writers in literature classes have is that they will be penalized for quoting too much in their papers. This is a legitimate fear. Plenty of students have gotten a paper back covered with red slash marks cutting out what they thought was their best evidence. There is also the fear of being accused of cheating or padding a paper with long quotations just to fill up space. And then there is the fact that plenty of writers *do* pad their papers with long quotations just to fill up space.

The best way to avoid quoting "too much" is to remember what the quotations are there for in the first place. One does not quote merely to demonstrate that one has read the text. Quotations in literary analysis serve a rhetorical purpose. They are intended to bring new information to the reader or to convince the reader to change her ideas about some point. Of course, that is the same reason they appear in the literary text in the first place—the author wants to instruct, entertain, delight, persuade, challenge, and affect the reader. The difference in our literary analysis paper is that the writer of literary analysis wants to instruct or persuade the

reader about something other than what the author intended for that language. For instance, in "The Tell-Tale Heart,"
Poe has his narrator speak the following lines:

> Above all was the sense of hearing acute. I heard all
> things in the heaven and in the earth. I heard many things
> in hell. How, then, am I mad? Hearken! and observe how
> healthily—how calmly I can tell you the whole story.

Poe uses these words to begin his story, to introduce us to
the narrator, to establish the narrator's state of mind, and
to introduce the themes of perception and insanity, among
other things.

A writer of an essay of literary analysis may quote Poe
in his essay to make *similar*—but not identical—points. He
may, for instance, suggest that the foregoing ideas were in
Poe's mind when he wrote the story. But that is really a different rhetorical end than Poe had in mind. Poe was never
writing about Poe, was he? He was telling a story about a
fictional killer; the essayist is writing a paper about an actual work of fiction. He might also use the foregoing passage
to make a point about Poe the man. He could make an argument about Poe's state of mind as he wrote the story, perhaps suggesting that these lines indicate that Poe was upset
or even unbalanced when he wrote "The Tell-Tale Heart."
Plenty of folks have made the argument. But making that
or any other argument means commenting on these passages
and instructing the reader to no longer think of these words
as only part of the plot of the story or a piece of character
development. The essayist has to ask the reader to think of
these words as part of his paper, now.

As writers, we have to remember that when we quote an
author we are trying to get our readers to agree with us,
not the author we quote! Remember that whenever our readers *might* not understand us, there is a good chance they *will
not* understand us! It is our job to make sure that they read
the quotations the way we want them to!

As a colleague of mine tells his students: your audience
is an idiot! What he means is that the reader will not understand the writer's ideas until the writer tells him what
those ideas are. We should never assume that our readers
will know why we have quoted a passage from the text unless we tell them *why* we have quoted that passage.

Once the language of a literary text becomes part of our
paper, we have an obligation to *frame* the discussion so the
reader will see these lines in the same context in which we
see them. That means that the obligation is now on us to
make our reading of the passage clear. To do so, I recommend
the following rule of thumb.

Explain the context and rhetorical purpose of the quotations you use in your paper. And make sure that your explanation strikes a balance with the quoted material. If, for instance, you quote five words from a text, give your reader at least five of your own words to explain why the quote appears at this point in your paper. If you quote twenty words, use about twenty of your own words to explain your reading of the text. Do not just drop in long (or even short) quoted passages with no context.

Consider the following example, using a passage from an essay by the crime writer Raymond Chandler. In his essay, Chandler, without explicitly mentioning his detective, Philip Marlowe, describes the kind of hero he would like to see in more detective fiction. In the essay quoting Chandler, the essayist tries to comment on Chandler's description:

> Raymond Chandler's hero is a man of honor. Chandler discusses this in his essay, "The Simple Art of Murder":
>> Down these mean streets a man must go who is not himself mean, who is neither tarnished nor afraid. The detective . . . must be such a man. He is the hero, he is everything. He must be a complete man and a common man and yet an unusual man. He must be, to use a rather weathered phrase, a man of honor, by instinct, by inevitability, without thought of it, and certainly without saying it. He must be the best man in his world and a good enough man for any world. . . . He will take no man's money dishonestly and no man's insolence without a due and dispassionate revenge. He is a lonely man, and his pride is that you will treat him as a proud man or be very sorry you ever saw him.
> Here we see Chandler's vision of the detective as honorable man.

The quotation does nothing here but stretch out the paper! This writer needs to trim the quotation and introduce it with enough of his own language to ensure that the text will become an integral part of *his* (not Chandler's) argument. Look at this revision:

> Although the detective genre is often thought of as being "only entertainment," and not about ideas, Raymond Chandler's novels are ultimately about honor. Marlowe may live in a corrupt world, but he is not a corrupt man. In "The Simple Art of Murder," Chandler describes his honorable hero with language that emphasizes both the corruption of the world and the incorruptibility of the man. "Down these mean streets a man must go who is not himself mean, who is neither tarnished nor

afraid," Chandler writes. Yes, the world of his books may be corrupt, but the hero is not. Chandler says his hero "must be the best man in his world and a good enough man for any world. . . ." Chandler's hero stands in opposition to the decadent world in which he finds himself.

In the revised passage, our writer has a solid paragraph. Even though it is a little shorter than the first version, he uses only a small portion of Chandler's passage. That means he has more material to borrow for later passages in his paper.

Also, he has bracketed the quote with his commentary of it. In the first passage, he leaves himself open to accusations of laziness and unoriginality. In the revision, he has taken a few minutes to make sure that the readers will see in Chandler's comments what he wants them to see.

What Is Paraphrasing?   Paraphrasing is another tool writers use to demonstrate their familiarity with others' texts and to build arguments based on those texts. When paraphrasing, writers restate the words of a text in their own words. A writer may paraphrase to clarify meaning or to ensure a smooth style.

How Many of the Words Must Be Changed?   To call a passage paraphrased, all of the major words in the passage should be replaced with new language. If paraphrasing a passage of ten words, your new passage should contain approximately ten words, all of your own composing. Of course, it may be difficult to find new ways to say "if" or "it." Generally speaking, we do not need to worry about every preposition and pronoun. Still, make an effort to restate the passage in language that is clearly different than that of the original passage.

Look at the following example. Ralph Waldo Emerson made the following statement in his essay, "Nature":

> Crossing a bare common, in snow puddles, at twilight, under a clouded sky, without having in my thoughts any occurrence of special good fortune, I have enjoyed a perfect exhilaration. I am glad to the brink of fear.

We could draft a word-for-word paraphrase merely by replacing each word with a synonym, but that would lead to a very awkward statement. It is better to be a little looser:

> While walking alone, even during cold and inclement weather in the darkness, regardless of his state of mind, he has been elated. He is awestruck by nature.

Why Paraphrase?   There are many reasons we may choose to paraphrase rather than include an exact quote in our essay. Often when we write about literature, we discuss the quality of the diction or word choice of the author. In such a case, we should clearly deal with the exact words of the writer. However, if we are dealing with a larger issue and merely wish to remind our reader of some key detail of a text, perhaps paraphrasing is the quickest way to get the information into our paper. Or perhaps we want to include a critic's observation and quickly move on to our own ideas.

Style considerations are another reason we may wish to consider paraphrasing. Paraphrasing is a tool we may want to rely on when a writer's language is so different than our own that it might be awkward to include the unedited quotation in our writing. Or perhaps we want to avoid featuring too many long quotations in a row; perhaps the rhythm of a sentence makes it difficult to include an exact quotation without extensive revision.

For instance, if I use the foregoing Emerson quotation in a paper about Emerson's nature writing, I might quote him word for word:

> Emerson is enthralled with nature, and he wants to make clear that when he talks about nature, he does not mean only those aspects of nature that are pleasing, like a beautiful flower or bird. He writes:
>
>> Crossing a bare common, in snow puddles, at twilight, under a clouded sky, without having in my thoughts any occurrence of special good fortune, I have enjoyed a perfect exhilaration. I am glad to the brink of fear. (6)
>
> Emerson wants us to imagine nature in more ways than the conventional.

On the other hand, I could just as easily do the job with a paraphrased passage:

> Emerson is enthralled with nature, and he wants to make clear that when he talks about nature, he does not mean only those aspects of nature that are pleasing, like a beautiful flower or bird. He writes that while walking alone, even during cold and inclement weather in the darkness, regardless of his state of mind, he has been elated and awestruck by nature (6).

There is certainly a sense of economy in the paraphrased passage, and I do not have to worry about blocking my quotation. On the other hand, the word-for-word passage retains all the power of Emerson's prose. Depending on the rhetorical demands of my paper, I can make either choice.

In any case, paraphrased material should be treated as borrowed information—we must tell our readers that the ideas discussed in a paraphrased passage are not our own, even if the diction is. So, while we do not enclose paraphrased passages in quotation marks, we do cite the passage using parenthetical documentation, just as we would with a word-for-word quotation.

Using Quotation Marks.   Use double quotation marks to indicate that the information within the marks are either conversation or borrowed from a text, as in the following example:

"To be or not to be."

Use single quotation marks within double quotation marks to indicate that you are quoting a passage that contains quoted material, as in the following example:

There have been many such comments made about Jones. One critic observes that he has been called "everything from a 'sinner' to a 'saint.'" (Smith 26)

The use of single quotation marks tells the reader that if she were to turn to page 26 in Smith's text, she would find the words "sinner" and "saint" already in quotation marks.

Using Quotation Marks with Other Punctuation.   One of the pieces of misinformation that many share is "all quoted passages must be introduced by a comma." Note that the preceding example uses quotation marks without a comma; this so-called "rule" is an exaggeration. However, there are guidelines we can follow to make sure that we clearly introduce whatever material we do borrow.

When we use a phrase to introduce a quoted passage, we do use a comma:

According to noted literary critic Lucindy Willis, "Good writing is a timeless treasure."
John Lennon sang, "Imagine no possessions."

Likewise, when we follow a quotation with a phrase, we also use a comma:

"Nothing comes amiss, so money comes withal," Shakespeare reminds us.

When we interrupt a quotation with our comments, we use commas.

"The moon," says lyricist Nick Cave, "is in the gutter."

These examples all rely on commas to introduce and set off quotations. All of the examples I have included use language intended to attribute credit for the passage being quoted.

Commas are not our only option, however. We may also use a colon (not a semicolon) when using a clause to introduce a quotation:

Herman Melville opens his novel *Moby Dick* with one of literature's most famous sentences: "Call me Ishmael."

However, we do not necessarily need any punctuation. The word *that* can serve as a comma:

Josh Billings says that "Nature never makes any blunders; when she makes a fool, she means it."

Colons are often used when we introduce longer borrowed passages. However, when we cite more than four lines of prose, we must also indent the passage ten spaces from the left margin (although we do not enclose the passage in quotation marks). Consider this example from the sample paper referred to earlier in this chapter:

In fact, he tells us about the killing not because we have forced him to or because we are his judge but because he wants to show off just how clever and sane he is. The famous opening lines tell us this much:

TRUE! —nervous —very, very dreadfully nervous I had been and am; but why will you say that I am mad? The disease had sharpened my senses —not destroyed— not dulled them. Above all was the sense of hearing acute. I heard all things in the heaven and in the earth. I heard many things in hell. How, then, am I mad? Hearken! and observe how healthily—how calmly I can tell you the whole story.

He is not forced to tell us this, he chooses to tell us.

Like the rest of our paper, this blocked passage should be double-spaced.

QUOTING POETRY AND DRAMA

So far all of our examples have come from prose works. Quoting from poetry and drama is similar in that we are required to give credit where credit is due and to use quotation marks to indicate which words we have borrowed. However, since poetry and drama are quite different than prose, there are other requirements when citing from these sources.

Quoting Poetry

When quoting poetry, make sure that you copy the poem as it appears on the page. Retain all capital letters as the poet intended them, for instance, and make sure to indicate line breaks. If citing only two or three lines, use a slash preceded and followed by an empty space (" / ") to show line breaks:

> Stephen Crane creates an assertive speaker when he
> writes, "A man said to the universe: / 'Sir, I exist!' "

If we quote more than three lines, we present the passage
as we do a long prose passage. Indent ten spaces and reproduce the poem faithfully.

> Crane's assertive speaker, unfortunately, receives an iron-
> ic response:
>> "However," replied the universe,
>> "The fact has not created in me
>> A sense of obligation."
> Crane is clearly not a very optimistic poet.

As with the quoting of a longer prose passage, this blocked
and indented quotation is double-spaced like the rest of the
paper. It is important to reproduce the poem as accurately
as possible, even when the poem has an unusual appearance. Consider the following passage taken from George
Herbert's "Easter Wings."

> Herbert shapes his poem to resemble wings, thus re-
> inforcing his metaphor:
>> Lord, who createdst man in wealth and store,
>>> Though foolishly he lost the same,
>>>> Decaying more and more
>>>>> Till he became
>>>>>> most poor:
>>>>> With thee
>>>>> O let me rise
>>>> As Larks, harmoniously,
>>> And sing this day thy victories:
>> Then shall the fall further the flight in me.

It may take some time, but when we deal with poetry, we
try to be accurate.

Using Parenthetical Documentation to Cite Poetry. Another issue a writer needs to take care of when quoting poetry is the citation form that poetry demands. Unlike prose,
poetry is not cited by page number. When citing poetry, cite
line numbers. So the preceding poem would be cited as
follows:

> (Herbert lines 1–10).

After the first such reference, one no longer needs to use the
word "line" in parenthetical documentation:

> Herbert asserts his faith with two simple words: "With
> thee" (6).

Quoting Drama

Drama, like poetry, puts different demands on us than does prose. When quoting dialogue from a drama, block the quotation, again ten spaces from the left margin. Include the characters' names, all in capital letters. The names should be followed by a period. After the first line, all subsequent lines of each character's dialogue should be indented an additional three spaces from the left margin.

> In this early scene from *The Tempest,* we see the relationship between Prospero and his magical slave, Ariel:
>
> **PROSPERO:** Hast thou, spirit,
>   Perform'd to point the tempest that I bade thee?
> **ARIEL:** To every article.
>   I boarded the King's ship; now on the beak,
>   Now in the waist, the deck, in every cabin,
>   I flam'd amazement. Sometime I'd divide,
>   And burn in many places; on the topmast,
>   The yards, and borespirit, would I flame distinctly,
>   Then meet and join.

I have tried to maintain the appearance of the text as it was on the page, retaining the text's spacing and capitalization.

Using Parenthetical Documentation to Cite Drama.   As with poetry, the page is not the key unit of drama. When we cite poetry, we generally cite line numbers. When we cite drama, we indicate act, scene, and line number using Arabic, not Roman, numerals. So the preceding passage would be cited as follows: (Shakespeare 1.2.194–201).

HOW DO I MAKE THE QUOTATION FIT IN MY PAPER?

Once you decide which information you want to borrow from the texts you write about, you need to incorporate that material smoothly into your paper. This means more than simply writing, "The author says." To make someone else's writing fit into your own, you sometimes need to change the language of one or the other (or both) to make sure the two make sense together.

For example, look at this passage from an essay I wrote about Poe's detective story "The Murders in the Rue Morgue." This story about the investigation into two particularly brutal murders introduced one of Poe's most famous characters, C. Auguste Dupin, and is often cited as the first detective story. I wrote:

> In "The Murders in the Rue Morgue," Dupin's first adventure, Poe has his detective expound on the power of

reason to dissipate chaos. Describing the singular nature of the murders, Dupin actually takes a kind of comfort in the unique "deviations" of these barbaric killings
that readers may find shocking:

> They have fallen into the gross but common error of
> confounding the unusual with the abstruse. But it is
> by these deviations from the plane of the ordinary, that
> reason feels its way, if at all, in its search for the true.

Even the fact that this passage was plucked out of a paper
you have not read does not entirely explain why it does not
make sense. Of course, I tried to prepare readers of this textbook for the quotation by telling them who Dupin was and
what "Rue Morgue" was about. However, the reader of this
textbook does not know the identity of the "they" mentioned
in Poe's passage. Dupin here refers to the police, but my reader may not know that. Even readers who have read the story
may not remember this passage. As a courtesy to my reader, I need to clarify this unclear pronoun. Read this revision:

> In "The Murders in the Rue Morgue," Dupin's first ad-
> venture, Poe has his detective expound on the power of
> reason to dissipate chaos. Describing the singular na-
> ture of the murders, Dupin actually takes a kind of com-
> fort in the unique "deviations" of these barbaric killings
> that readers may find shocking:
>
> [The police] have fallen into the gross but common
> error of confounding the unusual with the abstruse.
> But it is by these deviations from the plane of the or-
> dinary, that reason feels its way, if at all, in its search
> for the true.

By using brackets ([]) to enclose the words "The police," I
tell the reader that I am changing some of Poe's language
and inserting my own. With this new language, the passage
makes much more sense to my readers, who may not have
immediately recalled this passage. Such changes are frequently necessary to deal with pronoun use or tense changes
in quoted passages.

Elsewhere in the same essay, I referred to events in a
story by Raymond Chandler and found myself quoting the
story:

> The necklace was a gift from "the man [she] loved [. . .]
> [who] died in a burning plane."

The original passage reads as follows:

> The man I loved gave it to me. He's dead. There! He's
> dead! He died in a burning plane. Now, go back and tell
> my husband that, you slimy little rat!

The original passage is filled with passion and anger, but that is not what I want to discuss in my paper. I wanted to quickly refer to the relationships between the characters and remind my reader where the necklace came from. I wanted to do this without mentioning their names or getting too deep into the relationships. In the "Rue Morgue" example, I replaced a pronoun with a noun; in the Chandler example, I replaced one pronoun with another.

In both cases, it is important for me to make sure that my paper reads smoothly, even if that means changing the language of the authors I study. However, I cannot make these changes unless I inform my readers about the nature of the changes. Otherwise, I am misrepresenting the literary texts I study. Remember, these texts are my evidence. If my readers check the text and find that I have misquoted, they are likely to disregard much of what I have to say about the texts. After all, they might conclude, if he cannot even copy from the book accurately, his insights into the text cannot be very valuable.

Another way we indicate to readers that we have changed the texts we cite is the use of ellipses points, or periods separated by a space (. . .). Ellipses points are not needed for every omission we make. For instance, if I borrow only one or two words from a text, most readers will assume that there is more to the text than those one or two words:

> Woody Guthrie said the weapon used by the worst criminals was not a "six-gun" but a "fountain pen."

However, if I omit words from a text and end up with a sentence that may be mistaken for the unchanged words of the author, I owe it to the author and my reader to indicate what changes I have made. In fact, in the preceding example from the Chandler text, I make use of the ellipses to show that I have left information out of the text:

> The necklace was a gift from "the man [she] loved [. . .] [who] died in a burning plane."

But I cannot simply insert any number of points; ellipses follow strict guidelines. Use three spaced periods to indicate material has been removed from a sentence. Place these ellipses within brackets ([]) to indicate that you are adding the ellipses to the text and that they are not original to the quotation. If your ellipses appear at the end of the sentence, follow your closing bracket with a period:

> The necklace was a gift from "The man [she] loved [. . .]."

However, we usually will follow such a quotation with parenthetical documentation. In this case, the final period follows the citation, not the bracket:

The necklace was a gift from "The man [she] loved [. . .]" (Chandler 174).

If the ellipses indicate that you are omitting information from the middle of one sentence to the middle of another, simply insert the three ellipses:

The necklace was a gift from "the man [she] loved [. . .] [who] died in a burning plane" (Chandler 174).

Ellipses allow us to make borrowed material flow smoothly in our paper. Another way to ensure a smooth prose style is to avoid stand-alone quotes. You do not want sentences in your paper that are entirely made up of quoted material. You are assuming your audience will remember who said this and when. They may not. You are assuming that your audience will assign to these quotations the same significance you do. They may not. Consider the following example:

Raymond Chandler's Philip Marlowe is a latter-day knight who embodies all the best qualities of man in a corrupt world. "He must be [. . .] a man of honor, by instinct, by inevitability, without thought of it, and certainly without saying it." Chandler imbues all of the knightly virtues into Marlowe.

Who is the speaker of this quotation? Chandler? A critic? Marlowe? Another character in the work? Is the quotation an example of the idea just introduced or is it a refutation of it? Consider the following revision:

Raymond Chandler's Philip Marlowe is a latter-day knight who embodies all the best qualities of man in a corrupt world. To emphasize this point, Chandler says in his essay "The Simple Art of Murder":
"[The hero] must be [. . .] a man of honor, by instinct, by inevitability, without thought of it, and certainly without saying it."
Chandler transfers all of the knightly virtues onto Marlowe.

With this little phrase all of our questions are answered. We know who is responsible for the phrase and why it appears in this essay.

Once we go to all the trouble of including quoted material and editing it so it fits smoothly into our prose style, we want it to do its job. And in literary analysis, that job is making an argument. To maximize the effectiveness of these quotations, remind your reader that these passages are there to prove a point. End your discussion on your words, not theirs. It is your job to make your argument. Quoted passages will shore up your argument, but they will not be able to emphasize it like your own words.

Remember this paragraph from our discussion of "how much is too much"?

> Although the detective genre is often thought of as being "only entertainment," and not about ideas, Raymond Chandler's novels are ultimately about honor. Marlowe may live in a corrupt world, but he is not a corrupt man. In "The Simple Art of Murder," Chandler describes his honorable hero with language that emphasizes both the corruption of the world and the incorruptibility of the man. "Down these mean streets a man must go who is not himself mean, who is neither tarnished nor afraid," Chandler writes. Yes, the world of his books may be corrupt, but the hero is not. Chandler says of this hero, "He must be the best man in his world and a good enough man for any world [. . .]." Chandler's hero stands in opposition to the decadent world in which he finds himself.

I ended the paragraph with my own words. If I had left off the last sentence, I would be counting on Chandler to make my argument for me. But Chandler was not writing about Chandler, he was writing about Marlowe. Since I have a different argument than Chandler did, I need a different conclusion:

> Yes, the world of his books may be corrupt, but the hero is not. Chandler says of this hero, "He must be the best man in his world and a good enough man for any world [. . .]." Chandler's hero stands in opposition to the decadent twentieth-century world in which he finds himself.

Maybe my reader would get the idea anyway, but I do not want to take any chances, so I conclude my paragraph with *my* commentary on the source material.

CONCLUSION

Here we have tried to put together much of the material of this book into a discussion of writing one paper. We have also stopped to consider some of the mechanical issues of writing literary analysis papers. However, we have only scratched the surface of the thorny issue of research and documentation. Chapter 6 will discuss this issue.

Using Research and Writing the Documentation Page

WHY DO I DOCUMENT BORROWED INFORMATION?

In Chapter 5 we discussed plagiarism. One reason we document our sources is to avoid being charged with plagiarism. But that is not the only reason we document source material. The Works Cited page of a paper can serve rhetorical purposes as well. When a writer shows her readers all of her source material, she demonstrates how much work she has done in preparing her paper. She demonstrates her expertise. She demonstrates that she has given this subject some thought and that she has read the opinions of others.

And although it may seem a minor point, a writer should consider the effect of professional presentation when she completes an essay. When we present our ideas to our readers, we are really presenting ourselves. A well-organized paper speaks well of us. What your paper looks like is your reader's first inkling as to its content. If your paper appears messy and incomplete, you will begin fighting your reader's poor assumption about its content, even if the paper is brilliant. If your paper appears neat and well organized, you will begin benefiting from your reader's high assumption about its content, even if the paper is awful. Also, documentation is a simple matter compared to actually writing the paper. Documentation depends on straightforward rules and guidelines. A reader may assume that a writer who cannot handle the easy part of literary analysis should not be trusted with the difficult stuff!

HOW DO I DOCUMENT BORROWED INFORMATION?

The standard documentation format for dealing with literary texts is MLA style. While I will cover some basic aspects of

MLA style here, there are many other aspects left unaddressed. Consult the following book for more detailed information:

> Gibaldi, Joseph. <u>MLA Handbook for Writers of Research Papers</u>. 5th ed. New York: Modern Language Association. 1999.

When borrowing information, writers have an obligation not to merely mention *in* their texts that the information is borrowed. They have a further obligation to list at the end of their paper all of the books, journals, magazines, Web sites, and other sources from which they have quoted or paraphrased. In the MLA format, we call this a Works Cited page (or a Work Cited page, if the writer has borrowed from only one work).

Most students are familiar with the concept of a documentation page. Many have been responsible for writing such pages since the fifth grade. However, different formats demand different information. Students used to writing a Bibliography page and using footnotes in the body of their paper may find the MLA format confusing. However, it is really no more difficult than any other style. We can examine the basics using the foregoing example of the *MLA Handbook* itself.

This entry is for a book with one author, and we can see several basic pieces of information listed: the author's name, the title of the book, the edition, the city in which the book was published, the name of the publishing company, and the date of publication.

author's name   **book title**

> Gibaldi, Joseph. MLA Handbook for Writers of Research Papers. 5th ed. New York: Modern Language Association, 1999.

2nd and following lines indent 5 spaces   **edition (if 2nd or later)**   **city of publication**   **publisher**   **year of publication**

As this book is the fifth edition, that information is given. Had we been referring to the first edition, we would not note that in the entry; our reader will assume the book is a first edition. Of course, this is just one kind of book. In literary analysis we encounter many kinds of books: novels, collections of poetry or short stories, anthologies, books of criticism, reference books, textbooks, and dictionaries to name a few. We may also borrow information from magazines, literary journals, Web sites and CD-ROMS, even newspapers and personal interviews. The documentation formats for all of these kinds of sources are unique in their own way.

Identifying Titles

Very specific rules govern the appearance of titles in a literary analysis paper.

Book Titles.   Book titles should be underlined, and the title should be taken from the book's title page, not the cover. Capitalize first and last words and all important words in the title as well as words that follow a hyphen or colon. Nouns, pronouns, verbs, adjectives, adverbs, and subordinating conjunctions (such as *although* and *because*) all get capitalized. Unless they appear at the beginning or end of the title, the following parts of speech do not get capitalized: articles (*a, an, the*), prepositions (*in, on,* etc.), and coordinating conjunctions (*and, but, for,* etc.). For example:

Black Boy

A Handbook to Literature

Bitter Blood

Beneath the American Renaissance: The Subversive Imagination in the Age of Emerson and Melville

Memoir of James Jackson, The Attentive and Obedient Scholar, Who Died in Boston, October 31, 1833, Aged Six Years and Eleven Months

Underlining Titles.   Generally speaking, longer works are underlined. Of course, *longer* is a relative term. Another guide to use is this: works published independently (or works in an anthology that were originally published independently) are underlined.

The kinds of works whose titles are underlined include the following:

books

plays

long poems published as books

periodicals and pamphlets (newspapers, magazines, and scholarly journals)

films

television and radio programs (although the titles of individual episodes would be put in quotation marks)

records, cassettes, videotapes, CD-ROMs, DVDs, and CDs

paintings

long musical works (operas, etc.)

For example:

A Connecticut Yankee at King Arthur's Court (book)

Sandinista! (compact disc)

Biography (television series)

The War Prayer (long poem published as a book)

A Prairie Home Companion (radio show)

Apocalypse Now (film)

M Butterfly (play)

Newsweek (magazine)

American Literature (scholarly journal)

Titles in Quotation Marks.   Generally, *shorter* works are set apart with quotation marks. However, *shorter* is as relative as *longer*. If a work was published as part of a larger work, then use quotation marks to designate the title. The kinds of works that generally receive quotation marks include the following:

short stories

short poems

essays

magazine, newspaper, or journal articles

individual episodes of a television or radio series

short musical compositions (i.e., song titles)

book chapters

For example:

"A Good Man Is Hard to Find" (short story)

"Mending Wall" (short poem)

"Mark Twain" (episode of a television series)

"This Land Is Your Land" (song)

"Apocalypse by Imagination" (chapter title)

"The Art of Autobiography in Bound for Glory " (journal article)

Exceptions to the Rules.   Exceptions to these rules include the following:

Our own essay titles do not receive quotation marks on the title page of our own paper.

Titles of sacred writings, laws, and political documents are neither underlined nor put in quotations. For example:

Bible (sacred writing)

Genesis (sacred writing)

Exodus (sacred writing)

Koran (sacred writing)

Talmud (sacred writing)

Declaration of Independence (political document)

United States Constitution (political document)

The Use of Symbolism in Poe's Short Stories (paper written for a literature class)

Citing a Book Without an Editor

A citation for a novel or other book with one author is similar to the preceding example. This is especially true if the
novel does not list an editor or translator on the title page
or cover. Unless an editor's name is mentioned on the title
page or cover we do not need to mention the editor in our citation. The following citation for Lee Smith's novel, <u>Fair and
Tender Ladies</u>, is an example of such a citation:

```
Smith, Lee. Fair and Tender Ladies. New York:
     Ballantine, 1988.
```

Author's Name.   Again, start with the author's name, last
name first and first name last (entries will be alphabetized
by author's name on my Works Cited page). Follow with a
period, skip two spaces, and list the title.

Book Title.   Since this is a novel, underline the title. The
title is followed by a period and two spaces.

Italicizing and Underlining.   Since most computers can reproduce an italicized font, most instructors do not mind the
use of italics rather than underlining. However, MLA guidelines warn against use of italics as an individual computer
printer may reproduce such a font poorly. This chapter will
use underlining, as many students will choose that option.

City of Publication.   Next comes the city of publication. (List
the city, not the state; the "New York" listed previously is
"New York City," not "New York State.") If there is more than
one city, list the first city mentioned. If the city's name is
not a familiar one, one may list the state or country after
the city's name (i.e., Englewood Cliffs, NJ; Aukland, New
Zealand). The city's name is followed by a colon and a space.

Publisher.   Then comes the name of the publisher. The
writer may abbreviate the name of the publisher. For example, one need not include "Co., Inc.," or other such abbrevi-
ations. If the publisher's name includes the name of an
individual, mention the family name ("W. W. Norton and Co."
becomes "Norton"). Eliminate terms such as *Books* or
Publishers ("Ballantine Books" becomes "Ballantine"). All of
this information will be found on the title page or the copyright page, which follows the title page.

Date of Publication.   The publisher's name is followed by
a comma, two spaces, and the date of publication. This date
will be the most recent year found on the copyright page.

(Also note that the second and later lines of the entry are indented five spaces from the left margin.)

Books with an Editor and Later Editions

Works of great literary value will be reprinted in many editions. Often an editor will be credited on the cover and the title page. This editor is the person who prepared the text for publication. In such a case, the editor is credited as follows:

```
Melville, Herman. Moby Dick; or, The Whale. Ed.
    Charles Feidelson, Jr. New York: Bobbs-
    Merrill, 1964.
```

Similarly, if a work has been translated, the translator should be credited:

```
Arenas, Reinaldo. Graveyard of the Angels.
    Trans. Alfred J. MacAdam. New York: Avon,
    1987.
```

Citing a Drama

A drama that has been published as a book is cited like any other book:

```
Shaw, Bernard. Heartbreak House: A Fantasia
    in the Russian Manner on English Themes.
    Ed. Dan H. Laurence. Harmondsworth, Eng.:
    Penguin, 1984.
```

Citing Two Works by the Same Author

When citing two works by the same author on one Works Cited page, I need not repeat the author's name.

```
Smith, Lee. The Devil's Dream. New York:
    Putnam, 1992.
---. Fair and Tender Ladies. New York: Bal-
    lantine, 1988.
```

Substitute three dashes for the author's name. Of course, on a Works Cited page, both works would be listed first under *S* for Smith and then alphabetically by title.

Citing a Poem from a Collection by One Poet

To cite an entire collection of poems, once again, we treat the book like any other:

```
Berryman, John. Collected Poems: 1937-1971. Ed.
    Charles Thornbury. New York: Noonday Press,
    1989.
```

However, when a paper refers to only one poem, the author should cite that poem in particular:

> Berryman, John. "Surviving Love." <u>Collected Poems: 1937-1971</u>. Ed. Charles Thornbury. New York: Noonday Press, 1989. 54-55.

Notice that the entry ends with the page number on which this poem can be found. Do not include "pg." or "pp." or any other abbreviation for "pages."

Citing a Short Story from a Collection by One Writer

Such a work is treated very much like a poem from a collection:

> Chandler, Raymond. "Trouble Is My Business." <u>Trouble Is My Business</u>. By Chandler. New York: Vintage, 1992. 3-60.

Again, this entry includes page numbers. It is interesting because the title of the story is also the title of the book in which the story appears. When referring to the story, use quotation marks. When referring to the book, underline the title.

Citing a Work from an Anthology

Often in literature classes, students read from anthologies of works by many authors. Such works are compiled by editors. Students of literature will often find themselves writing this sort of entry. If one were to cite Walt Whitman's "Crossing Brooklyn Ferry" from a copy of <u>Concise Anthology of American Literature</u>, the entry would look like this:

> Whitman, Walt. "Crossing Brooklyn Ferry." <u>Concise Anthology of American Literature</u>. 4th ed. Ed. George McMichael. Upper Saddle River, NJ: Prentice Hall, 1993. 1128-1132.

Citing an Editor's Work from an Anthology

One of the nice features of anthologies is that they often include useful editorial information. For instance, many anthologies include brief biographies of the authors whose work is contained in the book. If a writer borrows such information, he or she needs to cite the work of the editor (or editors), not the subject of the biography. So if a writer borrows some information from the entry on the poet Walt Whitman, he or she cites the work of the editors, not Whitman himself:

> McMichael, George, ed. "Walt Whitman, 1819-1892." <u>Concise Anthology of American Lit-</u>

erature. 4th ed. Upper Saddle River, NJ:
Prentice Hall, 1993. 1061-1063.

Citing a Work with More Than One Author

If a work is credited to more than one author, the author
listed first on the title page and cover is credited first, first
name last and last name first. The second author's name is
not inverted:

Mairowitz, David Zane and Robert Crumb. <u>In-
troducing Kafka</u>. Cambridge, England: Totem
Books, 1994.

Cross-Referencing

Some collections (such as anthologies, for instance) are
so useful that one may borrow from several works in the
same book. In this case, cross-reference the entries. If the
writer wishes to use more than one work from the same book,
he or she cites the work of the editors as well as abbreviat-
ed references that steer the reader back to the full entry.

Hawthorne, Nathaniel. "Young Goodman Brown."
McMichael. 707-716.
McMichael, George, ed. <u>Concise Anthology of
American Literature</u>. 4th ed. Upper Saddle
River, NJ: Prentice Hall, 1993.
---. "Walt Whitman, 1819-1892." McMichael.
1061-1063.
Wheatley, Phillis. "On Imagination." McMichael.
407-408.
Whitman, Walt. "Crossing Brooklyn Ferry."
McMichael. 1128-1132.

Citing a Critical Essay from a Collection
of Essays

Citing a critical essay from a collection of essays is just
like citing a work of literature from an anthology. Usually,
such a book mentions an editor on the title page and cover,
as is the case with the following example:

Lewis, R.W.B. "Always Going Out and Coming
In." <u>Modern Critical Views: Walt Whitman</u>.
Ed. Harold Bloom. New York: Chelsea House,
1985. 99-125.

Like an entry for a work from an anthology, the writer of
the essay, not the editor of the book, receives primary credit. If using several works from this book, cross-reference them
as with the literature anthology.

Citing a Critical Essay from a Critical Edition of a Literary Work

A critical edition of a literary work is yet another kind of work that will likely turn out to be useful in a literary analysis paper. A critical edition is one that contains not only the work of literature itself (a novel or play, for instance) but also several articles about the work. Treat such a work like a novel with an editor if citing just the literary work, as this example shows:

Hawthorne, Nathaniel. The Scarlet Letter. Ed. Ross C. Murfin. Case Studies in Contemporary Criticism. Boston: Macmillan, 1991.

This book also happens to be part of a series. Cite the series name (without quotation marks or underlining) after the editor's name.

If a writer cites an essay from the book but not the work of literature, then he or she cites only the essay:

Ragussis, Michael. "Silence, Family Discourse, and Fiction in The Scarlet Letter." The Scarlet Letter. Ed. Ross C. Murfin. Case Studies in Contemporary Criticism. Boston: Macmillan, 1991. 316-329.

If the writer chooses to cite both the literary work and the essay, he or she cross-references, using the editor's name for the major entry:

Hawthorne, Nathaniel. The Scarlet Letter. Murfin. 21-201.

Ragussis, Michael. "Silence, Family Discourse, and Fiction in The Scarlet Letter." Murfin. 316-329.

Murfin, Ross C., ed. The Scarlet Letter. By Nathaniel Hawthorne. Case Studies in Contemporary Criticism. Boston: Macmillan, 1991.

Citing Reference Books and Dictionaries

A reference book—such as a dictionary or an encyclopedia—is different than a book of essays. Such books often list entries in alphabetical order, making the listing of page numbers unnecessary.

"Crockett, Davy (David) (1786-1836)." The Oxford Companion to American Literature. Fifth Edition. 1983.

This entry lists the name of the article in question. Since this reference book does not list the authors of individual entries, list the entry as an anonymous work. As such, it is alphabetized on the Works Cited page by the title of the entry, not the author. The editor's name need not be listed.

Citing an Introduction, Preface, Foreword, or Afterword

Like a critical edition, many other editions of literary works include information other than the work itself. A good edition of a literary work may include an introduction, preface, foreword, or afterword. Any of these sources may prove useful to the student working on a literary analysis paper.

> Buell, Lawrence. Introduction. Leaves of Grass and Selected Prose. Ed. Lawrence Buell. New York: Modern College Library. 1981. xix–xliv.

In this case, the writer of the introduction is also the editor, so he gets double credit. The term *Introduction* (or Preface, Foreword, or Afterword) is capitalized, but it is not put in quotation marks, nor is it underlined.

Citing an Article from a Literary Journal

Like a book, the entry for a scholarly journal follows the basic pattern of author, title, and publication information. However, since a periodically published journal is quite a different thing than a book, the publication information is different. Also, there are different kinds of journals, including those with and without continuous pagination.

Some journals continue pagination throughout the year: the first issue of each year begins with page 1. If issue 1 ends on page 234, then issue 2 of that year will begin on page 235. These two kinds of journals demand two different kinds of entries:

> Badenhausen, Richard. "In Search of 'Native Moments': T. S. Eliot (Re)Reads Walt Whitman." South Atlantic Review 57.1 (1992): 93–108.

After the title of the journal, list the volume number (57) and issue number (1) of the journal. Since this particular journal is one without continuous pagination, the writer needs to include both volume and issue number. If the journal uses continuous pagination, the writer lists the volume number, knowing that a reader could pick up all of 1992's issues and find only one page 29, for instance. Since this journal does not use continuous pagination, there will be several page 29s in 1992's issues.

If this journal used continuous pagination, the entry would look like this:

> Badenhausen, Richard. "In Search of 'Native Moments': T. S. Eliot (Re)Reads Walt Whit-man." South Atlantic Review 57 (1992): 93-108.

The entry would need to cite only the volume number, "57."

Citing an Article from a Magazine

> White, Robb. "Signs of the Times." Smithsonian Aug. 2000: 120.

Magazine citations require less information than scholarly journals. In the case of Smithsonian, which is a monthly magazine, the entry would need to include only the month and year of publication, not issue and volume. Page numbers are also cited.

Citing an Article from a Newspaper

> Yardly, Jonathan. "Alice's Adventures in Comix World." The News and Record [Greensboro, NC] 27 Sept. 1990. 19A.

The newspaper citation follows the same basic rules as most items on a Works Cited page, with some variation. Notice here that the entry includes the date and both section and page numbers for the article ("19A"). Since this is not a newspaper with a national reputation, the entry indicates the city in which it was published in brackets after the title. For obvious reasons, this would not be necessary when citing a newspaper such as The New York Times.

Citing Electronic Sources

The term *electronic sources* encompasses many kinds of sources, from information stored in a school library's computer on CD-ROM to sites established by universities, corporations, and other institutions to commercial sites to personal homepages. The Internet changes daily (even hourly) and the protocols for documenting Web sites are changing, too.

Also changing at this alarming rate is the very content of the Web pages themselves. When we document a print source, we can be sure that no matter when another reader finds that source, the words on that page will remain the same. This is not the case with Internet sources such as Web pages, which are regularly edited. Consequently, writers must give readers additional information if they hope to adequately document research. The kind of information one may need to document might include the date the writer accessed the information as well as the date it was originally published (if the text was first published in print) and the date it was originally posted on the Web (if that information is available). Researchers should also include the site's URL (Uniform Resource Locator) or Web address. However, these addresses change and are easily mistyped, so include other pertinent information to help readers get to the source material. As a result, documenting some electronic sources can be quite a challenge.

Joseph Gibaldi's MLA Handbook for Writers of Research Papers is particularly useful for dealing with the Internet, as it goes into great detail regarding many kinds of electronic sources. Andrew Harnack and Eugene Kleppinger's Online! A Reference Guide to Using Internet Sources is another very useful source for this kind of information. We will look at a few of the kinds of sources used frequently by people starting out on the road to literary analysis.

Basic Information in an Electronic Citation

Basic information in an electronic citation includes the author of the material being cited, the title of the "text" in question, the "medium" in which the material was located (CD-ROM or Internet site, for example), the publishing information/location of the information, the date the material was published, and (if an Internet site) the date on which the information was accessed.

Since so many variables are involved with Web sources, it is wise to download a copy of the material electronically. If the Web page is discontinued, the student still retains a copy of the material from which she borrowed.

Citing a Web Page

There are, of course, many kinds of Web sites to document. The Web features on-line books, on-line journals and magazines, on-line newspapers, scholarly databases, professional and personal sites, and the list grows daily. Let's look at a few examples.

A Personal or Professional Site.   Ideally, we would begin with the author's name, in reverse order for alphabetizing.

However, even this kind of basic information is often not available. The following example of a professional site is treated like an anonymous source.

> "Woody Guthrie." Woody Guthrie Foundation and
>   Archives. Woody Guthrie Foundation. 26
>   July 2000. <http://www.woodyguthrie.org/
>   biography.htm>

The entry begins with the title of the article (in this case, a biography of Woody Guthrie) and is followed by the title of the page. Next, the entry lists the institution associated with the site. Again, ideally, one would follow this with the date the page was "published." However, this information is frequently not given on Web pages. Then follows the date the writer accessed the information. Finally the entry lists the URL.

When listing the URL, the writer should be careful not to break the address up; try to include the entire address in one line of text. If the writer must break the address and continue it on the next line, he or she should break it at a slash ("/") and not insert a hyphen. To ensure accuracy in transcription, it might be a good idea to *cut* the address from the Web and *paste* it directly into the paper.

Citing an On-Line Text Also Available in a Traditional Edition.   Increasingly, literary texts are becoming available in on-line forms. Using these sources can be quite convenient. However, it is worth keeping in mind that traditional books are going to be more reliable, especially if they are published by a reputable publishing company and edited by a professional. When citing on-line texts, there are documentation protocols one needs to follow:

> James, Henry. Hawthorne. 1879. 1 Aug. 2000.
>   <http://eldred.ne.mediaone.net/hjj/nhhj1.
>   html>

In this case, the Web page gives no information regarding the source of the text. Had it done so, the entry would include that information after the title. The site does, however, list the date of original publication, so that information is included.

Citing an Article from an On-Line Magazine.

> Bacon, Katie. "An African Voice." Interview
>   with Chinua Achebe. Atlantic Unbound. 2
>   Aug. 2000. 4 Aug. 2000. <http://www.the
>   Atlantic.com/unbound/interviews/ba2000-08-
>   02.htm.>

As with a print magazine article, the entry cites author, title, magazine title, and publication information. Also included is the URL and two dates. The first is the date the article initially appeared. The second is the date the writer accessed the information.

Citing an Article from an On-Line Scholarly Journal.

Helming, Steven. "Failure and the Sublime: Fredric Jameson's Writing in the 80's." Postmodern Culture 10.3 (2000) 4 Aug. 2000 <http://www.iath.virginia.edu/pmc/current. issue/10.3helming.html>

The citation documents author, title, journal title, volume and number, date of publication, and date of access. The citation concludes with the URL.

Citing an Article Found on a CD-ROM Database.

"A Hobo's Unhappy Home: Letter from Okemah, Oklahoma. (Hometown of Legendary Folk Musician Woody Guthrie)." The Economist 28 June 1997. 91. InfoTrac. CD-ROM. Information Access. 7 Jan. 1999.

The entry essentially cites the magazine as if it were a traditional publication and then appends the information regarding how the writer found the article. First list the title of the database, then the medium ("CD-ROM"), and then the access date. Since this article is anonymous, it does not list the author's name but is alphabetized by title (under "H" for "Hobo's").

Citing a Publication on CD-ROM.

Spiegelman, Art. The Complete Maus. CD-ROM. New York: Voyager. 1993.

The CD-ROM is a permanent text, like a book. This edition cannot be revised the way a Web page can be, so the citation requires much less information than a Web page does.

Citing an Article from a Nonperiodical Publication on CD-ROM.

Chase, Gilbert. "Leadbelly." Encyclopedia Americana 10th ed. CD-ROM. Groliers, 1999.

Again, CD-ROMs are permanent documents, so do not include date of access. This particular CD-ROM, however, is made up of many articles by many writers. Fortunately, the CD-ROM gives author credits for each entry, as in the case of this biographical sketch of the blues singer Huddie Ledbetter, also known as Leadbelly.

Ideally, just before the name "Groliers," the entry would include the city in which the CD-ROM was "published." However, that information was not available. Citing electronic media means getting and citing all of the information available. Frequently, the researcher will not find all of the information that he or she would like to find.

THE PURPOSE OF PARENTHETICAL CITATION AND WORKS CITED PAGE

In the past, you may have been asked to use footnotes within a paper to indicate when you are borrowing directly from one source or another. Using MLA style for the most part means abandoning the footnote for the parenthetical citation. The parenthetical citation is an aside, contained within parentheses. This may seem odd if you are used to footnotes, but after a time, most students find the use of parenthetical citation a little easier to navigate than footnotes.

In MLA format, parenthetical citations have limited uses; they are not intended to give the reader all pertinent documentation information. They are intended merely to lead a reader to the Works Cited page, which is a separate sheet at the end of the paper. The Works Cited page, not the parenthetical citations, is intended to give your reader pertinent documentation information. Usually, the parenthetical citation offers no more information than an author's name and a page number. Since the parenthetical citations work only in conjunction with the Works Cited page, let us construct a fictional Works Cited page and see what parenthetical citations might be used to lead a reader to a given text. Although it is hard to imagine the paper that would be written using this collection of source material, we will stick to the works already discussed:

Smith 11

Works Cited

Arenas, Reinaldo. <u>Graveyard of the Angels</u>.
Trans. Alfred J. MacAdam. New York: Avon,
1987.

Hawthorne, Nathaniel. "Young Goodman Brown."
McMichael. 707–716.

Mairowitz, David Zane and Robert Crumb.
<u>Introducing Kafka</u>. Cambridge, England:
Totem Books, 1994.

McMichael, George, ed. <u>Concise Anthology of
American Literature</u>. 4th ed. Upper Saddle
River, NJ: Prentice Hall, 1993.

---. "Walt Whitman, 1819–1892." McMichael.
1061–1063.

Melville, Herman. <u>Moby Dick; or, The Whale</u>.
Ed. Charles Feidelson, Jr. New York: Bobbs-
Merrill, 1964.

Spiegelman, Art. <u>The Complete Maus</u>. CD-ROM.
New York: Voyager. 1993.

Wheatley, Phillis. "On Imagination." McMichael.
407–408.

Whitman, Walt. "Crossing Brooklyn Ferry."
McMichael. 1128–1132.

"Woody Guthrie." <u>Woody Guthrie Foundation and
Archives</u>. Woody Guthrie Foundation. 26
July 2000. <http://www.woodyguthrie.org/
biography.htm>

The Works Cited Page

A Works Cited page, of course, only lists the material actually cited (quoted or paraphrased) in a paper. It is the final
page in a paper, and writers should think of this page as part
of their paper. Students sometimes draft the Works Cited
page in a separate file. This is a mistake, as that file sometimes slips the student's mind, and she finds that she is handing in a research paper with no documentation information.
If you draft the paper as a whole, including the Work(s) Cited
page, it will not get lost, and its pagination, font, and heading will be consistent with the rest of the paper. Also,
changes made in the paper can immediately be reflected in
the Works Cited page, and vice versa.

The page, of course, is paginated as part of the essay. If
the argument ends on page 10, the Works Cited page is page
11 and should feature the writer's last name in the upper
right-hand corner, along with the page number.

Next, the writer writes the phrase "Works Cited" (not
"Works Cited Page"). Capitalize the first letter of each word.
This phrase is centered on the top line of the page. It is not
boldfaced, underlined, italicized, or written in a different font
or size. The list of Works Cited begins immediately afterward
on the following line. Like the rest of the paper, the Works
Cited page is double-spaced.

Works are listed alphabetically by author. If there is no
author, works are listed alphabetically by the first term to
appear in the entry. Usually, this is the title of the piece in
question. If there are two works by the same author, list alphabetically by author first and title second.

Parenthetical Citation

When quoting or paraphrasing from a text in the body of
the paper, include a parenthetical citation to lead the reader to the Works Cited page for more information about the
source in question.

Parenthetical Citation for a Work with One Author.   For
instance, if the writer of the preceding paper quoted from
the Hawthorne story listed previously, she would follow her
quote with a parenthetical citation giving the author's last
name and a page number:

> At this point in the story, Young Goodman Brown "passed
> a crook of the road" (Hawthorne 707).

She would follow the quotation with the author's name and
page number; she does not include a comma between the

name and page number, nor does she include an abbreviation for "page." The reader understands that she is referring to page numbers. Since there is only one work listed by Hawthorne, the paper's writer needs to list only the author's name; she need not mention the title. The period follows the citation, which is now as much a part of her sentence as is the quotation itself.

Parenthetical Citation When the Author Is Listed More Than Once on the Works Cited Page.   If our writer quotes from the McMichael essay on Walt Whitman, she faces a problem. McMichael's name appears twice on the Works Cited page. To head off any potential confusion, she needs to include an abbreviation of the title in question to clarify matters for her reader.

> One critic writes that "Whitman had an expansive oceanic vision" (McMichael, "Walt Whitman" 1062).

Of course, she could simplify matters a bit by referring to the author in the text of her sentence:

> McMichael writes that "Whitman had an expansive oceanic vision" ("Walt Whitman" 1062).

Since she mentions the author in the text of the sentence, there is no need to repeat his name in the citation. She does, however, need to retain the title since there are two works by McMichael in the list of Works Cited.

Parenthetical Citation for a Work Without an Author.   One of the works on our writer's Works Cited page has no author. If the writer quotes from that source, she obviously cannot list the author's name in her parenthetical citation. Since she knows that her reader will be looking at the left margin of her Works Cited page for her alphabetically listed source, she lists the term closest to the left margin, in this case, the article's title:

> The Woody Guthrie Foundation's Web page biography calls *Bound for Glory* Guthrie's "first novel" and "[a] semi-autobiographical account of his Dust Bowl years" ("Woody Guthrie").

This Web site has no page numbers, so she is only able to give a title.

Parenthetical Citation for a Work with More Than One Author.   If we quoted from Introducing Kafka by David Zane Mairowitz and Robert Crumb, we would be faced with the problem of wondering which name to cite in the parenthetical citation:

Apparently, Kafka's sense of humor was very dark. In fact, "[w]hen Kafka read passages from The Trial out loud to his friends, he is reported to have laughed uncontrollably" (Mairowitz and Crumb 95).

When more than one author is responsible for the work, include all the names in the Works Cited entry.

WHY USE RESEARCH WHEN WRITING A LITERARY ANALYSIS PAPER?

Research to Confirm or Refute a Theory

All of these rules about citing borrowed information imply that there is a value in doing research in the first place. What is that value, after all? Why should a writer not remain content with his own reaction to a literary text? We can imagine many reasons to use research to write a literary analysis paper. We may use research to confirm or refute a theory the writer has developed about an author. For instance, a reader of Herman Melville's *Billy Budd* may have noticed some similarities between that story and the poetry of Emily Dickinson. The writer may develop a theory that Melville was strongly influenced by his reading of Dickinson. Some research into Dickinson's publishing reveals that Dickinson did not publish enough poetry during Melville's lifetime to be much of an influence. There goes that theory—but better the research reveal that than write a paper that is so far off base. And perhaps further research will reveal a third writer who influenced both Dickinson and Melville, saving a nugget of the writer's original theory.

Research for Clarification

As we may do research to test a theory we have developed, we may also do research because we have no theory at all. This kind of research may be called research for clarification. Perhaps a reader of T. S. Eliot's The Waste Land is utterly lost in the complexity of the poem. That reader may do some research into the sources in the poem (many of which are mentioned in Eliot's notes). Rather than confirm a theory, this reader is merely seeking a starting point, a way into the poem. Or perhaps the reader will search for an article on the poem that suggests at least one possible reading.

Research as a Form of Exploration

In the same vein, a reader may do research as a form of exploration. That is, the reader may encounter a literary text—say, Gabriel Garcia Marquez's <u>Chronicle of a Death Foretold</u>—which he basically understands but for which he has not developed a satisfactory thesis of his own. He may want to see what others have said about the book. The previous example suggested looking into the sources of a work. A look into the criticism of <u>Chronicle</u> may reveal Marquez's sources, but it may also reveal other useful information. Perhaps he will find Marquez's own comments on the work, or an essay by a critic using Marxist philosophy to discuss its meaning. Maybe there is an essay arguing for a feminist or psychoanalytical reading of the book. One of the nice things about exploring the criticism of a text without an agenda is that just about everything a writer finds is potentially useful.

Research to Clarify and Define a School of Criticism

If we are inclined to write our paper from one critical perspective or another, we may do research to clarify and define a school of criticism. There are many schools of contemporary literary criticism that are complex and difficult to explain. For the student experimenting in literary theory, it may be useful to consult the experts on matters of theory.

Research to Fulfill an Assignment Requirement

Finally, students often conduct research to fulfill an assignment requirement. This may seem a trivial point to make, but it is an important one. A student who may well feel comfortable writing an essay based only on her reading of a text may find herself rounding up four sources because her instructor told her she must. This is hardly the most noble reason to do research, but it is a real and common predicament. When faced with this kind of an assignment, some students may be tempted to grab the first four (or however many are required) sources and insert quotations from them into their papers. Unfortunately, that kind of work rarely satisfies the person writing, reading, or grading such papers. It is, therefore, important for students to consider the purpose of research before treating it as a mere requirement.

We have discussed some of the reasons writers might do research: to confirm or refute a theory, to seek clarification, clarify and define a school of criticism, or to explore a topic. Of course, a paper assigned in a literature class is a little different than one written by a professional literary critic. The literary critic wants to explore literature because that is her job or her avocation. She does it because she wants to or because it is expected of her in a professional capacity. The student writes such a paper for educational reasons and because he is going to be graded on his work. This student's work will likely be evaluated in light of the following criteria:

- competency of the writing itself (i.e., spelling, composition, grammar, organization)
- competency of the writer's grasp of the subject matter (Does the student demonstrate that he has been paying attention in class? Does he show familiarity with ideas and concepts discussed in class?)
- originality of the thesis (Is the student thinking for himself or only repeating ideas discussed in class?)
- persuasiveness of the argument (Is the reader inclined to agree with the paper after reading it?)
- adherence to the assignment (Did the student understand the parameters of the assignment and attempt to follow those parameters?)

Most instructors are looking for these general qualities in an essay. In the case of a research paper, we can add:

- competency of the research itself (Has the student tracked down quality, relevant material?)
- gracefulness of the incorporation of researched material (Does the quoted and paraphrased material read naturally, or does it seem forced or tacked on to the paper?)
- documentation of the researched material (Has the student been careful to give full credit to the original authors of the borrowed material?)

When a student considers that her work will be held to such high standards, she should be careful to take time with her research and to not be satisfied with the first material to come to hand. She should be sure to look for material that will enhance her understanding of the literature and to enhance her ability to communicate that understanding to others. And if her work is going to be held to high standards, then she should be sure that she holds equally high standards when she considers the material that will go into that paper, and she should hold herself to high standards of accountability in conducting her research.

Tips for the Student Embarking on Research

Begin research early. That perfect article you think you will find so easily is likely to be missing or nonexistent. Do not wait until the last minute.

Keep photocopies of every page from which you quote or paraphrase—you may need them later. While in the library, make sure to take notes on journal articles, book chapters, and so forth. However, it is wise to also photocopy this material and keep all copies in a folder with your rough draft. If you are ever accused of plagiarism or sloppy research, you want to be able to demonstrate the validity of your research practices. This may cost a few dollars, but it is a good investment.

Cite every word or phrase you quote or paraphrase, using appropriate documentation. It is better to cite too much than not enough.

Begin writing your Works Cited page early. Do not wait until the day the paper is done. Write entries for works as you find them.

Write your Works Cited page in the same file as your paper. Do not keep the Works Cited page in a separate computer file. As I said earlier, this often leads to a lost Works Cited page.

Make sure you have documented all of your source materials before returning them to the library.

Consider the useful material to which you may already have access. Does your textbook feature an introduction, a bibliography, a glossary, or an afterword? Read these materials, looking for material to include in your paper and for clues to finding other materials.

Know your library. Every library has its strengths and weaknesses. Find out what your library can do to help you. Does the library keep bound journals? Does it subscribe to on-line databases? Does your library share interlibrary loan privileges with other libraries? How long does it take for material to arrive? Are there limits on your use of the system? Are you permitted to print unlimited pages from on-line sources, or is there a cutoff point?

Trust your librarians. Librarians are great people. These are people whose job is helping people find information. Do not be afraid to ask them questions. They are usually happy to help. Not only that—they want you to know how to find information.

Back up everything. Make sure you have copies of all of your work. If you are working on a computer, back up material and make hard copies. If you are using a computer in your school's lab, make sure to keep copies of your work (and your documentation) on a disk.

Some Broad Standards for Evaluating Source Material

Value relevance over convenience. Encyclopedias are convenient sources of great quantities of information, but they are not the kinds of source material that demonstrate careful research. What message does a paper dependent on an encyclopedia send to its reader? It does not speak well of the author's research ability.

Do not blindly trust the Internet! Over the centuries, readers have come to trust libraries as storehouses of worthwhile material, and libraries have earned their reputations. The Internet has not yet earned this level of trust. Readers assume that a good academic library buys journals that professionals on staff have evaluated and found credible. The material in these journals is often "peer reviewed." That is, these essays have been read and criticized by fellow professionals in the field. The Internet is different. Anybody who can afford an Internet connection can put up a site on Jane Austen. Anybody with the right software and decent design skill can make a site look professional. That does not mean that the site can be trusted. We know this, but we often forget while in the heat of getting our paper done, especially if the information on a Web site seems to support our ideas and gets our paper finished on time! Later in this chapter we will discuss specific criteria for judging Internet sites, but a healthy skepticism should always be your guide.

Use the most recent sources you can find. Although it is true that in the humanities, research stays valid longer than, say, research in biology or computer sciences, you want to set up some boundaries. Unless you are planning an exhaustive research project, try to focus on material written in the last twenty years. This is not to say that older material is never useful; however, recent research can expand upon or even debunk older material. A research paper on Edgar Allan Poe using material published in 1909 is going to be very different than one relying on material published in 1999.

Consider the publisher. Is this journal published by a familiar university? Have you ever heard of the author or any of the members of the editorial board? Is this book published by a reputable university press? Is this publisher one whose books you have used before? Have other instructors assigned this publisher's books in your classes?

Consider the author. Who wrote this essay or book? Do you know this person's reputation? Was her work recommended to you? Is the author identified on the book jacket or in the journal? Have you read other work by this person? As a student, the names of all literary critics may seem unfamiliar, but it cannot hurt to look. Also, as you do research in a particular field, you may notice that the same name keeps cropping up. For instance, if I do research on Ernest Hemingway, I may stumble across the name "Michael Reynolds" again and again. If I pursue this "lead," I will find out that Reynolds is a well-respected critic and biographer of Hemingway. Suddenly, I have a "toehold" in my research.

HOW DO I BEGIN MY RESEARCH?

If I have been asked to write a paper about Edgar Allan Poe's "The Tell-Tale Heart" and I have already written about this story or if I have taken careful notes about it, I should be happy. What I know about the story itself may guide me in my research. Even more, I know that Edgar Allan Poe is a very famous and well-respected writer. There should be plenty of material about Poe in a good academic library.

As to the story itself, since I have discussed it in class I know, for instance, that the point of view is important to an understanding of the story. I may then begin my research looking for articles written about this story's *narrative voice* or *narrator* or some related term. The terms *Gothic* and *romantic* appear in my notes. Those terms also can guide my research.

Narrow Your Search

In this age of computer databases, key terms become increasingly important. In fact, in the case of a writer as well known as Poe, there may be so many entries on him in a given search that narrowing the search with key terms will be useful.

So, I may begin my research by doing some note taking before I head to the library. I will want to take my assignment sheet (if I have one), my notebook, and my (annotated) copy of "The Tell-Tale Heart" with me to the library. I want to look at my textbook. Is there an introduction, bibliography, glossary, or other editorial material to guide me in my search?

Once I get all of this material organized, I can head to the library and begin my search. My initial notes might look something like this:

Edgar Allan Poe

Fiction

"The Tell-Tale Heart"

Horror/terror story

Gothic/romantic literature

Crime story

Narrative voice/point of view

This may not seem like much, but consider the following scenario. Perhaps I begin my research where so many students do (but obviously should not!): the Internet. I sit down and type "Edgar Allan Poe" into a search engine. What do I expect to find? One or two juicy articles?

When I tried it, I found 30,168 pages. Try alphabetizing all of them on a Works Cited page! As in much of life, quality is superior to quantity when we do research.

So, one of our goals is to narrow our search. We can start by looking in our library instead of on the Internet. When we search the Internet, we search the entire planet. When we search in our library, we search in a single location on the planet. Our search is narrower already!

What Sources Might Prove Useful?

Of course, libraries are big places themselves. There are many useful sources in most academic libraries. In fact, there are so many that we may find the library a daunting place. Knowing a few useful resources to get us started may make the place a bit more inviting. Let us categorize some useful kinds of sources and look at a few examples of individual sources.

Critical Biographies and Other Book-Length Studies. Biographical approaches to literary criticism have long been considered out-of-date. By biographical approach, I mean the consistent attempt to trace significant themes and events in a writer's work to his or her life. Virginia Woolf, Edgar Allan Poe, and Emily Dickinson have been major victims of this approach, causing some readers to look at their writing in an attempt to figure out what was "wrong" with these people.

However, critical biographies remain valuable resources for the student. A good critical biography attempts to strike a balance between the literature and the author's life. A well-written critical biography can include not just a chronology of the author's life but of the critical response to the work. The student working on a paper on Walt Whitman, for instance, can take a look at Justin Kaplan's or David Reynolds's biographies for historical context, critical insight, or even an indication of the critical consensus of a given poem. These books can be as big and intimidating as a library, but the student of literature needs to remember that the index of such a work can be an invaluable resource. The student writing about an individual poem can look up that poem in the index and read only those pages in the text. When doing a research paper (especially under a tight deadline), one should expect to read chunks of books—not necessarily entire volumes.

Of course, this use of the index is equally useful for book-length studies of literary works, figures, periods, and themes. Leslie Fiedler's <u>Love and Death in the American Novel</u> is a classic work on American literature, but it is also over five hundred pages long. For the student who has three weeks to write a paper on <u>The Adventures of Huckleberry Finn</u>, that may be a bit much to digest. However, a quick glance at the index shows me at least fourteen places in the book that deal with <u>Huckleberry Finn</u>, including one twenty-page section. Even intimidating resources can be helpful if used wisely.

Encyclopedias and Reference Books.   Elsewhere in this book I have suggested that encyclopedias should not be a major component of a good literary research paper. An encyclopedia can be a useful first stop in the library, but as a major source for research papers, it is of limited use. An encyclopedia contains a wealth of information, but the information is condensed and often at least slightly out-of-date. An entry on a major figure or event might be as little as a paragraph, and usually only a page or two at most. That should not be enough information to satisfy our curiosity. Also, encyclopedias—especially general-interest encyclopedias such as the *Encyclopedia Britannica*—cover many topics beyond literature. They do not have space to go into the kind of specific detail the student of literature ought to be looking for (such as in-depth interpretations of individual texts, for instance).

On the other hand, an encyclopedia can quickly define terms. If a student is told that he must write a paper about performances of <u>Macbeth</u> in the Globe Theater, and he has never heard of the Globe Theater, an encyclopedia may be just what he is looking for to get him started. However, he needs to quickly move beyond the encyclopedia. In fact, he may get help doing just that by consulting the bibliographies that accompany many encyclopedia entries.

He might also consult encyclopedias of literary biography that his library might have. But even books such as this are likely to be a little too general, a little too tightly focused on biography to be acceptable as his only (or major) source.

Reference Books and Dictionaries of Literary Terms. Even more helpful than encyclopedias are dictionaries of literary terms. When a student moves from a general-interest work such as the *Encyclopedia Britannica* to a more specifically themed work such as a literary dictionary, she narrows her search. These books define the terms often encountered in literary studies. These terms may seem familiar at first, but a reader may find that when applied to literary analysis, simple terms such as *text, comedy,* and *drama* take on specific connotations with which she is not familiar. The following are a few of the books one may turn to for help getting one's bearings in the language of literature. Most of these books can be found in a good academic library.

A Handbook to Literature. Hugh Holman, et al.,
    eds. (Prentice Hall)
The Penguin Dictionary of Symbols. Jean Che-
    valier and Alain Gheerbrant (Penguin)
A Glossary of Literary Terms. M. H. Abrams
    (Harcourt Brace)
NTC's Dictionary of Literary Terms. Kathleen
    Morner and Ralph Rausch (NTC Publishing
    Group)

Other Reference Books. Oxford has published a series of very useful books called the Oxford Companions. These books are handy dictionaries of authors, texts, and ideas central to a variety of fields of literature. Of course, other publishers (notably Cambridge) offer similar books. The Oxford series is particularly useful, however. The series includes the following and other books:

The Oxford Companion to Women's Writing in the
    United States. Ed. Cathy N. Davidson, et al.
The Oxford Companion to African American Lit-
    erature. Ed. William L. Andrews, et al.
The Oxford Companion to American Literature.
    (6th Edition) Ed. James David Hart, Phillip
    Leininger.
The Oxford Companion to English Literature.
    Ed. Margaret Drabble.
The Oxford Companion to Twentieth-Cemtury Lit-
    erature in English. Ed. Jenny Stringer.

Literary Theory and Criticism. Contemporary literary theory is often considered the toughest aspect of the discipline of literary studies. There are a few books out there that make this difficult material a little easier to navigate.

Literary Theory: A Very Short Introduction. by Jonathan D. Culler (Oxford)

Literary Criticism: An Introduction to Theory and Practice. Charles Bressler (Prentice Hall)

The Penguin Dictionary of Literary Symbols and Literary Theory. J. A. Cuddon (Penguin)

Marxism and Literary Criticism. Terry Eagelton (California University Press)

A Dictionary of Modern Critical Terms. Roger Fowler, ed. (Routledge)

A Handbook of Critical Approaches to Literature. Wilfred Guerin, et al. (Harper)

A Reader's Guide to Contemporary Literary Theory. Raman Selden (Kentucky University Press)

Book Series.   There are several very useful book series that offer the student researcher quick access to a handful of essays on a given topic as well as excellent bibliographic information. Some of these series, such as the Norton Critical Editions, are available in cheap paperbacks. Others, such as the Chelsea House series, are more likely to be found in an academic library (although the other series are often found in library collections as well).

Bedford Case Studies in Contemporary Criticism.   This series includes not only the text of a literary work but critical essays that consider the text from a variety of theoretical positions. This approach allows the student to see the theory in practice rather than read about the theory in the abstract. These books also contain other materials, including introductions, bibliographies, and glossaries.

Norton Critical Editions.   This series generally features the complete text of a major literary work, an introduction, context material (historical documents of the era in which the work was published, for instance, or early reviews), and a series of critical essays about the work. These little books can be an excellent start. There are many, many works in this series.

Bedford's Cultural Editions.   Like the Norton Critical Editions and Bedford Case Studies books, these editions feature both the literary text and essays and other materials. Rather than current criticism, these books focus on the historical context of the works in question and offer historical documents.

Bedford's Case Studies in Critical Controversy.   This series also features the text of a work as well as essays in criticism about the book. However, this series has a theme: controversy. Essays in these books focus on the controversial aspects of the work in question. What is nice about this approach is that it reminds the reader of just how widely divergent views of literature can be. Is <u>Huckleberry Finn</u> a bitter indictment of racism, or is it actually a racist novel that needs to be kept away from children?

Chelsea House Series in Modern Critical Views.   Harold Bloom's exhaustive Chelsea House Series does not include primary literary texts like the Norton and Bedford Editions do. The series features a chronological sampling of the modern criticism of major literary figures. Everyone from Albert Camus to Ursula K. Le Guin has been considered in this very valuable series. The Chelsea House Series is really an excellent first stop for the student beginning a big project on a particular text or author. Bloom's introductions themselves outline the history of the reception of the author or work in question and are themselves excellent resources.

MLA International Bibliography

Perhaps the most valuable resource for the student engaging in literary research is the MLA Bibliography. Found in most academic libraries, and now available in CD-ROM and on-line versions, the MLA Bibliography is the most complete catalog of articles and books in literary studies available today. The MLA International Bibliography features bibliographic information regarding tens of thousands of articles on all aspects of literature from scholarly journals and books published over the last several decades. Consequently, the student searching the MLA Bibliography must narrow his search.

For instance, if the student is looking for information on Poe, he might consider articles written in a certain time period. As we have previously discussed, it is probably wisest to start with the more recent publications, especially with a writer as well known as Poe. Next, the student may want to focus on Poe's fiction rather than his poetry. Of that fiction, he may decide on either horror or crime, or narrow his search to one particular story, such as "The Tell-Tale Heart."

Once these key terms are fed into the database, the MLA Bibliography will produce a list of article titles, some of which may or may not be located in journals or books in that student's library. The value of the MLA Bibliography is not that it delivers the articles themselves to the student. However, the bibliographic information it delivers will lead the student to those articles.

Internet Sites

The Internet is such an unstable entity that it is almost pointless to list Web sites here (although I will mention a couple). No doubt as I write this, hundreds of literature-related sites are being posted and hundreds more are being taken down. More important than memorizing one or two sites, though, is having a set of criteria for evaluating the sites out there.

Having a stable set of rules in mind is important while we navigate the Internet, for although it is a huge potential resource, it is an unruly one. Andrew Harnack and Eugene Kleppinger remind us why it is so important to be vigilant while surfing the Net:

> Consider this: not only is there no editorial board for most Internet publications, there also is no market force to drive incompetent or untrustworthy publications off the Web. (53)

Harnack and Kleppinger go on to suggest helpful ideas in keeping track of Internet searches. They wisely recommend that the student doing research bookmark useful pages and document important information for every site from which the student considers borrowing information (i.e., record author, title of document, URL, date of publication, date of access, etc.).

Harnack and Kleppinger also suggest evaluating each source by considering who published the page, evaluating how well and how fully the page has documented and represented its sources, whether or not the information can be verified in other sources, and how current the information is.

This may sound like a lot of work. It is. Essentially, the person evaluating a given Web page becomes an editor. In traditional publishing (books, magazines, newspapers, and journals) the editor verifies the information the author brings to the publisher. As Harnack and Kleppinger point out, there is no editor on the Internet.

One way to avoid all this work is to avoid using the Internet altogether, but that smacks a little of throwing away the baby with the bath water. Another solution is to only use sites with the URL designation "edu." This should keep the intrepid researcher away from all commercial sites. However, the "edu" does not always mean that the author of the site is an expert. Virtually anyone associated with an educational institution can get a site with this designation. And a commercial designation is not necessarily the kiss of death. There are plenty of useful commercial cites, such as The Atlantic Monthly's site, Atlantic Unbound <www.theAtlantic.com>.

One might scrupulously avoid all sites but those that originate from a source as reputable as any print journal (i.e., hypertext editions of print works or on-line scholarly journals such as Postmodern Culture <www.iath.virginia.edu/pmc/current.issue/>, which employ editorial boards just like traditional journals do). There are also link sites sponsored by reputable educational institutions. The fact that a university hosts a link site does not mean that all of the links are valid, but it is a first step. Two such link sites are:

> The University of California at Santa Barbara site called "Voice of the Shuttle" is an excellent and diverse compendium of links: http://vos.ucsb.edu/index.html

> Many academic libraries have set up Web sites featuring link pages. Check your library to see if it has established such a page. One such page is hosted by Southern Connecticut State University's Buley Library: http://library.scsu.ctstateu.edu/litbib.html

On-Line Writing Labs

Another valuable resource for the writer of literary analysis is the OWL (Online Writing Lab). Many colleges and universities have set up electronic, 24-hour labs to assist the student who needs help at 2 A.M. Does your school host such a site? Many of these sites feature useful "FAQ" ("Frequently Asked Questions") pages where the student may find a quick answer to a thorny grammar, style, documentation, or research problem. The homepage for Colgate's National Writing Centers Association links to a comprehensive list of hundreds of OWLS: http://departments.colgate.edu/diw/NWCA.html.

Evaluating Web Pages

It is still possible to use other sites as long as the researcher has a solid set of guidelines for evaluating the sites. Jim Kapoun of Southwest State University has devised a very useful guide to evaluating Web sites. You may have encountered this checklist in your Web travels. Kapoun's criteria are as follows:

Criteria for Evaluating Web Pages

EVALUATION OF WEB DOCUMENTS

Accuracy of Web Documents

- Who wrote the page and can you contact him or her?
- What is the purpose of the document and why was it produced?
- Is this person qualified to write this document?

Authority of Web Documents

- Who published the document and is it separate from the Webmaster?
- Check the domain of the document. What institution publishes this document?
- Does the publisher list its qualifications?

Objectivity of Web Documents

- What goals or objectives does this page meet?
- How detailed is the information?
- What opinions (if any) are expressed by the author?

Currency of Web Documents

- When was it produced?
- When was it updated?
- How up-to-date are the links (if any)?

Coverage of the Web Documents

- Are the links (if any) evaluated and do they complement the documents' theme?
- Is it all images or a balance of text and images?
- Is the information presented cited correctly?

HOW TO INTERPRET THE BASICS

Accuracy

- Make sure the author provides e-mail or a contact address/phone number.
- Know the distinction between author and Webmaster.

Authority

- What credentials are listed for the author(s)?
- Where is the document published? Check URL domain.

Objectivity

- Determine if the page is a mask for advertising; if so, information might be biased.
- View any Web page as you would an infomercial on television. Ask yourself why was this written and for whom.

Currency

- How many dead links are on the page?
- Are the links current or updated regularly?
- Is the information on the page outdated?

Coverage

- Is there an option for text only, or frames, or suggested browser for better viewing?
- If the page requires special software to view the information, how much are you missing if you don't have the software?
- Is it free, or is there a fee to obtain the information?
- Is there an option for text only, or frames, or suggested browser for better viewing?

Putting It All Together

- *Accuracy*. If your page lists the author and institution that published the page and provides a way of contacting him or her, and . . .
- *Authority*. If your page lists the author's credentials and its domain is preferred (.edu, .gov, .org, or .net), and . . .
- *Objectivity*. If your page provides accurate information with limited advertising and it is objective in presenting the information, and . . .
- *Currency*. If your page is current and updated regularly (as stated on the page) and the links (if any) are also up-to-date, and . . .
- *Coverage*. If you can view the information properly—not limited to fees, browser technology, or software requirements, then . . .

You may have a higher-quality Web page that could be of value to your research!

Table courtesy of Jim Kapoun, Southwest State University.

The Tell-Tale Heart by Edgar Allan Poe (1843)

TRUE!—nervous—very, very dreadfully nervous I had been and am; but why *will* you say that I am mad? The disease had sharpened my senses—not destroyed—not dulled them. Above all was the sense of hearing acute. I heard all things in the heaven and in the earth. I heard many things in hell. How, then, am I mad? Hearken! and observe how healthily—how calmly I can tell you the whole story.

It is impossible to say how first the idea entered my brain; but once conceived, it haunted me day and night. Object there was none. Passion there was none. I loved the old man. He had never wronged me. He had never given me insult. For his gold I had no desire. I think it was his eye! yes, it was this! He had the eye of a vulture—a pale blue eye, with a film over it. Whenever it fell upon me, my blood ran cold; and so by degrees—very gradually—I made up my mind to take the life of the old man, and thus rid myself of the eye forever.

Now this is the point. You fancy me mad. Madmen know nothing. But you should have seen *me*. You should have seen how wisely I proceeded—with what caution—with what foresight—with what dissimulation I went to work! I was never kinder to the old man than during the whole week before I killed him. And every night, about midnight, I turned the latch of his door and opened it—oh so gently! And then, when I had made an opening sufficient for my head, I put in a dark lantern, all closed, closed, that no light shone out, and then I thrust in my head. Oh, you would have laughed to see how cunningly I thrust it in! I moved it slowly—very, very slowly, so that I might not disturb the old man's sleep. It took me an hour to place my whole head within the opening so far that I could see him as he lay upon his bed. Ha! would a madman have been so wise as this? And then, when my head was well in the room, I undid the lantern cautiously—oh, so cautiously—cautiously (for the hinges creaked)—I undid it just so much that a single thin ray fell upon the vulture eye.

And this I did for seven long nights—every night just at midnight—but I found the eye always closed; and so it was impossible to do the work; for it was not the old man who vexed me, but his Evil Eye. And every morning, when the day broke, I went boldly into the chamber, and spoke courageously to him, calling him by name in a hearty tone, and inquiring how he has passed the night. So you see he would have been a very profound old man, indeed, to suspect that every night, just at twelve, I looked in upon him while he slept.

Upon the eighth night I was more than usually cautious in opening the door. A watch's minute hand moves more quickly than did mine. Never before that night, had I *felt* the extent of my own powers—of my sagacity. I could scarcely contain my feelings of triumph. To think that there I was, opening the door, little by little, and he not even to dream of my secret deeds or thoughts. I fairly chuckled at the idea; and perhaps he heard me; for he moved on the bed suddenly, as if startled. Now you may think that I drew back—but no. His room was as black as pitch with the thick darkness, (for the shutters were close fastened, through fear of robbers,) and so I knew that he could not see the opening of the door, and I kept pushing it on steadily, steadily.

I had my head in, and was about to open the lantern, when my thumb slipped upon the tin fastening, and the old man sprang up in bed, crying out—"Who's there?"

I kept quite still and said nothing. For a whole hour I did not move a muscle, and in the meantime I did not hear him lie down. He was still sitting up in the bed listening;—just as I have done, night after night, hearkening to the death watches in the wall.

Presently I heard a slight groan, and I knew it was the groan of mortal terror. It was not a groan of pain or of grief— oh, no! —it was the low stifled sound that arises from the bottom of the soul when overcharged with awe. I knew the sound well. Many a night, just at midnight, when all the world slept, it has welled up from my own bosom, deepening, with its dreadful echo, the terrors that distracted me. I say I knew it well. I knew what the old man felt, and pitied him, although I chuckled at heart. I knew that he had been lying awake ever since the first slight noise, when he had turned in the bed. His fears had been ever since growing upon him. He had been trying to fancy them causeless, but could not. He had been saying to himself—"It is nothing but the wind in the chimney—it is only a mouse crossing the floor," or "it is merely a cricket which has made a single chirp." Yes, he had been trying to comfort himself with these suppositions: but he had found all in vain. *All in vain;* because Death, in approaching him had stalked with his black shadow before him, and enveloped the victim. And it was the mournful influence of the unperceived shadow that caused him to feel—although he neither saw nor heard—to feel the presence of my head within the room.

When I had waited a long time, very patiently, without hearing him lie down, I resolved to open a little—a very, very little crevice in the lantern. So I opened it—you cannot imagine how stealthily, stealthily—until, at length a simple dim ray, like the thread of the spider, shot from out the crevice and fell full upon the vulture eye.

It was open—wide, wide open—and I grew furious as I gazed upon it. I saw it with perfect distinctness—all a dull blue, with a hideous veil over it that chilled the very marrow in my bones; but I could see nothing else of the old man's face or person: for I had directed the ray as if by instinct, precisely upon the damned spot.

And have I not told you that what you mistake for madness is but over-acuteness of the senses?—now, I say, there came to my ears a low, dull, quick sound, such as a watch makes when enveloped in cotton. I knew *that* sound well, too. It was the beating of the old man's heart. It increased my fury, as the beating of a drum stimulates the soldier into courage.

But even yet I refrained and kept still. I scarcely breathed. I held the lantern motionless. I tried how steadily I could maintain the ray upon the eye. Meantime the hellish tattoo of the heart increased. It grew quicker and quicker, and louder and louder every instant. The old man's terror *must* have been extreme! It grew louder, I say, louder every moment!—do you mark me well? I have told you that I am nervous: so I am. And now at the dead hour of the night, amid the dreadful silence of that old house, so strange a noise as this excited me to uncontrollable terror. Yet, for some minutes longer I refrained and stood still. But the beating grew louder, louder! I thought the heart must burst. And now a new anxiety seized me—the sound would be heard by a neighbour! The old man's hour had come! With a loud yell, I threw open the lantern and leaped into the room. He shrieked once—once only. In an instant I dragged him to the floor, and pulled the heavy bed over him. I then smiled gaily, to find the deed so far done. But, for many minutes, the heart beat on with a muffled sound. This, however, did not vex me; it would not be heard through the wall. At length it ceased. The old man was dead. I removed the bed and examined the corpse. Yes, he was stone, stone dead. I placed my hand upon the heart and held it there many minutes. There was no pulsation. He was stone dead. His eye would trouble me no more.

If still you think me mad, you will think so no longer when I describe the wise precautions I took for the concealment of the body. The night waned, and I worked hastily, but in silence. First of all I dismembered the corpse. I cut off the head and the arms and the legs.

I then took up three planks from the flooring of the chamber, and deposited all between the scantlings. I then replaced the boards so cleverly, so cunningly, that no human eye—not even *his*—could have detected any thing wrong. There was nothing to wash out—no stain of any kind—no blood-spot whatever. I had been too wary for that. A tub had caught all—ha! ha!

When I had made an end of these labors, it was four o'clock—still dark as midnight. As the bell sounded the hour, there came a knocking at the street door. I went down to open it with a light heart,—for what had I *now* to fear? There entered three men, who introduced themselves, with perfect suavity, as officers of the police. A shriek had been heard by a neighbour during the night; suspicion of foul play had been aroused; information had been lodged at the police office, and they (the officers) had been deputed to search the premises.

I smiled,—for *what* had I to fear? I bade the gentlemen welcome. The shriek, I said, was my own in a dream. The old man, I mentioned, was absent in the country. I took my visitors all over the house. I bade them search—search *well.* I led them, at length, to *his* chamber. I showed them his treasures, secure, undisturbed. In the enthusiasm of my confidence, I brought chairs into the room, and desired them *here* to rest from their fatigues, while I myself, in the wild audacity of my perfect triumph, placed my own seat upon the very spot beneath which reposed the corpse of the victim.

The officers were satisfied. My *manner* had convinced them. I was singularly at ease. They sat, and while I answered cheerily, they chatted of familiar things. But, ere long, I felt myself getting pale and wished them gone. My head ached, and I fancied a ringing in my ears: but still they sat and still chatted. The ringing became more distinct:—It continued and became more distinct: I talked more freely to get rid of the feeling: but it continued and gained definiteness—until, at length, I found that the noise was *not* within my ears.

No doubt I now grew *very* pale;—but I talked more fluently, and with a heightened voice. Yet the sound increased—

and what could I do? It was *a low, dull, quick sound—much such a sound as a watch makes when enveloped in cotton.* I gasped for breath—and yet the officers heard it not. I talked more quickly—more vehemently; but the noise steadily increased. I arose and argued about trifles, in a high key and with violent gesticulations; but the noise steadily increased. Why *would* they not be gone? I paced the floor to and fro with heavy strides, as if excited to fury by the observations of the men—but the noise steadily increased. Oh God! what *could* I do? I foamed—I raved—I swore! I swung the chair upon which I had been sitting, and grated it upon the boards, but the noise arose over all and continually increased. It grew louder—louder—*louder!* And still the men chatted pleasantly, and smiled. Was it possible they heard not? Almighty God!— no, no! They heard!—they suspected!—they *knew!*—they were making a mockery of my horror—this I thought, and this I think. But anything was better than this agony! Anything was more tolerable than this derision! I could bear those hypocritical smiles no longer! I felt that I must scream or die! and now—again!—hark! louder! louder! louder! *louder!*

   "Villains!" I shrieked, "dissemble no more! I admit the deed!—tear up the planks! here, here!—It is the beating of his hideous heart!"

Glossary
of
Literary Terms

aesthetics: The philosophy that considers the nature and expression of beauty. We may also use the word to describe our own personal conception of what is artistically valid or beautiful.

allegory: A literary work in which characters and events stand for abstract ideas. The literal reading of an allegory suggests a parallel symbolic reading.

alliteration: The repetition of the same consonant sounds at the beginning of words or in stressed syllables. Alliteration is a poetic device used to create harmony, unity, and musicality without necessarily using rhyme outright.

allusion: A reference in a work of literature to another work of literature; a passage of scripture; scene, character, or event from mythology; an historical event or personage; or the author's own life or experience.

analogy: A comparison between similar things. An analogy is often intended to help explain something by comparing it to something else with which the reader is familiar. Metaphor and simile differ from analogy in that a metaphor or simile is usually a more creative comparison.

assonance: Assonance refers to the repetition of similar vowel sounds. Like alliteration, assonance is often intended to create or reinforce a sense of harmony, unity, and musicality.

blank verse: Poetry written in unrhymed lines, usually of iambic pentameter. Shakespeare's plays are largely written in blank verse. Not to be confused with free verse.

canon: Those works that have been accepted as being of lasting importance. Often, we use the term to refer to those works traditionally taught in colleges and universities or contained in standard anthologies of literature. Virginia Woolf and William Shakespeare are canonical writers. Stephen King and Judith Krantz are not. The issue of what works should be accepted in the canon or whether a canon should exist as such has been hotly debated in recent years.

character: A person portrayed in a fictional text, be it drama, short story, novel, or even a poem or film or television program. When we speak of the creation and development of the traits of these characters, we speak of characterization. Different terms are used to describe different kinds of characters. These terms indicate the extent to which a reader accepts the character as a real representation of an actual person. Different kinds of characters include the stereotype, dynamic character, or stock character.

comedy: Generally, comedy refers to any literary work that amuses or deals with humorous subject matter. More specifically, a comedy is a dramatic work that is amusing or satirical in tone and that usually contains a happy resolution of the thematic conflict. Dramatic comedy is the counterpoint to tragedy. While a tragedy documents the reversal of fortunes of a character who goes from triumph to failure, a comedy ends with the protagonist in happier circumstances than we first met him or her.

dialect: A writer's attempt to mimic the language of a particular region through the use of distinctive pronunciation, grammar, vocabulary, or spelling. Usually, dialect differs from the standard literary language or speech pattern of its broader culture. Readers of Mark Twain are used to the dialect he employs to represent the language of the American South.

dialogue: In its simplest form, dialogue refers to any conversation between two people. In literary terms, we use the word dialogue to refer to the literary representation of such a conversation in a literary work, be it a drama or prose fiction, or poetry. There is also a genre of literature called dialogue. In such works, two characters carry on a conversation intended to reveal meaning to the reader. Such a dialogue usually concerns a philosophical topic.

diction: When we discuss a writer's choice and use of specific words in writing, we refer to the writer's diction. Careful attention to a writer's diction allows the reader to discern the tone of a literary work.

drama: A drama is a story written in dialogue, intended to be acted out by actors before an audience. Essentially, a drama is a play.

essay: A genre of literature. The essay is a short literary composition on a single theme, often presenting the personal opinions of the author. The essay is a very pliable genre, and can even read like a short story; however, an essay is understood to be a work of nonfiction, whereas a short story is understood to be fiction. When Henry David Thoreau describes the night he spent in jail in "Resistance to Civil Government," the reader is intended to believe that a real person named Henry David Thoreau actually engaged in the activity described in the essay. In Ernest Hemingway's short story "Big Two-Hearted River," we meet a fictional character we do not assume to be Hemingway himself. The essay is often used to make arguments and to persuade an audience to accept one point of view over another regarding the issue at hand.

exposition: In fiction and drama, information revealed (usually at the beginning of a work) that allows a reader to understand the work. Exposition may include setting, the relationship between characters, or other basic background information. Exposition revealed later in the narrative is called flashback.

fiction: Fiction refers to a narrative invented by the author and not intended to represent events that have actually occurred. The most well-known fictional forms are the novel and short story. However, drama and narrative poetry are also forms of fiction.

figurative language: Language that intentionally departs from the literal. Figurative language depends upon exaggeration and/or comparison. Hence, metaphor, simile, hyperbole, and personification are all forms of figurative language. These figures of speech are intended to be interpreted rather than understood to be taken literally. Thus, an expression like "it was raining cats and dogs" is clearly a use of figurative language.

figures of speech: Forms of figurative language such as metaphor, simile, hyperbole, and personification are all forms of figurative language.

flashback: A device often used in drama, film, and fiction that allows the author to reveal information or include narration that describes events that took place before the beginning of the story. Flashback is exposition that occurs after the beginning of the story.

foreshadowing: In a work of fiction, foreshadowing hints at events yet to come in the narrative. Foreshadowing may refer to a comment about the likely fate of a given character, or it may be as subtle as the description of a foreboding natural setting that implies dire consequences later in the work. In Steven Crane's "The Open Boat," four men trapped in a lifeboat discover four cigars but only three matches. Some readers suggest that the conspicuously missing match foreshadows the death of one of the men. In fact, one of the men does die at the end of the story.

free verse: Unrhymed poetry that is free of a regular beat or meter is called free verse. The best free verse (such as that by Walt Whitman, who popularized the form) is not without musical qualities. Free verse depends on the natural rhythms of speech for its musicality.

genre: A category of literary work, or any artistic composition, as in music or painting. A genre is marked by a characteristic form or content. Fiction is a genre of literature, and the novel and short story are both genres of fiction. Within these genres are the genres of science fiction, the Western, the detective story, etc. Drama and poetry are also genres of literature, and these genres also contain subgenres, like the epic poem or the tragedy.

hero/heroine: The main character in a literary work. In classical literature, a hero or heroine would be a person of mythological or legendary status. In modern literature, the hero or heroine is merely a person of admirable qualities.

hyperbole: Use of figurative language that depends on exaggeration. Used for emphasis.

iamb: A metrical foot consisting of an unstressed syllable followed by a stressed syllable such as in the word "insure."

iambic meter: Meter composed of iambs.

iambic pentameter: A poetic line of five iambic feet. In English, iambic pentameter is perhaps the most common poetic meter. The first line of Shakespeare's Sonnet 18, "Shall I compare thee to a summer's day," is written in iambic pentameter.

irony: Essentially, irony is the recognition of the difference between appearance and reality. This could mean using language to express a meaning different from or even opposite to its literal meaning. Such an expression (or even a figure of speech) that is marked by an intentional contrast between literal and intended meaning

is called verbal irony. We may also refer to situational
irony, which occurs in a story when events conspire so
that what actually occurs is the opposite of what might be
expected. In a literary work, situational irony may be
employed for humorous or other effect. Dramatic irony
refers to a situation in a work of fiction (often a drama) in
which a character unwittingly makes a statement the
audience or reader is intended to understand as ironic, or
in contradiction to the full truth. When a reader or viewer
knows more than the characters in a work of literature
themselves do about their current situation, we can say
that dramatic irony has occurred.

lyric: A short poem that expresses the poet's (or the
speaker's) emotions rather than narrating a story.

metaphor: A figure of speech in which two unlike objects
are strongly compared with each other. In a metaphor, the
comparison is made without using the words "like" or
"as." In fact, one could say that a metaphor is an
identification between two unlike objects rather than a
comparison (e.g., "He is a wizard at the computer,"
instead of "He is like a wizard when it comes to
computers"). As a result, a metaphor can be more
powerful than a simile, or comparison between two unlike
objects using the words "like" or "as."

meter: The pattern of accented and unaccented syllables
in the lines of a poem. These patterns create the rhythm of
the poem.

metrical foot: Meter is measured by the foot, or
arrangement of accented and unaccented syllables in the
lines of the poem. A poem's meter is determined by the
number of feet in a line. A line of one foot is called
monometer, two feet is called dimeter, three feet is called
trimeter, four feet is called tetrameter, five feet is called
pentameter. Much of English-language poetry is composed
in iambic pentameter, that is, lines consisting of five
iambs, or five couples of one unstressed and one stressed
syllable.

motif: An element or component in a decorative
composition. We may look for recurring motifs in a work of
fiction, poetry, or drama.

narration: The telling of a story. There are various modes
of narration. The person relating the events in a work of
fiction is usually called the narrator of the work. The
person relating the events in a work of poetry is usually
called the "speaker."

novel: A long work of prose fiction. A novel recounts the events that transpire to characters, and describes the setting of the story.

parody: A literary work that imitates another work in order to ridicule it. Usually this ridicule is achieved through exaggeration of style and structure. Frederick Douglass ends his 1845 *Narrative* with a poem titled "A Parody," which mocks the piety of slave owners who profess to be Godly even as they engage in the brutality of slavery. The poem is written in parodic imitation of a hymn.

personification: A figure of speech in which nonhuman objects or creatures are described in human terms (e.g., "eye-like windows").

plot: The arrangement of incidents in a narrative (be it novel, short story, poem, or drama).

poem: Literary compositions written in meter. Poetry is intended to be performed by the human voice, rather than merely read to oneself like a work of prose fiction.

point of view: In a piece of literature, the perspective from which a story is told. Generally, we speak of first, second, and third person points of view.

> **First person point of view:** Indicates that the narrator is himself or herself a character in the work being narrated. Stories told in this point of view use the pronoun "I." Since the narrator is involved in the action of the story, we may sometimes question how valid his or her observations may be.

> **Second person point of view:** Indicates that the *reader* is himself or herself a character in the work being narrated. Stories told in this point of view use the pronoun "you."

> **Third person point of view:** Indicates that the narrator is not a character in the work being narrated. Stories told in this point of view use the pronoun "he," "she," "it," or "they." Since the narrator is not a character in the work, this narrator can generally be seen as more reliable than the first person narrator. The third person narrator can be characterized as either *limited* or *omniscient*. A "limited" third person narrator reveals only some information (the thoughts of one character but not another, for instance). An omniscient third person narrator reveals far more information (the thoughts of all the characters, or the eventual fate of the characters, for instance).

protagonist: The main or principal character of a work of fiction or drama.

satire: A humorous work that mocks human folly in order to effect change (e.g., Jonathan Swift's "A Modest Proposal").

short story: A short narrative work of prose fiction, traditionally readable in a single setting.

simile: A figure of speech comparison between two unlike things that uses "like" or "as" (e.g., sly as a fox, sleep like a log).

symbol: Anything that represents or stands for something else. Often a symbol is something concrete that stands for something abstract. For example, fire may be fire and also symbolize passion. A symbol may be said to embody an idea. There are two general types of symbols: universal symbols that embody universally recognizable meanings wherever used, such as light to symbolize knowledge or a skull to symbolize death. There are also invented symbols that are given symbolic meaning by the way an author uses them in a literary work, as the white whale becomes a complex symbol in *Moby Dick*.